D0688366

BETWEEN BOARDS

Other Books

By Leona Rostenberg
English Publishers in the Graphic Arts 1599–1700
Literary, Political, Scientific, Religious & Legal Publishing, Printing & Bookselling in England, 1551–1700
The Minority Press & The English Crown: A Study in Repression 1558–1625
Bibliately: The History of Books on Postage Stamps

By Madeleine B. Stern
The Life of Margaret Fuller
Louisa May Alcott
Purple Passage: The Life of Mrs. Frank Leslie
Imprints on History: Book Publishers & American Frontiers
We the Women: Career Firsts of Nineteenth-Century America
So Much in a Lifetime: The Story of Dr. Isabel Barrows
Queen of Publishers' Row: Mrs. Frank Leslie
The Pantarch: A Biography of Stephen Pearl Andrews
Heads & Headlines: The Phrenological Fowlers
Editor: *Women on the Move* (4 vols.)
Editor: *The Victoria Woodhull Reader*
Editor: *Louisa's Wonder Book—An Unknown Alcott Juvenile*
Editor: *Behind a Mask: The Unknown Thrillers of Louisa May Alcott*
Editor: *Plots & Counterplots: More Unknown Thrillers of Louisa May Alcott*

By Leona Rostenberg & Madeleine B. Stern
Old & Rare: Thirty Years in the Book Business

BETWEEN BOARDS

BOARDS

New Thoughts on Old Books

LEONA ROSTENBERG

&

MADELEINE B. STERN

Allanheld & Schram  MONTCLAIR
George Prior LONDON

Published in the United States of America in 1978
by ALLANHELD, OSMUN & CO.,
19 Brunswick Road, Montclair, N.J. 07042,
and by ABNER SCHRAM LTD.,
36 Park Street, Montclair, N.J. 07042

Published in the United Kingdom in 1978 by
by GEORGE PRIOR ASSOCIATED PUBLISHERS LTD.
Rugby Chambers, 2 Rugby Street, London WCIN 3QU.

ISBN 0-86043-1541

Copyright © 1977 Leona Rostenberg and Madeleine B. Stern

All rights reserved. No part of this publication may
be reproduced, stored in a retrieval system, or trans-
mitted, in any form, or by any means, electronic, mechanical,
photocopying, recording, or otherwise, without the prior
permission of the publisher.

Library of Congress Cataloging in Publication Data

Rostenberg, Leona.
    Between boards.

    1. Book collecting.   2.   Bibliography--Rare books--
History.   3.   Antiquarian booksellers.   I.   Stern,
Madeleine Bettina   joint author.   II.   Ti-
tle.
Z987.R83   020'.75   77-15896
ISBN 0-8390-0208-4

Printed in the United States of America

Contents

The co-authors are identified by initials at the beginning of each chapter.

BETWEEN BOARDS

1

Mistress Folly's Life Cycle—
HABENT SUA FATA LIBELLI*

[LR]

This must be the house," we declared almost in unison as we confronted a large undistinguished row of flats on the Martius Strasse. We had promised our Erasmus collector that we would visit him the next time we returned to Munich to buy books.

A young girl in a white apron opened the door. "Guten Tag," she smiled curtsying just a wee bit, a subservience scarcely in vogue in the early nineteen–seventies. She ushered us into an extremely large room—amazingly bright despite the heavy overstuffed furniture, the bulky cumbersome couch draped with a Turkey shawl, the magnificent Oriental rug stretched across the parquet floor, an array of small tabarets loaded with pipes, lace curtains at the windows drawn back against the red portières. Interspersed among the eleven-foot shelving of books which skirted the three walls were engravings of Erasmus of Rotterdam after Dürer and Holbein and an excellent copy of the Quentin Metsys oil of the master copied from the original in the Louvre. We were mesmerized by the glorious array of octavos and quartos bound in pigskin, calf and morocco, the folios neatly arranged on the two lower shelves.

*Books have their fates.

"Hello there, my dear friends!" An arm around each of us broke our reverie.

"And hello to you. See, we came," we laughed enthusiastically. Our Erasmus customer faced us. He wore neither jerkin nor hose, *Schnabelschuhe* nor a biretta with a long goose quill. His suit was of excellent English tweed and his London-made shoes gleamed a dark rich russet brown. His sallow face broke into a thousand smiles as he extended his hand, kissing ours. "Willkommen, my friends. I am so happy you have come. Do sit down and make yourselves comfortable."

The English of our Munich customer Klaus Felix Schneperle von Wattenheym was almost faultless. But then had he not studied at Oxford hoping to recapture the experience of his great Erasmus— the scholar's stay with his Oxford Platonic friends, his residence in London with More? Wattenheym, or as we privately referred to our enthusiastic customer "Schnapps," had related his Erasmian odyssey on several occasions when he had visited us in New York in search of Erasmian related items.

We drank several cups of excellent coffee served in delicate Meissen by the smiling Fräulein, devoured a variety of *Kugelhopf* and chocolate squares and wistfully gazed upon a hazelnut torte covered with cream. "Schnapps" regaled us with questions about our recent purchases.

"Any Erasmus? Tell me at once!" "Schnapps" rose in the direction of his shelves.

"Let me show you some of my very fine copies. Have you ever seen the genuine first edition of *The Praise of Folly*—Paris, undated, probably ca. 1510? It is extremely rare. I have practically every edition and all fine copies. All but one," he amended, hesitating. "Did you know that Erasmus stayed with Aldus in Venice and in 1515 the great Venetian publisher issued *The Praise of Folly*? This might be a presentation copy. Here is the first English edition, London 1549. Have you ever studied the Myconius copy at the University of Basle? It has the original marginal drawings of Holbein. Just to see this marvel alone is worth a trip to Europe."

"You have wonderful books, Herr Wattenheym, stupendous."

"Ja, Ja," he agreed, "but there is one copy of *The Praise of Folly* that is not mine." His eyes misted as he stared beyond the portieres, beyond the lace curtains, back into time. We looked at each other. What was he talking about? What edition? What marvel??? He turned upon us almost violently: "Have you ever heard of the

Schürer- Pirckheimer- Dürer-Arundel-Hollar- Ratcliffe- Charteris copy of *The Praise of Folly*? The authorities say it is lost. Schmeisinger of Göttingen states catagorically. it never existed and Van Leeuwarden of Utrecht is convinced that for a brief time it had been taken by a Belgian administrator to the Congo. This is all ridiculous, *unsinn*. It exists. I repeat emphatically, it exists. I discussed its whereabouts with my dear friend, the late E. P. Goldschmidt of London and I have analyzed it for hours with Domizlaff. He is cynical. By the way do you know a young Erasmian, an American? He studied my collection. Ah yes, Charles Whitehurst—you Americans address him as Chuck. I think he teaches now at some American university on the East coast, somewhere not too far from the city—Long Island."

"Long Island," we interrupted, "we know it well, we summer there." Lost in the past, he paid little heed to us.

"This Whitehurst is well-informed. We have discussed my *Folly*. He is a droll man but a good scholar."

We glanced at our watches. "Schnapps" would never end. We were lost in Mistress Folly's cycle and were longing for the climax— dead, buried or alive! "We'll look for it," we exclaimed gaily as we walked toward the door. "Schnapps" shook his head sadly. His hand was limp as he kissed our fingers. "Poor 'Schnapps,' " we mused walking in the direction of the dealer Domizlaff. "Can such a copy really exist?" we queried each other, "one that belonged to the collector Pirckheimer, Dürer and Wenceslaus Hollar??? How come we have never heard of it? He is off his rocker," we concluded. "And who is this Whitehurst, teaching in Long Island of all places . . . ?"

We purchased two fine Luthers from Herr Domizlaff, declined a liqueur and paused to discuss Wattenheym's *grande folie*. Domizlaff smiled indulgently: "I must admit he is very serious about this copy. Of course Schürer published many editions and Pirckheimer was a great collector. Who knows? There is much magic in books. Need I tell you that almost anything is possible in our profession?" He smiled wryly as we bade him farewell: "You are resourceful ladies. Go find it for him."

* * *

Within the year "Schnapps" came to New York for a sale of early sixteenth-century books. During lunch with us he discussed in detail the story of his long-sought copy of the 1511 edition of *The Praise of Folly*.

"I know it is in the States. It was brought here by an English collector during the last century. I spent a few days down at Southampton with my friend Chuck Whitehurst. We discussed it." He lingered over coffee, rambling on about this fabulous copy. Mady and I glanced at each other, skeptically indulging the ravings of a mad bibliophile. Could such a copy possibly exist?

The story which is now revealed to a public audience for the first time may be read for what it is worth. It reflects the great honor accorded a work by the Stupor Mundi, Erasmus of Rotterdam, the vicissitudes endured by a single book in the course of four and a half centuries, the callous indifference of the ignorant and mercenary, and above all the passion of great bookmen. *Habent sua fata libelli*. It is an amazing tale—so amazing that it taxes credulity, and sometimes, even now, my partner and I are inclined to disbelieve it. Believe it or not—*lege et gaudebis* (read and you will rejoice).

* * *

Erasmus of Rotterdam was extremely weary after his lengthy journey on horseback from Italy to the Channel. His thoughts returned to Italy, its refinements and barbarisms. Did not the Roman pontiff Julius II think more of battle than of the Christian soul? Had not Christ's vicar on earth personally led his forces against those of the proud Venetian Republic? In so enlightened an age Italian venality and corruption had outraged the great scholar. He eagerly anticipated his journey to England, a fair land, which he had visited eleven years earlier in 1499.

Then Erasmus had derived much pleasure from tutoring the young Lord Mountjoy—"so gracious and charming a youth I would follow him to hell." He had savored the relaxation of English country life at Bedwell in Hertfordshire, Mountjoy's estate, and had received much acclaim at Oxford where he had been entertained by the foremost English scholars, John Colet, Thomas Linacre, William Grocyn and the gracious, genial, brilliant barrister Thomas More.

Now, eleven years later, Erasmus again crossed the turbulent Channel waters to the realm of a new young monarch described by Mountjoy as one who "favors the learned. I venture to swear on my life that even without wings you would fly over." The renowned humanist had scarcely flown over. It had been a tiring, tedious trip and as he drew close to the English shore his mind was not on the "wise, just and good" Henry VIII but rather on stupidity and insincerity—the folly of man. Upon arrival the exhausted traveler remained a short time at Bedwell, rooming later with Andreas Ammonius, a secretary of Henry VIII, who proved to be not merely delightful company but an excellent poet. Yet Erasmus longed for the companionship of his old friend More and eventually repaired to his home. Here the two scholars, joyful in mutual understanding, debated the merits of new lectures and texts in Greek much to the annoyance of Dame Alice, More's second wife who preferred a conversation more pertinent to daily needs. It was during this stay with More that Erasmus suffered a severe attack of lumbago. Mental diversion would distract him, ease his pain. His thoughts turned to a satire on folly, man's doltish behavior and levities which had preoccupied him during his lengthy trip from Italy across the Channel. Folly could become the heroine of a short text as well as a pun on the name of his host, Thomas More—*Moriae Encomium*—*The Praise of Folly*.

The author was well aware of the "fool" literary genre. He was familiar with the popular *Ship of Fools* of the Swiss jurist Sebastian Brant, who had described 112 kinds of fools, and with the *Stultifera Navis*, a revised text by the scholar-publisher Jodocus Badius Ascensius. Badius was of the opinion that Brant had not permitted a sufficiency of women aboard ship and supplied the deficiency adding six ships reserved for female fools alone.

Erasmus's heroine Folly satirizes all classes of society. The immured scholar who has passed his boyhood and youth in pursuing the learned disciplines has

never tasted so much as a little pleasure, always frugal, impecunious and austere . . . afflicted by pallor, leanness, invalidism, sore eyes, premature age, white hair, dying before the appointed day. He has never lived.

As for the priesthood, while Erasmus considered it "best to pass over them in silence" he scarcely did so.

They are protected by a wall of scholastic definitions, arguments, corollaries and implicit and explicit propositions. Furthermore, they explain as pleases them the most arcane matters, such as by what method the world was founded and set in order, through what conduits original sin has been passed down along through generations and how long the perfect Christ was in the Virgin's womb. The men . . . generally call themselves "the religious" and "monks"—utterly false names both—since most of them keep as far away as they can from religion. They reckon it the highest degree of piety to have no contact with literature, and hence they see to it that they do not know how to read.

Veneration of the saints, Christian superstitions and ecclesiastic hierarchy become the butt of the author's venom:

One saint assists in time of toothache, another is propitious to women in the time of travail, another receives stolen goods. But why should I launch out upon this sea of superstition? The whole of Christian life everywhere is full of fanaticism of this kind. Our priests allow them, without regret, and even foster them, being aware of how much money is wont to accrue from this source.

As Folly scathingly defrocked the ecclesiast, she little spared the pomposity of lawyers and scientists. The jurists pile

. . . glosses upon glosses, opinions upon opinions, thus contriving to make their profession seem the most difficult of all. Near these march the scientists revered for their beards and the fur on their gowns . . . knowing nothing in general they profess to know all things in particular though they are ignorant even of themselves.

Folly also rebukes the ever credulous rulers who "diligently hunt, feed some fine horses and sell dignities and offices for profit devising daily measures which drain away the wealth of citizens and sweep it into their own exchequer."

The learned world of England and the Continent applauded Erasmus's brilliant fantasy, this enchanting *jeu d'esprit*. A copy of the manuscript was immediately shipped to Paris where it was published without date by Gilles de Gourmont. The first dated edition of *The Praise of Folly* appeared in Strasbourg in 1511 published by the author's "very own dear friend" Matthias Schürer, scholar and intimate of scholars.

Matthias Schürer was born into the vigorous Alsatian printing trade about 1470 at Schlettstadt. Here he attended the local academy moving on later to the University of Cracow where he received a Master of Arts degree. Filled with humanistic ardor, he returned to Strasbourg to be engaged by several master-printers as assistant. He strove for excellence in transcription and style and the elegance of a well-turned Latin phrase. Begging the reader's indulgence for any possible errors in an edition of *Germania* by the doyen of Alsatian letters, Jacob Wimpheling, he declared: "Am I an Argus endowed with one hundred eyes? Can one see all?"

In 1508 Matthias Schürer opened his own printing establishment, resolving to disseminate writings of current Italian and German scholars and handy editions of the classics. The latter program had doubtless been inspired by the trade-list of the great Venetian publisher Aldus Manutius, who had begun to circulate the classics in pocket format.

A year after entering business Schürer added to his list of available publications a revised edition of the *Adages* of Erasmus designed "for the use of scholars." A reprint followed in 1510 and shortly thereafter he issued *The Ship of Fools* of the influential Strasbourg divine Geyler of Keysersberg. This work appeared in January 1511 and there can be little doubt that its success and the prestige of the great Erasmus influenced the Strasbourg publisher to issue in August 1511 the first dated edition of *The Praise of Folly*. The title-page of this slim 84-page small quarto volume, set in Roman type, was unadorned, reading simply *Moriae Encomium Erasmi Roterodami Declamatio*. A terse note to the reader states that it is the text of Erasmus, the "Ornament of Germany," a work evoking the greatest admiration. "If you will buy and read it, I wager you will be well rewarded for your investment." Circulating in an edition of 1,000 copies and priced at a demi-gulden, it could only bring countless joy to the author's ever-increasing reading public.

Erasmus of Rotterdam, the foremost scholar of Europe, was bound to the Strasbourg publisher, Matthias Schürer, by personal ties. The *stupor mundi* had twice visited Strasbourg and been received with heady adulation by the city's Literary Society of which Schürer was a member. In humanistic hyperbole the great humanist was hailed as "the son of Apollo nourished by Minerva" to which Erasmus replied that "Agamemnon would have indeed considered himself most fortunate to have won the praise of such Nestors." Matthias Schürer at this time must be counted among the younger Nestors to whom the "Son of Apollo" was to write: "Did I not love my Matthias so greatly I would be justly said to bear iron and steel in my heart. There is nothing I would not do for you." Erasmus of Rotterdam did much for the publisher Matthias Schürer since many of the texts he wrote or edited bore the imprint of the Strasbourg craftsman.

Erasmus and Schürer enjoyed the company of several *illustrissimi,* among them one Beatus Rhenanus, born also at Schlettstadt, a small community not far from Strasbourg. As a student, Beatus Rhenanus had studied at Paris where he worked a short time for the distinguished Parisian publisher Henri Estienne I. Upon his return to Strasbourg he was employed as reader and corrector by Schürer, later to be engaged by Erasmus as supervisor of the publication of a collected edition of his writings. Like many humanists, Beatus Rhenanus was a versatile man, a good scholar, the owner of a fine library and the author of a *History of Germany.* He also cultivated important people personally and through a large and varied correspondence.

There can be little doubt that he was familiar with the reputation of a distinguished Nuremberg jurist and senator of the "Golden Corinth of the North," a collector and writer who eventually would compose a paean of German history. Willibald Pirckheimer was a wealthy patrician of Nuremberg; he had inherited and increased his father's library. Like Beatus Rhenanus, he enjoyed a correspondence with the *decor Germaniae,* Erasmus of Rotterdam, several of whose volumes graced the patrician's collection at Neunhof.

It was entirely within the province of Schürer's corrector and reader, Beatus Rhenanus, to suggest that the publisher send a copy of the recently issued *Praise of Folly* to another admirer of the Dutch humanist. The Nuremberg jurist and bibliophile Willibald Pirckheimer could only rejoice in so delightful a gift.

Selecting a well-inked copy printed on very white paper without blemishes, Matthias Schürer decided upon an appropriate inscription for the eminent recipient. In a fine hand he had learned from an Italian writing master, while attending the University of Cracow, he wrote on the title-page:

Summo viro D. Bilibaldo Pircaimero sereniss. urbis Noricae Consilario dono dedit Matthias Schurerius Mag. Artium Argentinopolis mense Decemb. Anno. M.D.XI.*

It was judicious on the part of the Strasbourg publisher to mention his degree *Magister Artium.* Pirckheimer would realize that this was no gift from a poor ignorant printer!

Upon receiving this attractive volume several months later, Willibald Pirckheimer would doubtless have preferred an inscription from the great Erasmus, but he surely was most pleased to add to his fine collection a publisher's presentation copy of the 1511 edition of *The Praise of Folly.*

---

*Matthias Schürer, Master of Arts of Strasbourg, presents [this book] as a gift in the month of December in the year 1511 to the most exalted gentleman, Master Willibald Pirckheimer, counselor of the city of Nuremberg.

Master Pirckheimer's library at Neunhof had been begun by his father Johann and greatly enlarged by his son during his student days at Padua and Pavia where he studied law. His bibliophilic ardor is described in an encomium by his grandson Jerome Imhof: "As soon as a fine and beautiful book appeared in Italy whether at Rome, Venice, Mantua, Florence, Milan or elsewhere he had to acquire it—no matter the cost—texts today which rank as treasures—especially those published by Aldus Manutius."

Despite his many civic responsibilities, Pirckheimer at no time neglected his library. His agent at Pavia, young Anthony Kress, was instructed to acquire new publications, but was warned at the same time to be wary of incomplete texts. "These booksellers are a tricky race," wrote his patron. "Buy no more Greek books. I have found defects."

As the collection expanded it included notable works in juris- prudence and philology, grammar and rhetoric, history, mathe- matics, astronomy and astrology, theology and *belles-lettres* as well as Hebraica. Apparently Willibald Pirckheimer was a universal man, a member of the new breed who could tolerate if not embrace all creeds. Both reform and orthodox texts were represented in his collection. Fortunately an inventory of Pirckheimer's library exists, albeit in abbreviated form, citing some of his treasures: the first two editions of the *Ninety-Five Theses* of Martin Luther of Wittenberg, the hot-headed monk whose violent anti-Roman fulminations would plunge Christian Europe into religious war. Eight books by Desi- derius Erasmus are listed. Strangely enough, however, the inventory fails to cite the 1511 presentation copy of the Schürer edition of *The Praise of Folly*.

Young Kress was only one of Pirckheimer's scouts. The Nurem- berg bibliophile employed other agents, among them the cleric Johann Cochlaeus and that friend of Schürer and Erasmus, Beatus Rhenanus, who had originally suggested the presentation of *Folly*. One of Pirckheimer's book scouts towers far above all others and even rivals in genius the author of *Folly* himself.

Like his patron, Albrecht Dürer was a native of Nuremberg and early in his career was regarded as one of the greatest of living artists. During his 1506 trip to Italy he had written to Pirckheimer from Venice regretting his inability to find books for him. "There is nothing of significance by the Italians in the field of history pertinent to your studies. It is always one and the same."

It was as an artist that Albrecht Dürer best served Willibald

Pirckheimer. A few years after the young jurist's return from Nuremberg, Dürer executed a woodcut portrait of Pirckheimer which scarcely flatters this flat-nosed, muscular patrician in his rich fur-trimmed mantle. As the Pirckheimer library grew it required a bookplate and it was Dürer who, in 1502, executed the design: the Pirckheimer arms intertwined with those of his wife, the former Christine Rieter, and the motto *Inicium Sapientiae Timor Domini* (Reverence for the Almighty is the beginning of Wisdom). The great artist was to dedicate to "his especially dear master and friend Willibald Pirckheimer" two of his notable treatises, *Underweisung der Messung* and *Vier Bücher von menschlichen Proportion.*

Of greater bibliophilic significance is Dürer's artistic contribution to his "dear" Pirckheimer's library. His miniatures embellish, among others, Pirckheimer's copies of Aesop, Aristophanes, Theocritus, Homer and Josephus. Was not Erasmus's satire, *The Praise of Folly*, inscribed to Willibald Pirckheimer, worthy of illustration by the most celebrated of German artists? Would it not be appropriate for Albrecht Dürer to embellish a few of the wide, clean margins with copies of the buffoons and fools he had executed for *The Ship of Fools* by Sebastian Brant? And so, on the margins of b2 recto and e3 recto of the Pirckheimer copy of *The Praise of Folly* Albrecht Dürer inked his superb woodcuts of the "Fool who does not follow advice" and "Arrogance who became an ass." In addition, Pirckheimer added his bookplate executed by Dürer and since the little volume had journeyed so successfully from Strasbourg to the shelves at Neunhof, he tipped in a fine impression of the artist's St. Christopher. Perhaps one day the little book would again venture forth and need protection by the patron of travelers!

Matthias Schürer's gift had been sent unbound. A binding would remain the personal choice of a collector as discriminating as the Nuremberg patrician. Willibald Pirckheimer sought the help of Hieronymus Hölzel, a Nuremberg printer and binder, who had been engaged as craftsman to the city's Literary Society. After some discussion it was decided that *The Praise of Folly* would be bound in full pigskin, the front cover bearing a full-length blind-impressed portrait of the great Erasmus surrounded by rolls of buffoons and fools. The back cover would bear the Pirckheimer coat of arms with the motto "Reverence for the Almighty is the beginning of Wisdom." The Nuremberg goldsmith Hans Krafft was engaged to apply a fine embossed clasp and hinges. Willibald Pirckheimer could proudly display to his friends—the Tuchers and Behaims and other members of the Nuremberg patriciate—one of the finest books in the "Golden Corinth of the North"—indeed, in the Empire itself.

The city of Nuremberg where Pirckheimer died in 1530 was to witness a century torn by religious differences succeeded by the brutal decades of the Thirty Years War. When peace was finally restored to the Empire in 1648, Nuremberg had lost her position as a leading city.

Meanwhile Willibald Imhof the Younger had inherited his grand-father Pirckheimer's library. During the distress of the Thirty Years War his heir Hans Hieronymus Imhof, experiencing some financial difficulties, decided to sell fourteen of the volumes illus-trated by Dürer to a Dutch collector named Overbeck for the amount of 300 crowns. Oddly enough the Schürer presentation copy of *The Praise of Folly* was not among this lot. It remained in the original collection although a visitor to the Imhof home writing in his diary in 1634 remarked that this splendid little volume looked weary: "The clasp is quite loose, appearing as if the volume had been picked up carelessly. One of the fine gold pins holding the clasp is missing."

Thomas Howard, Second Earl of Arundel, has been dubbed by Horace Walpole the "Father of Vertu" in England. Young Howard had made a brilliant marriage having successfully courted Alathea, heiress of Gilbert Talbot, Earl of Shrewsbury, whose great wealth helped restore Arundel House, the seat of jousts and masques, to its former glory. It also helped Thomas Howard indulge his passion for travel, art and books. In 1636 as Earl Marshal of England he was sent by Charles I to Vienna there to negotiate with the Emperor regard-ing the restitution of the Palatinate to the homeless Prince Frederick and his wife, a former English princess.

During his lengthy trip Howard visited several German cities where he paused to inspect and purchase works of art. From Frankfurt, in December, 1636, he dispatched a letter to his agent in Rome:

I wish you saw the picture of the Madonna of Dürer which the Bishoppe of Wirtzberge gave me last weeke as I passed by that way, and though it were painted at first upon an uneven board and is varnished, yet it is worthe more than all the toyes I have gotten in Germanye, and for such I esteeme it having ever carried it in my owne coach since I had it.

There is little doubt that while in Nuremberg the "Father of Vertu" examined the fine library which had once belonged to Willibald Pirckheimer and gazed with ardor upon the presentation copy of *The Praise of Folly* whose clasp hung loose. It is certain that in his enthusiasm for the collection, he purchased from Hans Hieronymus Imhof for 350 crowns the remaining books that had once belonged to Willibald Pirckheimer—including the *Folly*. The volumes were removed from their shelves and dispatched in crates—not in his Lordship's coach—to the family seat, Arundel House.

It was during this same continental tour that Thomas Howard visited Prague where he found himself attracted to the delicate drawings of a native-born artist, Wenceslaus Hollar, who was enticed by the Second Earl of Arundel to accompany him to England where for better pay he might practice his fine art of engraving.

Hollar was to become one of the most prolific artists in England, developing a new technique of etching. According to that indefatigable observer of English virtuosi, John Aubrey, Hollar spent most of his time "draweing and copying rarities which he did etch." Although Thomas Howard had brought Hollar to England, he did not reside at Arundel House but rather found employment with a print dealer, Peter Stent of Guiltspur Street without Newgate, a specialist in art books, prints and engravings. Stent was a tough, miserly employer paying his gifted artist only four pence an hour, the time being determined by an hourglass. Hollar executed a variety of plates for his tight-fisted employer, portraits of English noblemen and noblewomen including one of his patron, the Second Earl of Arundel. A self portrait of Hollar depicts a rather morose individual who doubtlessly longed for the more familiar alleys and lanes of his native Prague. His hours were long and the promised pay meagre.

During an occasional holiday Wenceslaus Hollar visited Arundel House where he might view the great gallery of paintings and the fine library and become acquainted with his Lordship's librarian Francis Junius who had arrived from Leyden in 1621. Junius, known also as Du Jon, was a fine scholar with a thorough knowledge of Anglo-Saxon as well as the history of art.

The librarian from Leyden and the artist from Prague had much in common. Both were aliens and both were enamored with art, the one as historian, the other as consummate practitioner. It can be said with little doubt that Francis Junius showed the homesick Hollar many of his Lordship's splendidly illustrated books, among them the extra-illustrated copy of the 1511 edition of *The Praise of Folly*. There the systematic librarian had entered below the inscription of Matthias Schürer the exact location of the new acquisition—"C2/3"— indicating that the book had been placed in Case 2, shelf 3. The Czech artist feasted upon Dürer's illustrations on b2 recto and e3 recto, the marvelous plate of St. Christopher, the handsome binding. He deplored that the back cover was worn and scuffed.

The book was a great treasure and since his difficult but highly artistic employer Peter Stent would appreciate a volume illustrated by the great Dürer himself, Wenceslaus Hollar borrowed it, planning to show it briefly to the Master of the shop on Guiltspur Street without Newgate. The small quarto would be immediately and safely returned to the library of Arundel House. His promise was never kept. In November 1666 Wenceslaus Hollar was appointed His Majesty's "Scenographer and Designer of Prospects," a post which took him to distant Tangiers where he was to survey and etch the newly won English naval base under the command of his former patron's grandson Lord Henry Howard. A year earlier on September 29, 1665 it was recorded that "Peter Stynt on Pye House Corner Picture Seller died ex peste."

The great Plague had hit London before June 20, 1665. Activity in the city came to an almost immediate standstill. Citizens fled the capital for the country. In the thickly concentrated area of booksellers' row close to St. Paul's, contagion spread rapidly. Among the victims was the seller of prints Master Stent, who, having unsuccessfully confronted the competition of able and younger dealers, had moved from Guiltspur Street to Pye House Corner. The effects of a plague victim were hastily removed and deposited in front of the house to be burned before the dread disease spread. The prints and maps, the landscapes, the delicate engravings of Wenceslaus Hollar and several of the books published and owned by the late Peter Stent were taken from his premises for immediate destruction. Among the unhappy lot of loose plates and volumes was a small quarto text, its clasp gone, its back cover detached.

In all disasters scavengers abound. Hawkers of pamphlets and prints, books, broadsides and squibs conducted their precarious existence. Among those who at various periods traded in stolen or illicit tracts, foreign corantos or anti-government news-sheets were a number of female hawkers—May of Shoe Lane, Mother Tuck, Widow Douce and the notorious Alice Fowler. Frequently the female hawker was a dealer's widow who had inherited a few books and tracts. Her practical knowledge and cunning were occasionally extensive. She knew of dealers' needs and interests and in the booksellers' world—a network of alleys and lanes—she could transfer prohibited or stolen pamphlets and tracts from dealer to customer.

Little is known about the background of Judith Jones. Obviously she was strong and healthy, having escaped the violence of the London Plague. She lived a precarious existence within the confines of booksellers' row and it was not until 1680 that she earned some brief immortality when she was arrested by the Messenger of the Press for selling anti-Jacobean pamphlets at the Amsterdam Coffee-House.

Before Judith Jones suffered the ignominy of public arrest she scoured the city for tracts or prints of interest to the more established members of the book trade, and it was during her search for merchandise that she espied outside a printseller's dwelling on Pye House Corner the abandoned legacy of one of its tenants, the late Peter Stent. She riffled through Alexander Browne's *The Whole Art of Drawing*, some landscapes and maps—all of value. Her ragged slipper kicked a small volume printed in a strange language unintelligible to Judith Jones. As she glanced at the pages she saw a few illustrations and a plate of a giant carrying a child on his shoulders. The front cover of the book was bloated since there had been heavy rain and many of the pages clung to one another. It bore no back cover.

Pye House Corner was deserted. It hung under the pall of disease. She threw the little book and several loose plates into a sack and hurried away, fearing arrest.

Arriving at her dingy lodging in Bartholomew Close, Judith Jones scrutinized her recent loot. She could decipher the letters HOLLAR affixed to a plate which showed an elegantly attired English gentlewoman carrying a muff which matched her tippet. She hesitantly opened the small book gazing with some perturbation at the plate of the giant and child. Alarm beset Judith Jones. Surely this was a papist work. If it were found in her possession she would be immediately apprehended by a Messenger of the Press, clapped into Bridewell and condemned by the government as a papist whore-monger. Her decision was immediate. She would offer the plate to a printseller.

There would be no serious problem in its disposal. After all it had belonged to the late Peter Stent who, it was reputed, had boasted members of the nobility among his clientele. Deftly she extracted the plate of the giant and child from the little volume.

The following morning Judith Jones found the shop of a printseller "next to the Sign of the Drake close to Palsgrave's Tavern, without Temple Bar." Its master, William Faithorne the Elder, sold not only prints and drawings of many artists but also those he himself had executed. Encouraged by his brother-in-law, the successful John Martyn of The Bell, now printer to the august Royal Society, Faithorne had set up at The Drake as an artist and dealer in prints. His stock of portraits, views and maps and several books on the fine arts filled the shop which had become an attractive rendezvous for a distinguished clientele which included the scientist Hooke and the diarist Evelyn.

William Faithorne the Elder immediately recognized the identity of the engraver who had executed the plate offered him by Judith Jones. Further inquiry produced from Mistress Jones's sack the book from which the plate had been extracted. Leafing through the volume Faithorne observed a large tear on b2 and signature 3 was heavily dampstained. He was convinced that the little fool in the margin of e3—which, alas, had lost its head—was also the work of Albrecht Dürer. He purchased the book from Judith Jones who thanked him warmly for the shilling, two-penny he paid her. Faithorne's brother-in-law John Martyn had performed many services for him and so as a token of affection and appreciation he presented the small quarto to the Master of The Bell.

John Martyn's widow Sarah survived his demise in July 1680. The following June she concluded an agreement with Robert Scott of Princess Arms, internationally recognized importer and bookseller, for the sale of her late husband's stock.

Robert Scott was considered by the cognoscenti of Restoration England "the greatest librarian [bookseller] in Europe, an expert... and a conscientious good man, the only person of his time for his extraordinary knowledge of books." During his long and successful career Scott had published a variety of miscellaneous texts which attracted to his premises a large and distinguished clientele, including Hooke, Wren, Sir John Hoskins, President of the Royal Society and Richard Pearson, Under-Keeper of the Royal Library at St. James's. One of his most faithful and affectionate customers was the effervescent Secretary of the Navy, the diarist, Samuel Pepys, to whom Scott had written: "I love to find a rare book for yu."

Whether or not Scott realized that the 1511 Strasbourg edition of *The Praise of Folly* with its impressive presentation inscription was among a lot he had acquired from the widow Martyn must remain conjectural. He was a busy man, catering to his customers' needs, buying and selling books in large quantities.

At all events, in 1687, Robert Scott decided to auction off his stock of 25,000 books. "Grown old and much worn by the multiplicity of business . . .and [beginning] to think of his ease," he consigned the 8,808 lots to Robert Walford in whose rooms at The Bear in Ave Maria Lane near Ludgate, the sale began on February 13, 1687/88. The auction lasted "day by day the first five days of every week, till all books are sold, from Hours of Nine in the morning Till Twelve, and from Two Till Six in the Evenings."

Hezekiah Ribble of Montagu Street attended a morning sale during the week of February 20th. He had carefully inspected a small lot of foreign books among which he had found a worn volume by an author especially dear to him, Erasmus of Rotterdam. Its subject interested him extremely since he believed that man had always courted Mistress Folly who now reigned supreme at the licentious, extravagant, Frenchified, papist-minded court of James II. It is true that the copy was quite battered, the front cover badly scuffed, although Hezekiah Ribble could vaguely perceive the likeness of the great Erasmus from a print that hung in his modest home. Versed in Latin, he deciphered the presentation inscription and assumed it had been addressed to a wealthy patron. Competition for the lot desired by Hezekiah Ribble was not spirited. Customers sought lively novels and slim elegant folios, some books of travel, perhaps a row of classics rather than esoteric Latin texts. Hezekiah Ribble was a man of modest means who ministered to an Anglican congregation on Montagu Street. Much of the Reverend Master's time was spent around St. Paul's where he hunted reasonable items in the booksellers' shops. None that he purchased brought him more pleasure than he derived from his copy of *The Praise of Folly*. The volume was carefully preserved in a small box since he could ill afford to have it appropriately recased. Ribble cherished it until he died when it, along with a few household goods, passed to his eldest daughter Elizabeth, wife of Sampson Shrew, a prosperous butcher with a stall and shop on Vine Street.

In time, the large bedstead, mattress, feather pillow and a box of pewter plates and books, the property of the late Sampson Shrew, were inherited by his daughter Maria who had married her father's assistant Phineas Trott. Phineas was a man of some enterprise who expanded the business of his late father-in-law, displaying in his shop and stall glassy-eyed rabbits hung on wooden pegs, woodcocks, cutlets, a variety of small birds, quarters of well-hung venison, livers and kidneys for tasty pies. Two apprentices assisted in the cutting up and wrapping of meats. On a shelf in the back of the shop Phineas, a frugal tradesman, had placed a pile of books, the leaves of which could easily be torn out and used for the wrapping of purchases. In this way Phineas avoided the heavy tax imposed upon paper by the government of His Majesty George III. He also whetted the literary taste of a customer who might find a choice cutlet wrapped in a page of Latin prose or English verse.

On a pleasant morning in August, 1774, John Ratcliffe, a Southwark chandler, requested Ralfe Gubbins, Trott's second assistant, to select for him a small duck liver since he planned to dine alone. As Gubbins tore a leaf from a small book, Ratcliffe stared at the young man shocked by his indifference to and desecration of literature. John Ratcliffe was an avid bibliophile owning thirty Caxtons and a variety of incunabula.

"What do you have there, boy? Permit me to examine the volume." An uncommon excitement bestirred the soul of the Southwark chandler as he glanced at a page which he deciphered with some effort:

For what avails it to load the belly with all those fine wines, savory dishes, and rare meats, if similarly our eyes and ears, our whole souls do not batten on laughter of jests and witticisms?

John Ratcliffe gazed wrathfully at Ralfe Gubbins, at the liver which seemed to shrink, and the lifeless rabbits hanging limply from their wooden pegs.

"Permit me to speak to your master." For a few pence he purchased the entire volume from which the blood-stained leaf had been extracted. He carried it home, placing it for a time next to one of his thirty Caxtons. Although his knowledge of Latin was limited, Ratcliffe realized he had purchased a book by the great Erasmus, and that it contained an unusual bookplate. He would discuss his acquisition at the next Thursday morning meeting of his friends—the antiquaries John Croft and John Topham, Dr. Anthony Askew, the politician James West and Dr. Johnson's acquaintance, Topham Beauclerck—who gathered at his Southwark home to discuss the pleasures of bibliophily.

James West had come to town from his country seat at Alscott, Preston-on-Stour. He had come not just to discuss old books with his bibliophile cronies but also to consider the many problems regarding the growing unrest in the American colonies. In London he also enjoyed friendly relations with members of the Charteris family of Portland Square. The company of young John Frederick St. Helier Charteris was particularly agreeable for he had acquired a fine collection of the classics and humanities. West decided to invite him to the forthcoming Thursday gathering of bookmen at the home of John Ratcliffe. Young Charteris was deeply impressed by the Southwark chandler's superb Caxton collection, especially the 1482 edition of *Troilus & Cresidye* and the 1478 *Canterbury Tales.* The morning passed in enjoyable discussion of dealers, sales and acquisitions. Dr. Askew wondered why his host appeared bemused.

"Gentlemen, I believe that I have discovered a most uncommon book," Ratcliffe declared.

From a pile of quartos resting close to two Caxtons he drew a book without binding. Mr. Topham Beauclerck and James West examined it, handing it over to John Frederick Charteris who easily read the faded inscription:

Summo viro D. Bilibaldo Pircaimero sereniss. urbis Noricae Consilario dono dedit Matthias Schurerius Mag. Artium Argentinopolis mense Decemb. Anno. M.D. XI.*

His eyes lit up.

"Gentlemen, it is a presentation copy to one Pircaimer of Nuremberg by a certain Schurer of Strasbourg, anno 1511." Rereading the inscription, studying the bookplate and the title, he pursued:

"It is indeed *The Praise of Folly* of Erasmus with the bookplate of its owner. What a shame such a splendid little book is so scarred and battered."

John Ratcliffe smiled indulgently. He admired collectors, particularly young collectors. As Charteris bowed farewell, the Southwark chandler handed him the volume: "'Tis yours to cherish, Charteris."

---

*Matthias Schürer, Master of Arts of Strasbourg, presents [this book] as a gift in the month of December in the year 1511 to the most exalted gentleman, Master Willibald Pirckheimer, counselor of the city of Nuremberg.

John Frederick St. Helier Charteris was extremely pleased with his gift. He studied the book, the contents of which were brilliant and witty. On the right of the entry made over one hundred years earlier by Francis Junius he inscribed his name and that of the donor: "Charteris. October 1774. Given me by John Ratcliffe." His copy of *The Praise of Folly* required rebinding and he promptly repaired to the shop of the bookbinder Roger Payne located on Leicester Square.

Young Charteris paid little attention to the bookbinder's unkempt hair, unattractive visage and filthy attire, but spent his time in the selection of the appropriate leather—a straight-grained bright red morocco to be illuminated with ornamental devices of alternating stars and crescents. The sheets were to be resewn in silk and the backs lined with leather. Having given Master Payne exact instructions about binding in the bookplate, Charteris anticipated his newly recased copy of *The Praise of Folly*.

The love of books and fine bindings was a Charteris family trait, along with a predilection for travel. Those attributes were bequeathed by John Frederick Charteris to his grandson James Francis—along with his library—and by the early 1850's the young man had become a prominent collector. Much of his time was spent at the shops of the four leading London booksellers, Thorpe, Rodd, Rich and Pickering from whom he purchased books of travel and exploration, classics and odd volumes. As for the finely bound Erasmus satire, James Francis admired it as much as his grandfather had, appreciating both its contents and its provenance. Upon one occasion he showed it to the Keeper of Printed Books of the British Museum, Anthony Panizzi, who, though impressed by the associative significance of the volume, was saddened by its internal condition. In spite of its defects, young Charteris confided that he would take it with him to America where he planned to travel some day. "The book is very meaningful to me."

During one of Charteris's visits to the Museum in September 1855 Panizzi introduced him to an American bookseller Henry Stevens, agent of Mr. James Lenox of New York. Their conversation naturally revolved about books and collectors as well as American customs, climate and cities. Charteris mentioned his planned visit to America, remarking that if the country proved congenial he might make it his permanent residence. With Stevens's recurrent visits to London, their friendship ripened and Charteris's resolve to cross the seas strengthened.

At length, in 1857, James Francis Charteris sailed aboard the

"Great Western" to New York. In his pocket were two letters, one given to him by Henry Stevens and addressed to Mr. James Lenox, 53 Fifth Avenue, New York City, the other directed to Mr. Abraham Candy, Main Street, East Hampton, Long Island. Within the small trunk in his cabin were a miniature of his mother, a second edition of *The Pilgrim's Progress* of John Bunyan and *The Praise of Folly* of Desiderius Erasmus. During a patch of rough weather Charteris recalled Erasmus's allusion to the saint invoked at the time of shipwreck.

Mr. Lenox was very pleased to welcome this agreeable young Englishman who spoke so warmly of his London agent Henry Stevens. Knowing of his host's great collection, Charteris had brought with him two books which he considered worthy of discussion, his copy of the *The Pilgrim's Progress* and *The Praise of Folly*. Mr. Lenox showed extreme interest in the second edition of *The Pilgrim's Progress*, showing Charteris the first of the same year and the fourth edition where London was spelt Dondon.

"Do let me show you my copy of the great Mazarine Bible. It is as far as I know the only copy in this country," remarked Mr. Lenox, pulling down the unsurpassed Gutenberg Bible which he had purchased through Henry Stevens at Sotheby's for five hundred pounds. "And this is the Wicked Bible," he continued, "since as you know, the careless printer omitted the word "not" in the Seventh Commandment which now reads 'Thou shalt commit adultery.'" The time passed quickly as Charteris studied folios relating to the great explorations, the first editions of *Paradise Lost* and *Areopagitica*, the many splendid volumes which formed the growing library of James Lenox.

Since September in New York proved exceedingly warm for the London born James Francis Charteris he made inquiries about a possible visit to Abraham Candy of East Hampton, Long Island, to whom he had a letter of introduction. Informed that the town situated between ocean and bay enjoyed a most salubrious climate, Charteris decided to take the train to Bridgehampton, continuing to East Hampton by the horse-drawn omnibus of Messrs. Hackett & Fithian.

Charteris found the company of Abraham Candy quite agreeable. An Englishman, Candy had taught for some time at the local school, the Clinton Academy. Seeking a more lucrative income, he had opened a boarding house on Main Street where Charteris remained for several months. Actually he found the lovely town with its pond and willows, its great sycamores, its beautiful beaches, its rural hinterland far more delightful than Candy's guests. Walking and roaming the countryside he relished the Indian names, Apaquogue, Montauk, Shinnecock, the shells that littered the shore line, the gulls and terns, the ducks and mallards that inhabited beach and stream.

With the approach of winter, Charteris decided to seek a more equable climate in the South and, wishing to travel unburdened, left some of his possessions with Abraham Candy. Among them were his *Pilgrim's Progress* and his *Praise of Folly*, both of which Charteris promised to reclaim upon his return.

At his Main Street boarding house after the Civil War Candy had engaged a one-armed veteran named William Gardner, who for a time had served as Keeper of the Montauk Light House. Despite his handicap Mr. Gardner was an extremely genial gentleman who enlivened the inn with oyster suppers and dances in the parlor. Like most American hostelries, however, this one had its ups and downs and these eventually included new management and renaming. In 1902 the inn that Abraham Candy had opened was put on the market.

After its sale that same year a few trunks and packages found in the basement of the old Main Street caravansery went unclaimed. On one of them the name James Francis Charteris was faintly—scarcely—discernible.

Just how this particular package came to rest some seventy years later amid the clutter of Harriet Prescott's attic, Harriet Prescott herself could not explain. She herself habitually blamed the disorderly condition of her home upon her husband and her husband's forbears who "could never part with anything." One of the Prescotts, she knew, had been a town officer in the early 1900's and in the course of his "duties"—and the gratification of his acquisitive instincts—had appropriated any and all unclaimed gear or tackle, household effects or packages that survived fires, deaths—and inn sales. In every woman's life, however, there comes a time to part with excess impedimenta and for Harriet Prescott that time came when Mr. Prescott built a brand new ranch house in the Springs.

"Thank goodness we'll have no more attic," Harriet happily sighed. Before moving she had all the old Prescott "junk" removed from the attic. Her grandson Paul began to linger over the numerous boxes and a small trunk. "Don't bother with them Paul. I don't know what's in them and what's more I don't care. It's all old Prescott trash. Just do me a favor, put them in the car and take them for once and for all over to LVIS on Main Street. They'll find plenty to sell at the fair. I just don't want my new house cluttered up."

* * *

It had been our eleventh summer at Barnes Landing, East Hampton. We both wrote in the morning, swam, beached, explored, watched the seascapes and breathed in the beauty of the town. It was a particularly brilliant August day, this of the 1972 LVIS (Ladies Village Improvement Society) Fair.

"We'll go in the afternoon," we decided. "After all, we've never found anything much. This way we can write in the morning, have a swim and maybe we won't go at all." I interrupted, "Who cares about all their trash." After lunch our bibliophilic consciences began to prick. "We should go. Maybe we'll find two mint copies of *Tamerlane.*"

So off we drove to the LVIS Fair grounds adjoining the Episcopal Church on Main Street across from the Clinton Academy where Abraham Candy had taught over one hundred years earlier. Mady found a Dorothy Sayers paperback and I indignantly refused a copy of Kenneth Roberts' *Oliver Wiswell.* "The little lady states it's a first and wants $25.00." We shepherded our darling dachshund Cocoa Leona out, carefully avoiding the crowd milling about the soft ice cream stand.

East Hampton, known for many things, is also the backdrop for the wildest, largest, most prestigious and most awful cocktail parties. Our hostess had forgotten most of the guests' names. It did not matter, because most of the guests had forgotten her name. On the lawn we found, chewing a blade of grass, a rather dejected youngish man who introduced himself as Chuck Whitehurst. As we returned names he looked at us rather sharply:

"You're booksellers, no?"

"Yes, and your name sounds so familiar. Are you Klaus von Wattenheym's friend?"

"Sure thing, and he certainly has been on my mind this past week." We straightened up with some foreboding.

"How come you gals didn't go to the LVIS Fair last week?" He looked at us intently. "Boy! I found a book there. I think it's the book Klaus has been searching . . ."

We interrupted: "You mean his Erasmus really exists?"

"I'm not sure, but I think this may be it."

"Where is it?" we demanded violently.

"Where is it?—exactly where it should be. On its way to Klaus."

We smiled wistfully. Perhaps one day we would again visit old "Schnapps" and see the little book written by Erasmus, presented by its publisher to a great collector, embellished by Albrecht Dürer— the book that had traveled twice across the sea and withstood the ravages of time and the vicissitudes of man. We were thoughtful as we considered the centuries it had survived and the passions it had aroused.

"C'mon, cheer up," Chuck smiled, taking our hands. "The book is where it should be. Let's drink Folly's own toast." He raised his glass and clicked ours. "'And so farewell. Applaud . . . live . . . drink . . . O most distinguished initiates of Folly!'"

2

A New Found Land:
America in Strange Places*

[MBS]

Although she eluded us, Mistress Folly finally reached the shores of America. Other books, more specifically related to the scene than Erasmus' great satire upon humanity, have tarried for a while in our bibliopolic net. Americana is a magic word to the American antiquarian bookseller, and even we, who have never specialized in the field, can appreciate the veneration with which dealers, collectors and librarians hail the early books of exploration, of American manners and customs—works that trace the long history from the discovery of a new continent to the building of a young nation.

Most of those books, in whatever language they were written, wherever they were published, are direct and straightforward insofar as their titles convey some notion of their contents. Indeed the words *Nova Insula* or *Nouveau Monde*, if not the golden word *America* itself frequently appear in the title, alerting the reader to the riches that will follow. Those great and obvious books come without disguise, their glories all exposed. Such volumes—desired objectives of prowling scout and prestigious bookseller—are often rare and almost always valuable.

*For a Short Title List of books referred to in this chapter see pages 173–199.

Leona Rostenberg—Rare Books does not join the heated competition for the acquisition of those tempting beauties. The reason for our absence from that race is not that we love such books less but that we love others more. Those we love are more modest, secretive, appearing often in strange guises. The Americana we dote upon are the books that do not bear on obvious title-pages the words *Nova Insula* or *Nouveau Monde* or *America*, but whose texts none the less concern the brave new world.

To come upon anything unexpectedly—gold in a dungheap; a footprint on a desert island—sends a thrill along the spine. To come upon America unexpectedly, in a book that promises to deal with French trade or the beauties of Florence, political theory or the obsequies of a king, generates intense excitement. As we riffle the pages we become discoverers of an America in hiding. It goes without saying that, had we not examined the books we are going to discuss, we would not have found our treasures. Indeed we would have missed not only the American references but the keenest pleasure of the antiquarian bookseller who deals in no ordinary "merchandise" and whose study of his "wares" should never be perfunctory or routine.

We stumbled upon the "hidden" continent in prehistory when we glanced through a seventeenth-century work on antiquities and migrations by the German Waldenfels. His ethnological observations based upon Scripture seemed belabored and dull until we spied an oasis in the desert of Teutonic erudition: Japheth and his "founding" of America, not to mention the West Indies and the Austral Land. Our next unexpected encounter with the continent, chronologically speaking, came with a sixteenth-century romantic novel by the Italian Teluccini who lived at the Court of the Duke of Ferrara. In his spare time, when he was not serving Alfonso II, he produced an effusion in forty-three cantos entitled *Artemidoro*. Its hero happened to be the son of the Emperor of America who flourished in the year 220. *Artemidoro* revealed as much about late Renaissance concepts of the distant new world as about the author's vivid imagination.

The discoverer of that new world, Cristoforo Colombo, has a way of popping up in unexpected places. We have come across dozens of books of the sixteenth to the eighteenth centuries—Italian encyclopedic tomes or regional histories—in which his voyages creep in. In Maffei's encyclopedia devoted to science and medicine, printing and illustrious men, music and geography, a notable passage concerns

Columbus' second voyage. Interiano's detailed history of Genoa from the Middle Ages through the Renaissance gains distinction for its lengthy allusion to the navigator and his expedition to the new world under Spanish patronage. Sixteenth-century histories of Spain, such as Tarapha's, detailed political surveys of its monarch Philip II, such as Mainoldus', find space for the discovery, the new islands of the Atlantic, Spanish sovereignty over Hispaniola and Cuba, Jamaica and Florida.

Even more unexpectedly, readers of Torquato Tasso's *Jerusalem Delivered* will find in Canto XV an interesting reference to Columbus and America. For that reason, the great epic poem which has stirred so many imaginations over the centuries now stirs ours. Why should Columbus have figured at all in a grandiose poem narrating the First Crusade and modeled upon Virgil's *Aeneid?* Completed in 1574, when Tasso was only thirty, it was sent in manuscript to a number of distinguished literary men all of whom saw fit to make a variety of suggestions for emendations and corrections. Time passed; the *Gervsalemme* remained in manuscript on a shelf; the poet's health declined. Eventually, becoming subject to delusions, Torquato Tasso was sent to the madhouse of St. Anna where he remained for several years. Early during this incarceration, part of the *Gervsalemme* was published without his permission and in 1581 the entire poem was published, no remuneration going to the author.

Three hundred eighty-four years later, Leona and I visited a white clapboard house in Jamaica, Long Island, to buy a small library that had been assembled by an Italian interpreter at the turn of the twentieth century. We have told the story of our finds and our ecstacy at some length in *Old & Rare.* We did not mention, however, that among the books that regaled us—some hidden under crumbling issues of the *Daily News*—was a beautiful copy of Tasso's *Jerusalem Delivered* where, in the Fifteenth Canto, the poet had taken occasion to pen a noble prophecy of the future Columbus. We learned, when we studied the epic more closely, of Tasso's deep interest in discovery and of his hope that someday he would write another epic devoted entirely to Cristoforo Colombo. Tasso's Columbiad was never written, but his passion for the great navigator lives on in Canto XV. Having paid our respects to Columbus in the *Jerusalem Delivered*, we moved our copy on, from a village in Queens to a university in the midwest.

Not long after the publication of Tasso's epic poem, in 1583 the first speech was delivered before the Accademia della Crusca by the Florentine playwright Giovanni Maria Cecchi. In the course of his *Lezione,* most of which analyzed a sonnet by Francesco Berni, Cecchi took occasion to discuss "Cristofano Colombo, e sua storia," a "storia" that had apparently fired the imagination of the Italian Renaissance world.

Preparing a bio-bibliographical study of Renaissance Florence, Filippo Valori went so far as to adopt Columbus as a fellow citizen for the sake of including him in his regional survey. Panciroli, publishing his *Rerum Memorabilium Libri Duo,* devoted his book to the lost discoveries of the ancients and the second to modern discoveries unknown to the ancients. The voyages of Columbus, along with the explorations of Vespucci and Magellan, found a place among such *Memorable Things.*

The Columbus "storia" continued to stir the minds of seventeenth-century writers. The Genoese poet Ceba, writing *Rime* to his compatriots, addressed a poem to Columbus. A eulogy of the navigator appears out of the blue in a work on Italian university life by Passerino: the *Schedarivm Liberale.* Search and ye shall find. Columbus, who landed so unexpectedly in a new world, lingers on in many unlikely places.

After weeks of suffering, Philip II of Spain died at the Escorial on September 13, 1598. A funeral oration delivered at his obsequies by Fabrizio Bosso reviews the late monarch's achievements—his preservation of the faith, his war against the infidels. Then, referring to Philip's expansion of his holdings in East and West, the orator takes occasion to mention the way to the new world: "ad Nouum terrarum orbem iter." Indeed, the monarch's own Testament to his son Philip III, a copy of which we had in Dutch translation, advises his heir to hold on to those new western isles which the Spanish discoveries had added to the Spanish empire.

Those discoveries also appear in unexpected books. The Swiss geographer Joachim von Watt wrote an *Epitome* of the three parts of the world, specified in his title as Asia, Africa and Europe. Persistent readers of that thick octavo who survive to page 544 will find in the next twenty pages a discussion of "the largest of the islands," America, and the Spanish voyages there. A Latin tract of 1583 entitled *Commonefactio* refers to the division of the American continent between Spain and Portugal. An incisive study on the nature of government—*De Repvblica*—by Gregoire, law professor at Toulouse, happens to mention the upset of the Spaniards in Hispaniola through the influence of the god Zuni. Though omitted from the title, *Teatro Histórico, Politico, y Militar* by Luis Lamarca, the great Spanish navigator Hernando Cortes is there, his voyage to Cuba, his conquest of Mexico, the capture of Montezuma, the defeat of the Aztecs. The Spanish role in America, from the early discoveries and explorations to the Jesuit missions, has infiltrated any number of books. *Caveat lector!* Between the lines of many an innocent-looking volume, a Spaniard may be hiding. Chances are, he has a tale to tell of the western world.

Watch out for the Dutchman too. Our little pamphlet, the *Brevis Assertio Et Apologia . . . Portugalliae Regis* of the mid-seventeenth century, fulfilled the promise of its title insofar as it discussed the career of John IV of Portugal who expelled the Spanish garrisons and helped promote Portuguese commerce in Brazil. But it did more than that, for it alluded also to the Brazilian struggle with the Dutch, a struggle that resulted in the Netherlands' loss of Brazil in 1654.

Our searches once resulted in the acquisition of a far earlier and more important book about Brazil—a *pièce de résistance* of hidden Americana. Leafing through a foreign dealer's catalogue one frosty winter day, Leona spied the following lengthy Latin title: *Libri Dvo Apologetici ad Refvtandas Naenias, & coarguendos blasphemos errores, detegendaque mendacia Nicolai Durandi qui se Villagagnonem cognominat.* This translates freely and in abridged form as: *Two Books refuting the blasphemous errors and lies of Nicolas Durand who is called Villegagnon.* Its author was one Pierre Richer and its year of publication 1561. On the surface, this seemed to be a not too thrilling Protestant polemic in which the author was likely to indulge in equal amounts of theological hairsplitting and vituperous name-calling. But the seemingly dull title had contained a name that started the sparking in Leona's *Finger-Spitzengefühl.* The name that brought the wild bibliopolic look to her eyes was Villegagnon. As we have mentioned in *Old & Rare*, we had recently attended the great Thomas Streeter auction at the Parke-Bernet Galleries where we had witnessed the sale of a nineteen-page pamphlet about that same Villegagnon for $25,000. Of course that pamphlet, which had been purchased for the Newberry Library, was no hidden Americanum for its title-page boldly announced that it concerned the navigation of the Chevalier de Villegagnon to the lands of America. "Our" Villegagnon, whose lies Monsieur Pierre Richer was exposing, had sailed to Brazil where in

1555 he had tried to establish a French settlement—an ill-fated undertaking that ended in disaster.

The work with the lengthy Latin title was immediately ordered. Would we be successful in obtaining it, or would some other bookseller or librarian on the prowl ferret it out ahead of us? If we did get it, would it contain any reference at all to Villegagnon's exploits in Brazil? Suspense mounted. Eventually, at the unpredictable whims of the postal service, the package arrived. It turned out to be a prize indeed. Richer's polemic was filled with extraordinary details of the explorer's life and character, his behavior in Guanabara or Brazil, even his letter from the New World to Calvin. Climaxing all, the book contained a marvelous illustration depicting Villegagnon in the guise of a monster. The seemingly dull tome on Protestant theology, found on a winter's day in a foreign dealer's catalogue, was transported the next spring to the Newberry Library. It was fitting company for the $25,000 pamphlet from the Streeter collection.

We have mined several American bonanzas in eighteenth-century French books. An interesting account of Guinea on the west coast of Africa by the French voyager Loyer describes the Gold and Ivory Coasts but is preceded by a preliminary account of a voyage to the American islands. An anonymous survey of French agriculture and economics entitled simply *Essai sur Les Moeurs du Temps* launches an attack upon those "American savages" who are unfamiliar with literature, discusses the blacks employed by Europeans in the colonies, and analyzes the motives behind the European struggle for American territory. A French Revolutionary *Discourse* on the project of a national bank takes occasion to mention Franco-American trade in 1789.

Even in minor nineteenth-century books about France there may be hidden American nuggets. Any *Notice* of the Duke of Orleans who ascended the French throne as Louis Philippe in 1830 would be apt to contain American references, for in his salad days the future monarch visited the new world and stayed with Washington. Earlier, in his *Reflections on the Present State of Affairs on the Continent,* the English diplomat Morton Eden, Lord Henley, offered his estimate of Napoleon's rise and conduct. The work becomes an Americanum since the author saw fit to discuss also "the black republic in Hayti . . . the whole system of American and West Indian politics . . . undergoing a rapid change; the increasing power of the United States."

Serendipity lays bare many a hidden reference to the British role in that "increasing power." The seventeenth-century periodical, *Le Mercvre Hollandois*, for example, was edited by a journalist, Pierre Louvet, ostensibly to report events in the Low Countries. A careful or, if you prefer, a serendipitous reading will reveal all sorts of references to the new world, notably the English capture of the Empire City in 1664 which gave the metropolis its name:

Le 8. Septembre les Anglois s'emparerent de la nouvelle Hollande dans l'Amérique sans beaucoup de résistance des Hollandois, & le nommerent la nouvelle Yorck.

During the same century, a volume entitled *The Dutch Vsvrpation,* which surveys Dutch-British relations, alludes on scattered pages to English colonial rule in America and on page 6 recalls that "[Elizabeth] made many naval expeditions into America, and there did much infest the King of Spain, sinking his ships, burning his Towns, battering down his Forts and Castles, interrupting all his Trade and Commerce there."

Commerce with the West Indies; the fishing trade in North America; the export of ships, iron and other stuffs from the colonies into England all pepper the pages of eighteenth-century books whose titles seem never to have heard of America. *Remarks upon the Present Negotiations of Peace . . . between Britain and France; Constitutional Queries, Humbly Addressed to the Admirers of a late Minister;* McKinnon's *Observations on the Wealth and Force of Nations*—each harbors such references, elaborating the British role in the development of colonies and nation. Even in denouncing that role, the French jurist Chas in his *Réflexions sur l'Angleterre* elucidates it.

British books relating to the military occasionally yield surprising American references. Robert Jackson's *Systematic View of the Formation . . . of Armies,* which is primarily a study of the English army during the Napoleonic Wars, deigns to mention the American troops. More concealed is the American reference in that delightful military satire by Francis Grose, *Advice to the Officers of the British Army.* Grose, who was known as an "antiquarian Falstaff," had served as quartermaster with the Hampshire militia where the only account books he kept were his right and left pockets—one for receipts and the other for payments. His experience led him to write his humorous sketch of the British army which satirizes, à la Swift, every rank. His book, the sixth edition of which was published in 1782, a year after Yorktown, is enriched with an engraved folding frontispiece showing a group of officers gazing at their own reflection in a mirror. A map of America hangs on the wall.

A map of America—visible or invisible—played a part in many a European war, and books on those wars may well be finecombed for American allusions. Our *Catalogue of the Damages for which the English Demand Reparation from the United-Netherlands,* published in 1664 after the Dutch-English naval wars, yields a specially fruitful harvest. It refers to the vessels captured on the coast of America—one named the "May Flower," another the "Speedwell." The wars of the eighteenth century in Europe had their American repercussions if not their American counterparts. Books on the War of the Austrian Succession, for example, may well go into such subjects as the Assiento, privateering off Jamaica, Spanish commerce in the West Indies, the British in Canada, the loss of Cape Breton Island to France—spanning a multitude of inter-connecting events in the network of history.

When it comes to the Seven Years War, the hope for American allusions is even stronger, since that war was also fought out on the American continent as the French and Indian War. Our copy of Louis XV's declaration of war against England on June 9, 1756, marking the formal beginnings of the Seven Years War, cites as a causal factor English aggression regarding French possessions in America. Our *Letter Addressed to Two Great Men on the Prospect of Peace* contains the Bishop of Salisbury's comments on terminating that war and makes frequent allusions to English and French holdings in America.

The treaties that ended, or seemed to end, the wars of Europe may overlook the new world in their titles, but not in their articles. The Treaty of Utrecht, which ended the War of the Spanish Succession, and which we had in an Italian version of 1713, specifies the cession of colonies in Hudson's Bay and Nova Scotia, Newfoundland and Acadia to England. The Convention signed by Spain and England at the Prado in 1739 relates to the boundaries of Florida and Carolina. The many signatories of the Peace of Aix-la-Chapelle in 1748 consider not only the affairs of Europe but trade in the new world, the West Indies, and the Ile Royale, a French island off the coast of Newfoundland.

The unexpected surfacing of America in books on European history, its wars, its treaties of peace, engenders excitement in the discoverer for he has perceived a small connection in the interminable course of global struggle and dissension. If the discoverer is a bookseller, he has also, quite possibly, made a find. Even more exciting, to us at any rate, are those unexpected American references we have stumbled upon that relate less to history and politics than to culture and resources—to things and people American. Of these, surely the most American is the American Indian.

In how many strange places the brave has waited in ambush! Who would expect to find in a book of forty-five armorial and ornamental cartouches designed in 1685 by Charles Mavelot, engraver to the French court, a plate depicting two American Indians? Yet there they are—on Plate 31 of our *Nouveau Livre de différens Cartouches*—a reminder of the far-reaching interests of the *Grand Siècle*.

Similarly, in *The Life and Adventures of Mr. Bampfylde-Moore Carew, commonly called The King of the Beggars,* the western savage would seem an unlikely intruder. The "King of the Gypsies," however, was transported to America where, pretending to be a Quaker, he enjoyed the friendship of many Indians. They figure colorfully in Carew's story and heighten the interest of a not uncommon book.

The American Indian has, of course, been the object of many poetic musings. One of the more interesting was our folio volume, *The Prince of Peace, and Other Poems,* published by Edmund Cartwright in London in 1779. Edmund Cartwright was one of those fascinating eighteenth-century English characters who are entitled to a biographical digression. The *Dictionary of National Biography* describes him a bit cagily as "the reputed inventor of the power-loom." In a conversation with the better known inventor Arkwright, he remarked that it should be no more difficult to invent a weaving machine than it had been to create an automatic chess-player. He proved his point by constructing and patenting a power loom and by establishing a factory for weaving and spinning. The versatile Mr. Cartwright wove more than wool; he wove verses too. In 1779, the year he was appointed rector of Goadby Manor in Leicestershire, he wrote a poem suitably entitled for a doctor of divinity, *The Prince of Peace.* Its contents were less suitable for a patriotic Englishman, for they deplored the war with the rebellious American colonies.

We were not yet aware of that interesting fact when, in a small village in the Netherlands where we annually return to buy books, we saw for the first time a copy of Mr. Cartwright's *Prince of Peace* and were immediately attracted by a vignette on the title-page. Despite the serenity of the title, the vignette was anything but serene for it depicted what certainly appeared to be murderous Indian braves attempting to scalp settlers in a wilderness. We bought Mr.

Cartwright's ode. When we returned home we examined it with the usual searching intensity and found to our delight that the verses contained several exciting allusions not only to the American Revolution but to the Indians, among them the following delectable quatrain:

> Lo! Now arous'd to savage war,
> Their horrid rites begin; the chiefs advance:
> Hark! their wild orgies echo from afar!
> Their songs of death, that time the warriour dance!

Throughout *The Prince of Peace* we found extravagant descriptions of the antithesis of peace, and having discovered our hidden Americanum in the Low Countries, we proudly passed it on to that great repository of Americana, the John Carter Brown Library.

As a character in novels the American Indian is perhaps still more ubiquitous than as a theme in poetry. Usually, the title-page signals his presence. In the romance of Louis Sébastien Mercier, *L'Homme Sauvage,* however, the title might refer to any of the savage forms assumed by humanity. In effect it refers to the American Indian Williams who sends to Lord Baltimore a report on Indian life in America. One of the most colorful expressions of that life occurred in our romance *Florello, Histoire Méridionale* by Loaisel de Tréogate, published in Paris in 1776. While the title did not betray the native's presence, the frontispiece did, for it depicted an Indian attacking a white woman. The romance itself was devoted almost in its entirety to American Indians and, as it turned out, it became a precursor to the better-known and more obvious work of Chateaubriand.

The Indians, whether abhorred as despicable murderers or hailed as noble savages, were regarded as wonders of the new world. There were others: marvels of the west glimpsed by adventurers and bruited abroad as sources of wonder, themes of enchantment. The very physical nature of the new world was such a marvel—its rocks and stones, its minerals and caverns, its mines and mountains. And so the geology of the American continent crops up in such books as the sixteenth-century *La Minera Del Mondo* or the eighteenth-century *Principales Merveilles de La Nature.* In 1602 a German savant Keckerman wrote a dissertation on the earthquake that had erupted the year before in Europe and Asia. He amplified his detailed discussion of earth tremors and vibrations with some interesting comments on the submerged islands of the Atlantic, America, Cuba, Jamaica and Peru.

At the end of the seventeenth century, an Italian physician wrote an exhaustive treatise on fire called *Pyrologia Topographica* delving into terrestrial and subterranean fire, lava and sulphurous eruptions, the nature of the earth's core. He found place in his disquisition not only for Mount Etna but for the craters and eruptions in America.

The herbs, balsams and panaceas of America created as much of a stir across the sea as American silver mines. Did not the German knight Ulrich von Hutten write his *Holz Guaiacum* in 1519, assuring the European world that the resin from the trunk of the American guaiacum tree would cure ills from gout to rheumatism, from skin diseases to syphilis? In the same century did not Leonardo Fioravanti, after whom a balsam was named, include in his medical and scientific compendium accounts of the herbs and remedies from Peru, New Spain and the West Indies?

One of Fioravanti's western marvels was tobacco, whose literature forms a library in itself. Tobacco crops up in so many strange places that it could occupy a lengthy chapter of its own. It would hardly seem to belong in Bonardo's *La Minera Del Mondo,* but it is there nonetheless. In America, the author tells us in 1585, the Indians smoke the "herba Negotiana" in the following manner, with the following results:

In America gl'Indiani pigliano il fumo dell' herba Negotiana, e lo pigliano per un corneto di pietra, e oltra che si scaldano, come se stessero dentro a stufe, se ne ritardano le fame, & estingono la sette, rallegrano gli spiriti, e con vn grato sonno s'adormentanno, e sognano i più bei sogni, che si possa dire, & imaginare.*

By the time tobacco became part of the business of export-import, it appeared upon many a seemingly dull tax list such as *The Rates of the Excize of New Impost* of 1649 where, along with silks and spirits, sugar and drugs from the English Plantations, the noxious weed is rated for excise. Perhaps the most surprising references to tobacco were found by us in an unusual book called *Le Carnaval de la Barbarie et Le Temple des Yvrognes,* purportedly published in Fez in 1765. The work consisted of two verse narratives as the title indicated, one on the Carnival of Barbary, the other on the Temple of the Inebriates. But those poems

---

*In America the Indians take the smoke of the herb Negotiana [nicotine] and they take it by means of a small stone pipe and besides getting warmed as if they were in an oven, their hunger is held off, their thirst is quenched, their spirits raised, and they fall into a pleasant sleep and dream the most beautiful dreams that can be imagined.

were followed by a prose narrative on Bacchus that happened to mention the importation of tobacco from the West Indies and the smoking of a Mexican tobacco in Nicaragua—an infernal smoke. Instead of listing the curiosity in a catalogue of French literature, we offered it to the great Arents Collection of Tobacco housed in the New York Public Library, a monument to the weed that came out of the new world.

Other less tangible aspects of American life have fired the European imagination with the result that many provocative allusions to American culture and government are encountered unexpectedly. Does not the *Collection of Several Pieces . . . Never before printed* by John Locke contain that philosopher's comments on "The Fundamental Constitutions of Carolina"? Does not the distinguished eighteenth-century thinker George Berkeley include in his *Miscellany, containing several Tracts on Various Subjects,* "Verses on the Prospect of Planting Arts and Learning in America"? The French philanthropist Piarron de Chamousset projected in his *Vues d'un Citoyen* of 1757 a grandiose utopian scheme for a communal home and social security, care for the aged and child care, insurance aimed at the ultimate abolition of poverty. His fascinating book becomes more fascinating, however, for it also contains a chapter on the colonization of Louisiana by abandoned children. Before the American Revolution, in 1770, the anonymous author of *A Candid Enquiry into the Present Ruined State of the French Monarchy* analyzed the collapse of France, referred to the French and Indian War, and commented upon the political ideology that had been "provoked by the discovery of the new world [which] hath produced so great a revolution in the maxims of state."

The discovery of the new world, the revolution it produced, the way of life it developed—American geography, American taste, American attitudes, American curiosities may be surprised in any number of unlikely texts. Our *Bibliographia Historico-Politico-Philologica Curiosa,* a comprehensive work on historiography by a German historian Boeckler, has a section on Americana. Another seventeenth-century volume with an equally imposing title, *Propositiones Mathematicae ex Geographia de Aestu Maris,* a maritime study, happens to consider the possibility of an isthmus near Mexico joining the Atlantic and Pacific, and mentions not only Chile, Peru and the Philippines, but California. Indeed, a careful examination of the global map that adorns the title-page will reveal the outlines of the future state.

Of no little maritime interest is a less pretentious French pseudo-scientific treatise, *La Corrvption dv Grand et Petit Monde*. Here the author develops the remarkable theory that the Flood caused America's separation from the rest of the world. Thanks to that separation, whatever its cause, Charles II of England, delivering a *Speech to both Houses of Parliament* in 1664, could suggest that fanatics be transported to his colonies overseas.

Though they were scarcely fanatics, many members of the Moravian or United Brethren did transport themselves overseas to America. Accounts of their settlements in Pennsylvania and New Jersey, New York and Rhode Island, Maryland and North Carolina, their work among the Indians, and the practice of their faith in the new country are often tucked away in the pages of books that trace the history of the Unitas Fratrum or Evangelical Brethren.

American gold is deposited in many a literary European mine. The works of the great French Renaissance potter Bernard Palissy, explaining his *Art de Terre,* were republished in 1777. That late edition is of enormous interest because it contains a dedication from the publisher to Benjamin Franklin, a dedication said to have been suppressed before publication and hence found in only a few copies. Another French scientist of a later century, Maupertuis, wrote a treatise on generation entitled *Vénus Physique* occasioned by the appearance in Paris of a white Negro, an albino. Along with his comments on foetal formation and pre-natal influence, the author presents his thoughts on African and American blacks. An eighteenth-century medical *Rapport* on the "Mal Rouge de Cayenne" or elephantiasis, having exhausted the subject of elephantiasis in French Guiana, goes on to discuss leprosy in America.

Sometimes American gold is found not in the text of a book, not in its title, but in its imprint. Books published in Cap Haitien or in St. Christophe are exciting Americana simply because they emerged early on from the primitive presses of a new country. Our *Considérations sur l'Artillerie . . . des Pays-Bas* described the state of the Dutch army and would have been simply another in a long line of military treatises had it not been published in St. Christophe—St. Kitts. The manuscript, written by a Dutch sea captain, had reportedly been found after a hurricane and printed on that Leeward Island.

To us the most exciting Americana imprint belongs to a book which, except for its date, has no imprint at all. John Dod's *Plaine And Familiar Exposition Of The Tenne Commandements* was published, according to the title-page, in 1617. It happened to have been published in Leyden by the Elder William Brewster prior to his departure for the new world. The Pilgrim Press had been set up in secret in that city where the Pilgrims sought refuge before they sailed aboard the "Mayflower." There, under the leadership of the Elder Brewster, twenty titles were issued of which Dod's *Exposition* was the third. This Pilgrim Press—indeed all Pilgrim Press imprints—are part of the American heritage and though they nowhere mention America, they are American incunables.

To the American, all books about America are to be desired. Yet that which is encountered unexpectedly becomes far more desirable. Such an America is treasure indeed, for it makes us all discoverers.

3

Adventures of a Literary Sleuth

[MBS]

If everyman is a potential discoverer then everyman is also a potential detective. Sleuthing ranks high in the Rostenberg Antiquarian Credo and rightly so, for, at its most challenging, all research involves detection. Detection applied not to crime but to books has a special lure. It demands, at the least, two indispensable abilities: the ability to ferret out those "small facts upon which," according to the master detective Sherlock Holmes, "large inferences may depend;" the ability to recognize those "large inferences" for what they are whenever and wherever they are found—perhaps another version of that *Finger-Spitzengefühl* which Leona described so well but spelled so poorly in *Old & Rare*.

Literary sleuthing demands a physical as well as an intellectual movability. While much of the process involved may be armchair deduction, it is not all that comfortable, for the chase and the perils thereof usually precede the stage of sedentary rumination.

"Are they ambulatory?" asked a library director contemplating a tandem-style lecture by the authors of the recently published *Old & Rare*. It was an apt question. Thoreau may have traveled widely in Concord, but the literary sleuth must venture farther afield before settling down with his finds.

We have been, and I am happy to say still are, ambulatory. As dealers on the hunt for books and as writers after those "small facts upon which large inferences may depend" we have thus far survived the perils of the sleuthing chase, further details of which will be inimitably reported by my partner in a subsequent chapter. For now it is sufficient to mention that we have been utterly lost in some Lowland place near Loosdrecht when we should have been flying to Paris. We have been at once enchanted and bewildered as, leafing through seventeenth-century French pamphlets and eighteenth-century *Arrets,* we sat uncomfortably in an impossible cave cut into the Rue Dauphine in Paris' Sixth Arrondissement—its presiding genius no Aladdin but a fellow dealer. We have waited in a Florence railway station for the little train that never came and boarded instead a taxi to journey all the way to Milan. We have been caught in several frustrating strikes, most notably that of Paris in 1968. But even during that great strike when all movement was curtailed, we were ambulatory, fleeing—oh, irony of ironies—from La Belle France to Das Vaterland! Our most recent picaresque peregrination involved a circuitous journey from New York to Atlantic City where we were to deliver a lecture. We started out in a car that had been generously placed at our disposal. We arrived at our destination in the back of a truck from which I had to be lifted by degrees. In between, two other ill-fated vehicles had figured in this hazardous excursion. Needless to say, the subject of the Atlantic City lecture was "Adventures of a Literary Sleuth."

The "ambulatory" state applies to the mind of course as well as to the body. The moving mind sees connections and builds bridges. An observer at a recent book fair described a transaction she had witnessed at our booth. A customer had asked for Florence Nightingale's *Notes on Nursing.* We lacked it but offered instead a remotely related book by Dr. Home on gunshot wounds and their suppuration. The book certainly accounted for much of the nursing of the period. The observer commented, "They were asked for Nightingale and came up with bandades." Well, to be asked for Nightingale and come up with bandades is not such a bad idea if one lacks Nightingale. Certainly it shows an ambulatory mind at work.

All the sleuthing abilities mentioned—the ability to ferret out the small fact, to recognize the large inference, and to perceive connections—were put to use by my partner after a recent purchase.

Indeed, the purchase itself resulted from the combination of active *Finger-Spitzengefühl* and lively mental ambulation.

The chase had taken us to a small town in Holland and we had just completed our hunt through the shelves when Leona spied a small stack of books on the floor. "What's that?" she asked, drawn for some strange reason to one insignificantly bound quarto volume midway in the pile.

"Oh, that's new stock. I haven't had a chance to look through it yet."

"May I see it?" the sleuth persisted. Very quickly she leafed through the volume, said decisively, "If you'll price it we'll have it," glanced at me and walked out.

"I think there may be something there," she murmured, a deduction my own ambulations had already reached.

Just what the "something" was became apparent several months later when Leona spent a frosty, cloud-ridden winter afternoon with the quarto volume. It consisted of some sixteen Latin orations, treatises and dissertations, most of them indifferent speculations upon life, death and the varieties of human experience. But two of the sixteen were different. They had been written in 1598 and 1602 respectively by a Dutch patriot-savant who had traveled to England, admired her Queen and applauded her victory over the Spanish Armada. All this would have been sufficient to justify their purchase. But as she studied the texts of the two orations Leona saw the "small fact" and was able to connect it with the "large inference." Both treatises discoursed at length about a gentleman cited as "ille Draco," quickly identified by the sleuthing bookseller as none other than that great Elizabethan world-traveler, Gloriana's swashbuckling admiral, Sir Francis Drake. Having made copious reference to his exploits, the orations went on to dilate upon Spanish power in the West, the depopulation of the Indian natives, and events in the New World.

The winter afternoon had been fruitful. Just how fruitful became apparent after Leona examined the only "complete" bio-bibliography of Sir Francis Drake. Neither oration was mentioned in it. She had discovered two works containing hitherto unrecognized references to Francis Drake and the world to which he had sailed. She had, glancing at a volume in a stack on the floor, sensed a presence. She had ferreted out a small fact, connected it with a large inference and realized the importance of that inference. She had, in short, ambulated and sleuthed.

In my own double life as bookseller and as writer, those techniques are daily put to work. The furniture of the sleuthing mind includes much seemingly useless information, but once that mind starts ambulating, connecting and inferring, the useless information takes on meaning. Sometimes the researcher, especially in my general field of biography, is after a small fact or a lost letter, a name or a pseudonym; sometimes the quest is for an entire corpus of papers. Sometimes the search is successful; often it leads nowhere. But always the hunt gives life and the chase, whatever its perils, exhilarates.

Many years ago, after the publication of my first biography, Leona and I were vacationing with my proud mother in Colorado Springs. The porch was the pre-prandial rendezvous for the hotel denizens including ourselves, and although the conversation was seldom literary it whiled away the expectant moments before meals. Upon the occasion in question I was sporting, I remember well, what I thought an especially chic pair of slacks and a very snappy sombrero. As I lounged on the porch admiring my own appearance, I overheard the following exchange between a buxom guest and my mother:

Guest: "Is your daughter a rider?"

Mother, with great pride: "Indeed she is a writer."

Guest: "Is she riding in the rodeo?"

In the course of the many years during which I have indeed been writing in my own rodeo, I have had ample occasion to experience the excitements of literary sleuthing.

One particular search was for nothing more momentous than a lover's name. If my detection proved successful it would supply me with material for only a few sentences. But I wanted that name and was ready to dig deep for it.

The book upon which I was working was *Purple Passage: The Life of Mrs. Frank Leslie,* a copy of which would one day be enhanced by Sir Max Beerbohm's caricatures [see Chapter 9]. Now it was in the research stage. The exploits of Mrs. Leslie, a deliciously feminine feminist, a combination nineteenth-century *femme fatale* and high-powered publishing magnate, were difficult to trace. She ran through four husbands during her flamboyant lifetime, not to mention several minor extra-curricular cavaliers. But truth, when it concerned her age and her affairs, was not her forte. Her remarks to interviewers were extravaganzas of inaccuracy, and since mine was to be the first full-length biography of that provocative woman, it would take considerable digging to reach the truth through the layers of fluff.

At the height of her career, when she was married to Frank Leslie, the great newspaper and magazine publisher, a violent excoriation and exposé of her earlier life appeared. It was designed to ruin her utterly. According to that exposé, she had had in her early days an affair with an unidentified Congressman from Tennessee who had bought a house on Seventh Street, New York City, in her name. I was consumed with the desire to identify that Congressman.

In 1857, the year in question, the State of Tennessee had sent eleven Representatives and two Senators to Congress. Which of the thirteen gentlemen had been my heroine's? The only clue was the house that had been purchased in her name. I had, therefore, to examine the conveyances of the Seventh Street property in New York's Hall of Records. The first indenture I examined—that of April 29, 1857—revealed nothing beyond the fact that my then impecunious twenty-year-old subject had paid $9,000 for the ground and dwelling at 37 Seventh Street. The Congressman's name was conspicuous by its absence. I had to look further.

The next indenture was of interest mainly for its date—September 15, 1857—indicating that she had not held the property long in her name. On that day she had sold it to a merchant, one Perez D. Gates, for the purchase price of $9,000. Again no mention of a Congressman from Tennessee. He was still in hiding. Yet I was certain he must have wanted that property eventually in his own name.

I dug deeper and, with the third indenture, struck oil. On December 2, 1857, my shy lover emerged. On that day Mr. Perez D. Gates sold the property to William M. Churchwell of Tennessee. The rest was easy. William M. Churchwell turned out to be not only of Tennessee but the president of a bank and a railroad, an *"hombre interesante,"* and an erstwhile Congressman from Tennessee. My discovery was trifling, providing me with details for but a single paragraph. Still, the Congressman's anonymity had challenged, the sleuthing had excited, and I had beaten Mr. William Churchwell at his own game.

It was the search not for one small fact but for a whole body of information that started me upon quite a different chase. In this particular drama the Prince of Serendip played a leading role.

Some years ago, before the feminists had organized, I decided that the biographies of about a dozen nineteenth-century American women who had been first to enter the various arts and sciences, professions and trades would make a useful and absorbing book. I stipulated three requisites for my "women firsts": priority firmly established; a colorful career; adequate available and preferably heretofore unused source material. My standards were high and difficult to achieve. Naturally I was on a constant lookout for candidates.

Researching one of the chapters, I scoured the pages of a nineteenth-century American weekly devoted to women's emancipation titled *The Revolution.* When I turned to the issue of January 5, 1871, my heart stopped beating though my mind fortunately remained ambulatory. There I read the heading: "A LADY OCULIST—MRS. BELLA C BARROWS." The article beneath titillated. Mrs. Barrows, I learned, had "heroically struck out a new path for her sex . . . in thoroughly fitting herself for the profession of an oculist." Born in Vermont, she had married a missionary and spent some time with him in India. After her husband's untimely death there, she had returned to America and begun her medical studies. Then she remarried. Her new husband who had the unlikely name of June Barrows had served as Seward's private secretary. At the time of her second husband's illness, Mrs. Barrows had taken his place, thus becoming the first woman to work in the United States Department of State. Subsequently she had gone to Vienna to continue her medical studies and, having returned to this country, was prepared, in 1871, to hang out her shingle as the first American woman ophthalmologist.

Here was a subject after my heart and according to my need. Priority should not be difficult to establish; the colorful nature of her double career was already apparent; I needed only adequate original source material. I pursued Mrs. Barrows through a variety of biographical dictionaries and contemporary memoirs, city directories and local newspapers—to little avail. My findings were time-consuming but meager. Then, instead of ambulating, my mind did a hop-skip-and-jump. Mrs. Barrows had come from Vermont and her husband's name was June Barrows. Had I not, several years before, in connection with some other literary sleuthing, corresponded with a man named June Barrows Mussey who lived in Vermont? The recurrence of name and place must be more than coincidental.

By now, I learned, Mr. June Barrows Mussey had moved to Germany. With the variety of cardiac palpitation associated with detection I sent him an airmail letter asking if he had ever heard of Bella or Isabel Barrows. His reply arrived on the wings of the Prince of Serendip. To substitute another cliché, my shot had landed on target. He had indeed heard of Isabel Barrows. In fact, she was his grandmother. Moreover, Mrs. Barrows had written an unpublished autobiography. Would I care to see it?

Within ten days that charming autobiography, *Chopped Straw or The Memories of Threescore Years,* was on my desk. I was engrossed, enthralled by the story of Isabel Barrows, America's first woman stenographer for Congressional Committees and first woman ophthalmologist, a great human being who had begun life on a Vermont farm and ended it with a single-handed effort to free a prisoner in Czarist Russia. Mrs. Barrows—and her grandson—had provided me with source material for a chapter in my *We the Women* and for a full-length biography for teen-agers.

When the Prince of Serendip joins forces with Mr. Sherlock Holmes the combination is unbeatable. In the case I am about to relate—"The Adventure of the Body of Letters" it might be called—the reward consisted not of a single fact or even a single unpublished memoir, but an entire corpus of previously unused correspondence.

The case began, as it usually does, with a book. Leona Rostenberg—Rare Books had acquired the English translation of a history of the Russian Revolution of 1762 by Claude Rulhière. This informative little study would have been simply another bread-and-butter book in late edition of 1798 except that it had been published not in London but in Boston by one Joseph Nancrede, who announced at the end of the volume that he was offering "new works and scarce tracts, many of which were never seen before in America." The chase was on, not for Monsieur Rulhière and not for Peter III of Russia, but for Joseph Nancrede of Boston.

The chase led first to the *Dictionary of American Biography* which contained some intriguing information about Mr. Nancrede's life, but by no means all. Born in France, Nancrede had served in the Army of Rochambeau at Yorktown. He became so enamored of this country that he set up in Boston as bookseller-publisher, introducing much of French thought to America. The latter part of Nancrede's life, however, was practically unknown. The account in the *Dictionary of American Biography* whetted but did not satisfy the appetite.

My appetite is sometimes insatiable. Since Nancrede did not die until 1841, age 80, the latter part of his life stretched in my imagination like a vast unexplored continent. After a decade of remarkable productivity, how had he passed the remainder of his long life? What precisely had he done after 1804 when he auctioned off his stock in Boston and returned to Paris? Where were all the letters he must have received during a more or less literary career?

Toward the end of his life in Paris, I learned, Nancrede had befriended a young French-Canadian exile, Louis-Joseph Papineau, regarded by many as a radical agitator. And in Paris, in the cold winter of 1841, Nancrede had died. Since the end often explains the beginning, I began at Nancrede's end and, in the hope of tracing his activities during the "Great Hiatus" between his departure from America and his death, sought out his Last Will and Testament. This terminal document frequently supplies clues to what has preceded as well as to what has followed a death. With the inestimable help of Mme. Nicole Felkay, Conservateur d'Archives de Paris, Nancrede's final intentions were discovered among the Déclarations des Mutations par Décès. There my Franco-American bookseller-publisher had disposed of his possessions—his money, his investments, his property—the accumulations of a long lifetime. But for the literary sleuth one bequest transcended in interest all the others, that by which Joseph Nancrede left to his French-Canadian friend Louis-Joseph Papineau his books and papers. These were surely the testimonials to his intellectual life and to his lasting achievements. And with this direct clue to follow, I must find them.

The mind must now ambulate to Papineau and his activities. Three years after Nancrede's death, Papineau, writing to his wife, had mentioned the Nancrede "brochures" which he was having bound and the "archives" which he was having copied. Subsequently, after his exile had ended, Papineau returned to Canada. Had he carried with him the papers entrusted to him by his old friend Joseph Nancrede?

The literary sleuth must now be metamorphosed into persistent nuisance. The question was posed to almost every sizable Canadian library: Had the papers of Joseph Nancrede, 1761–1841, been placed on deposit by Louis-Joseph Papineau or his descendants? At about the fifteenth try the hunter found the quarry. Papineau proved a faithful legatee. The bulk of Nancrede's correspondence was now part of the Papineau Papers housed in the Public Archives of Canada. It included letters from Lafayette and John Jay, Louis Philippe and Joseph Bonaparte, Joel Barlow and William Cobbett, Timothy Pickering, William J. Duane, Moreau de Saint-Méry—a host of big and smaller wigs who played a part in Joseph Nancrede's eventful life. Thanks to this legacy and the sleuthing that had traced it, that life could now be illumined.

Literary sleuthing sometimes results in discoveries that are as strange if not stranger than fiction. My research in phrenology, for example—that curious "science" of the mind that took the place of psychoanalysis for nineteenth-century America—netted several eyebrow-raising finds. One of them was the discovery that Mark Twain, who scoffed so contemptuously at "bumpology," remained, if not to pray, at least to sit upon three different occasions for an examination of his head! The third analysis, made in March 1901, had been published the following month but the record had gone unnoticed by Twain's many biographers and critics. Yet this neglected phrenological portrait afforded an interesting insight into Twain's character and the literary sleuth was happy to rescue it from . oblivion.

In the same way the sleuth rescues all but chimerical books from oblivion. I think now of that "queer old book" picked up at a stall by Sherlock Holmes—the *De Jure inter Gentes*—published, as he said, in Latin at Liège in the Lowlands in 1642. A queer old book indeed. This was actually one of the most extraordinary volumes in the Holmes treasure room, as I was able to establish when I reconstructed the great detective's library.

Published anonymously, it had been authored by the English civilian Richard Zouche. Prior to Holmes' find, the first edition was universally thought to have been printed at Oxford in 1650 under a variant title of vast influence since it suggested to Bentham the felicitous phrase "international law." And here, in an aside uttered in the course of *A Study in Scarlet,* Holmes had disclosed the existence of a heretofore unknown pre-first edition! It was almost as if he had been in league with Thomas James Wise! My own trifling contribution was the full identification of this work which Holmes had found among the stalls of Ludgate Hill and dismissed so casually though it was a treasure fit to stand beside the first edition of Grotius.

Even the lustre of this pre-first edition of Zouche fades when compared with the great *Praise of Folly* whose history Leona traced so meticulously in Chapter One. Both books reflect the skills and the results of literary detection and both tend to prove that for the literary sleuth much may be improbable but nothing is impossible.

Nowhere in that writing rodeo of mine has this been more pointedly borne out than in my researches into the life and writings of America's best loved author of juveniles, Louisa May Alcott. As a result of Louisa's own sense of propriety and her inclination to gloss bravely and brightly over the harsher facts of life, her history is punctuated with metaphorical question marks and dots for omission. So too are the bowdlerized journals edited by Ednah Cheney and strewn with unelaborated references and unidentified initials. A biographer of the wholesome spinner of wholesome tales known as the Children's Friend must ambulate carefully between the Scylla of ignorance and the Charybdis of doubt.

One episode in Louisa Alcott's early life lasted only seven weeks but it had been a devastating experience and to be reconstructed accurately it required documentation. This was the period of extreme Alcott poverty in the mid-nineteenth century when the nineteen-year-old daughter had gone "out to service" in Dedham, Massachusetts, and been paid $4 for her seven weeks of drudgery. The drudgery had included digging paths through the snow and fetching water from the well, splitting the kindling and sifting the ashes, polishing the master's muddy boots with the blacking hose and playing audience to his maudlin attentions. The name of that employer had never been disclosed. I felt I must identify him.

Repeated efforts to extract the name from local historians were either unanswered or received with professions of helpless ignorance. It was only after my biography had appeared in print that a Dedham reader stepped forth and freely offered the information I had sought so persistently and so futilely. Local sources, withheld by embarrassed descendants from a prying biographer, were common knowledge to him, and thanks to his intervention I learned that the Honorable—*sic*—James Richardson, respected citizen, orator and lawyer of Dedham, Massachusetts had been the villain of Louisa Alcott's salad days.

There were other well kept secrets in her career. One that especially intrigued both Leona and myself was the secret of her clandestine literary life. Louisa Alcott's journals, a few of her letters, and *Little Women* itself were peppered with clues to the " 'thrilling' tales" she had written to "keep the family cosey." In 1862 she had confided to a young friend that she intended to

illuminate the Ledger with a blood & thunder tale as they are easy to 'compoze' & are better paid than moral & elaborate works of Shakespeare so dont be shocked if I send you a paper containing a picture of Indians, pirates, wolves, bears & distressed damsels in a grand tableau over a title like this 'The Maniac Bride' or The Bath of Blood A Thrilling Tale of Passion.

Jo March of *Little Women* had begun

to feel herself a power in the house, for by the magic of a pen, her 'rubbish' turned into comforts for them all. *The Duke's Daughter* paid the butcher's bill, *A Phantom Hand* put down a new carpet, and the *Curse of the Coventrys* proved the blessing of the Marches in the way of groceries and gowns.

If Jo March had plunged into "the frothy sea of sensational literature," surely her progenitor had done so also.

But what were the titles of her *Maniac Bride* or *Bath of Blood,* her *Duke's Daughter* or *Phantom Hand?* Where had they been published? Under what name had their authorship been concealed? The stories, if they existed, had apparently been written during the 1860's. It was in the 1940's that Leona and I asked ourselves those questions.

Then, spurred by a conversation with that delightful collector of Alcottiana, Carroll A. Wilson, which has been described in *Old & Rare,* we ambulated to the Houghton Library. We were both on the prowl—I for small facts and large inferences, Leona for a pseudonym and a lurid literary life. Seated at a desk side by side, we delved through piles of manuscript and mountains of family letters, reading, copying, searching, checking, comparing, connecting. Suddenly, in those austere and silent purlieus, Detective Rostenberg emitted a warwhoop—a barbaric yawp. She had come upon five brief letters from a Boston publisher to Louisa Alcott, letters that disclosed the pseudonym, the titles of three of the thrillers, and the name of the periodical that had issued them. She had plumbed the depths of Jo March's frothy sea of sensational literature. She had penetrated the secret of *The Maniac Bride* and *The Bath of Blood.* She had removed the mask from the Children's Friend.

All five letters had been written in 1865 and 1866 by a publisher who assured the Louisa Alcott of pre-*Little Women* days: "You may send me anything in either the sketch or Novelette line that you do not wish to 'father', or that you wish A. M. Barnard, or any other man' to be responsible for, & if they suit me I will purchase them." Specifically he referred to three gaudy titles: "V. V.," "The Marble Woman," and, most appropriate of all, "Behind a Mask." The periodical in which they had appeared was apparent from the letterhead where *The Flag of Our Union* waved.

Leona had made the discovery. Now she must sleuth to fill in the bibliographical details. At that time, during the early 1940's, the best file of *The Flag of Our Union* was in the Library of Congress. To wartime Washington, therefore, she repaired, having paved the way with the necessary correspondence and been carefully apprised of the library's hours, rules and regulations. The moment arrived. She presented her call slip for the appropriate volumes of *The Flag of Our Union*. With those familiar and all but unbearable anticipatory palpitations she awaited their arrival, only to be informed that the periodical had been placed in safe keeping for the duration of the war.

Despite this frustration, Leona was able to piece the installments together from scattered issues in other libraries, and in 1943 she announced her extraordinary discovery in an article entitled "Some Anonymous and Pseudonymous Thrillers of Louisa M. Alcott" published in *The Papers of the Bibliographical Society of America*. The revelation made a bit of a splash among scholars. Carroll Wilson wrote a charming note of appreciation. Librarians finding the Ten Cent Novelette, *V. V.,* by "A. M. Barnard" bound in durable cloth with "Pamphlets Various" promptly disbound it and deposited it in their rare book rooms under the name of Louisa May Alcott. Booksellers sent forth their scouts with instructions to search and seize. Biographers, bibliographers and publishing historians duly took note of the fact, now clearly proven, that Louisa May Alcott had indeed written sensation stories anonymously and pseudonymously. The sleuthing had been neat and productive. Eventually it would result in the publication of two additional volumes of Alcott stories: *Behind a Mask* and *Plots and Counterplots,* in whose flamboyant pages are presented nine suspenseful tales of manipulating heroines and feminist anger, mind control and madness, hashish experimentation and opium addiction—all by the Children's Friend.

Thanks to Leona's sleuthing at the Houghton Library, the hitherto unsuspected complexities of a literary life had been revealed and, as a recent review put it:

recognition was given to one of the most interesting facts in American literature . . . that [the] authoress of the preeminently gentle and respectable "Little Women" had also been the impassioned writer of a series of secret blood-and-thunder shockers appearing in the sensational magazines of Midvictoriantide.

Not all the Alcott researches have been so fruitful. Not all the adventures of the literary sleuth end successfully with the netting of a long-sought fact, the identification of a pseudonym, or the harvest of a cache of letters. In research and detection nothing is elementary, and neither blind faith nor unsubstantiated hope merits a place in the intellectual or emotional equipment of the sleuth.

My Alcott hopes ran high when, after months of dickering, I was finally able to track down and set up an appointment with a woman who promised to be an outstanding source of information. She had gone to school with Louisa Alcott's artist sister May and hence was as close an extant connection to the "Little Women" as I could hope to find. She was staying at the Colonial Inn in Concord, Massachusetts, whose porch alarmingly resembled the one in Colorado Springs where my literary inclinations had been confused with equestrian prowess. At all events, there she was—seated on a porch rocker, a shriveled, white-haired woman with snapping blue eyes—my eye-witness to the life of the Alcotts, my living link with the past.

As it turned out, she was more than a mere source; she was a fountainhead, gushing forth reminiscences to which my eager pen could scarcely keep pace. The memories and revelations flowed from her for hours—a torrent of spring. Then, when her voice died down and her marvelous recollections had been safely trapped in my voluminous notes, I rose to thank her. Smiling archly, with just the faintest hint of slyness, she murmured, "Oh, I could go on telling you stories—I do enjoy talking so much—but none of them would be true you know. I really don't remember anything any more." And she chuckled softly.

May Alcott's schoolmate, like Louisa Alcott's elusive teakettle, the story of which was told in *Old & Rare,* forms a caveat to the literary sleuth. To authenticate a reminiscence, to ferret out small facts and make large inferences, to see connections, to ambulate mentally—these are the tasks of detectives who work with books. The wider their frame of reference and the keener their skills, the more productive their detection. They need two guardians as well: a firm and unwavering scepticism at their right hand and the Prince of Serendip at their left. Then their adventures will be all but limitless, for the books that possess them are the record of life itself.

4

Feminism is Collectible*

[MBS]

Sleuthing had uncovered the fact that Louisa May Alcott, America's best-loved writer of juveniles, had written in secret sensational stories with a strong feminist slant. In many of the books by and about women that we had bought, catalogued and sold, we had found a similar, previously unrecognized slant. In fact, it appeared to us that if behind every man there is a woman, behind every woman there is a feminist. Certainly the feminist movement that gathered such momentum during the 1960's had its roots deep in the past. It seemed essential to point this out both to militant feminists and to avid collectors.

The result of that conviction was "Feminism Is Collectible," a talk that proved so popular that I was subsequently invited to several libraries and institutions to give variant versions of my feminist discourse. Here follows the sixth and most complete variation on that provocative theme. I sincerely hope it will attract as many readers as earlier versions attracted listeners; I hope that it will broaden the scope of feminists, and expand the libraries of collectors.

*For a Short Title List of books referred to in this chapter see pages 173–199.

Feminism, like every other "ism," is collectible, for its long history has been recorded in groves of books and pamphlets, newspapers and periodicals, broadsides, letters—and probably papyri. Feminist literature did not emerge fullblown in 1978 or in 1878. Feminist doctrine of today stems from feminist doctrine of yesterday and the day before yesterday. The current sexual revolution could not have been launched had not earlier sexual revolutions been fought on bloody or bloodless battlefields. Without the bridges that span yesterday and today there could be no marchers.

Those bridges are books: books by women; books about women; and finally militant feminist literature. Not merely during the last decade but during the last five centuries such books have been written—all of them in one way or another, obliquely or overtly, attesting to the great age of the so-called "new" Eve. Indeed, women's lib probably began with Adam's rib and the "new" Eve is as old as time.

There is an enormous corpus of books by bluestockings and novelists, poets and dramatists, travelers and scientists, educators and philosophers who happened to be women. Gathered together they form an army of feminists whose militancy is muffled but can still be heard. A shelf of books by early bluestockings throws light upon the problems and ambitions of early women. The very first composition by a woman ever printed belongs on that shelf: the *Centones* of Falconia Proba, a fourth-century bluestocking who rearranged the lines of Virgil's *Aeneid* so that they would narrate the stories of the Bible. This strange tour de force may not have much overt bearing upon feminism but it certainly elucidates the workings of a fourth-century erudite female mind. And since it was the first work by a woman to achieve print, it deserves a place in a feminist library. Our copy of the 1513 edition of that unusual effort was most interesting. It had belonged to the German printer-scientist Jacob Koebel, who appended to it a fourteen-page manuscript on Falconia's life and work. A year or so later, Koebel printed an edition of the *Centones* with his own preface, and so an early male champion of women joined forces with the earliest woman on a publishing list some four hundred sixty years ago.

The Renaissance was a fruitful time for learned women especially in the Italian city-states. Their writings belong in the bluestocking division of the feminist library for, while there is no militancy here, there are persistent reminders of the stature and strength of the "weaker" sex. Cassandra Fedele, a Venetian prodigy born in 1465, became famous for her extraordinary learning, corresponded with notable contemporaries from Louis XII of France to the Queen of Hungary, and delivered orations on the liberal arts. A collection of her *Letters and Orations* restores to our distant eyes the Rialto of Venice as it was viewed once by an intellectual woman. Cassandra's contemporaries epitomize as she does the flowering of the Italian Renaissance and woman's place in it: Olympia Morata; Vittoria Colonna whose verses won the praise of an unchauvinistic Michelangelo; Isabella Sforza whose thoughts on the attainment of peace of mind were published by the great House of Aldus Manutius in 1544.

If sixteenth-century Italy yielded a tribe of bluestockings, seventeenth- and eighteenth-century France germinated a host of women novelists of the parlor, the kitchen and the bedroom schools. The stories they wove on rich and colorful canvases belong in a feminist library because, properly read, they offer insights however indirect into women's trials and tribulations and women's methods of escape. In the stories of gallantry and sentiment, the fairy tales and imaginary voyages, the allegorical romances and the romantic allegories spawned by the Mss. Aulnoy and Conti, Durand and Fontaines, Molière and Scudéry, Villedieu and La Fayette (author of the *Princesse de Clèves*), we can still find the feminist reactions and responses of earlier centuries. As for nineteenth-century England, an entire library of women authors could be assembled, most of them so obvious that they have won stars in undergraduate reading lists. The less obvious are sometimes more interesting. One thinks of Mary Anne Clarke, great-grandmother of Daphne Du Maurier and mistress of the Duke of York. She exploded a nineteenth-century variety of feminist anger in her autobiographical novel *The Rival Princes* in which she exposed the secret intrigues of fashionable English society. Has any one here in America thought of studying the first Beadle Dime Novel from the feminist viewpoint? *Malaeska: the Indian Wife of The White Hunter* was written not by a trailer in buckskin or a scout of the Great Plains but by a New England woman fifty years old named Ann Stephens. Her tale of an Indian princess married to a white hunter is not only a collector's item but, like more factual narratives of Indian captivity, a valuable sourcebook in feminist problems.

The oblique is usually more exciting than the direct. Leona's discovery of the pseudonymous thrillers written by Louisa May Alcott before and during the composition of *Little Women* has been related as one of the "Adventures of a Literary Sleuth." An analysis of those blood-and-thunders discloses a feminist anger quite unexpected in the author of wholesome juveniles and indicates that there are connections everywhere, even between Louisa May Alcott and Betty Friedan. Louisa's stories of revenge and mind control, madness and drug addiction are recommended for a feminist library either in the excessively scarce original paperback or serial versions or in the recent reprints.

On a shelf close by the women novelists the women poets should be placed. Since the obvious ones are known to all readers of this chapter, I mention only a few of the less obvious who have intrigued us. From the Isles of Greece I choose not Sappho but rather Corinna who, it is said, instructed Pindar; or Telesilla of Argos who led a band in the war with Sparta. From France I nominate another woman warrior, another case of "arms and the woman." Like Telesilla of Argos, Louise Labé, known as *La Belle Cordière* of Lyons, fought at the siege of Perpignan, formed a fine library, and gathered the erudite society of Lyons around her. She also wrote poetry that included a debate between folly and love, with both of which she was apparently familiar. My representative from Italy is the sixteenth-century Neapolitan Laura Terracina who produced forty-six cantos all devoted to a criticism of Ariosto's *Orlando Furioso.* As for England, the mind boggles at the number of minor women poets. My own suggestions might be Hannah Cowley, known variously as "Anna Matilda" or "The Tenth Muse," and Katherine Philips, known as "The Matchless Orinda." Here in America, I select one poet only— no, not Anne Bradstreet—but Phillis Wheatley. Phillis was not only a woman but a black, sold at auction in Boston in 1761 at the age of seven. Purchased by John Wheatley, she was educated in her master's home and wrote verses of such talent that they won the admiration of the local intellectuals. In 1772 she made a trip to England where she was enthusiastically received by the Countess of Huntington to whom she dedicated her *Poems on Various Subjects.* The first collected edition of her verses appeared in 1773 with testimonials to their authenticity by the Governor of Massachusetts and others. In 1801 her poems were republished as an appendix to a most interesting book entitled *The Negro Equalled by Few Europeans,* the major part of which is devoted to a novel about the blacks. Today Phillis' book has taken her place on the auction block.

Women dramatists, though fewer in number than women novelists and women poets, make a lively section in a feminist library. Isabella Andreini, "the first actress of Europe," was also a student of literature, poetry and philosophy as well as a dramatist. She began her pastoral play, *La Mirtilla,* as a child, and though it borrows perhaps from Tasso it looks forward to Molière. Our 1594 edition belongs on the feminist shelf. In 1701 a play entitled *The Czar of Muscovy* appeared between boards, the work of one Mary Pix who shaped a tragedy out of the career of an impostor czar. Later in the century Lady Elizabeth Craven, an emancipated and colorful Englishwoman known for the "daring" of her private life, wrote words and music for several plays, one of which was printed at Walpole's famous Strawberry-Hill Press. In between those two barnstormers and before and after them, the long line of women dramatists—from Aphra Behn to Fanny Kemble and on to Lillian Hellman—could take the spotlight in a library of books by women. Here too belongs, although it is not a play, the *Effusions of Fancy* by Elizabeth Wright Macauley whose life was nicely balanced between acting in London and preaching in the provinces. Sarah Bernhardt did no preaching, but offstage she did collect books and the catalogue of her *Bibliothèque,* sold in Paris in 1923, must be added to the theatrical division of collectible feminism.

There are in fact so many media in which women have written and so many subjects that have engaged their attention that the possibilities for collecting seem unlimited. Women sports-writers? Start, if you can afford to, with Lady Juliana Berners whose *Boke of Saint Albans* on hunting and hawking is one of the most sought-after incunables. Women letter-writers? Though they wrote under the names of De Stael and Sévigné, Pompadour, Récamier and Maintenon, their name is really legion. Women travelers may never have been hired by Baedeker or Michelin but they recorded journeys that were global. Here in America after only a *Summer on the Lakes,* Margaret Fuller wrote her first book with its poignant comments upon pioneers and settlers, women and Indians. After a posh journey to California, Mrs. Frank Leslie recounted her *Pleasure Trip from Gotham to the Golden Gate.* The reformer Eliza Farnham wrote of both the midwest and the far west from personal experience. American women who do not disdain to sleep on a table with a bag of salt for a pillow make intrepid travelers and their travelogues reveal as much of themselves as of the countries they visit.

Women scientists have left their written records: we think of the first woman botanist of North America, Jane Colden. Did not the Marquise de La Vieuville de Saint-Chamond write an éloge of Descartes in which she analyzed his scientific and philosophical system? Jane Squire, whose *Proposal to Determine our Longitude* (1743) was a pioneer work on the subject, was probably the only woman who ever wrote on longitude. Women educators have transcribed their projects and experiences: Sarah Trimmer, an advocate of industrial education who wrote *The Oeconomy of Charity;* Mrs. Dawbarn who in 1805 published a book on early progressive education which she called *The Rights of Infants.* Women philosophers have reported their provocative thoughts: Madame Necker on divorce; her daughter Madame De Stael on suicide. Women have published their views on government. The *Instructions* of Empress Catharine II with its liberal provisions for Russian laws was characterized by Voltaire as the finest monument of the century. A less exalted woman, Rachel Fanny Antonina Lee, who had been the heroine in a criminal trial and the subject of a chapter in De Quincey's *Auto-biographic Sketches,* wrote *An Essay on Government* in 1808 which won an accolade from Wordsworth.

Eve writing is a many-faceted woman. If her name was Margaret Fell she gave us in the seventeenth century *An evident Demonstration to Gods Elect* and *Women's Speaking Justified,* the first defense of women ministers in England. If her name was Hester Chapone she gave us *Letters on the Improvement of the Mind, addressed to a Young Lady,* a work placed by many "next to the Bible." If she was Mary Hopkins Pilkington—the cult of the middle name had begun by 1799—she produced *A Mirror for the Female Sex* for use in "ladies' schools." If she was Julia Evelina Smith she gave to the world the first English translation of the entire Bible by a single individual. The labor of many years, this was published in the Centennial year of 1876 to prove woman's capabilities.

Patricia Ballou, a Barnard librarian, recently introduced me to the extraordinary Miss Smith. One of five sisters from Glastonbury, Connecticut, Julia Evelina grew up less in the odor of sanctity than in the aura of erudition, and her study of the Bible was an intellectual rather than a spiritual undertaking. By 1847, when Miss Smith was fifty-five, she launched into the monumental labors of translating the Old and New Testaments into English and by the time she had finished she had translated it five times: once from Latin, twice from

Greek, and twice from Hebrew. The Hebrew had been self-taught. Although her version had been completed within seven or eight years, it remained in manuscript in several boxes until the Centennial year of 1876. When it was finally published, one or two wits referred to it as the "Alderney" Edition of the Holy Bible. For this there was good reason.

During the late 1860's and early 1870's, the two surviving Glastonbury maids had entered the feminist arena, with their Alderney cows. Assessed for what they considered a disproportionate share of taxes, since, as women, they had no representation in Glastonbury government, the Smith sisters refused payment. The town fathers, in retaliation, marched seven of their fine Alderneys to the Glastonbury signpost and auctioned them off to cover delinquent taxes. As one commentator put it, "Though Miss Julia, the older of the two sisters, is the one who raised the cows, Miss Abby is the one who raised the breeze." The breeze was raised in several directions, by lawsuit and by platform speeches. As far afield as Chicago, souvenirs appeared on the market made from the hair of the Glastonbury cows, and when Julia Smith's Bible was published, the critics produced a curious blend of "cows and Biblical lore, dairy products and Greek and Hebrew."

During the Centennial year, Julia Evelina Smith published her remarkable work at her own expense through the American Publishing Company of Hartford, a firm whose major claim to fame is Mark Twain's association with it as a director and as author. The book, sold by subscription, was in all likelihood set into type by women compositors and sold by women canvassers. In May 1876, 1000 copies of Miss Smith's Bible emerged from the binderies, proof of what one woman could accomplish. If the sisters had raised a breeze with their cows, Julia Evelina raised a whirlwind with her Bible. In 1879, in her deep eighties, she married an octogenarian admirer of her work, and she lived on until 1886, "the only woman in the world's history to translate the entire Bible into any language." The life story of Julia Evelina Smith and her Bible naturally intrigued us and we were delighted to be able to supply the Library of Congress with a copy and at the same time to contribute to its *Quarterly Journal* an article entitled "The First Feminist Bible: The 'Alderney' Edition, 1876."

Women editors have produced newspapers and magazines, enough to form an entire library of feminist periodicals. It might include *The Anglo Saxon Review* edited by Lady Randolph Churchill and cased in a sumptuous replica of a Stuart binding. It should include *The Lowell Offering,* a magazine written entirely by women employed in the mills of Lowell, Massachusetts. It must include *The Dial,* edited by Margaret Fuller, a periodical that became the medium for the freest expression of thought. Frances Wright's *Free Enquirer* would join *The Dial* on those shelves, a magazine that advocated the equal distribution of wealth and liberal divorce laws. Later in the nineteenth century there was Susan B. Anthony's *The Revolution* and there was *Woodhull & Claflin's Weekly,* the turbulent medium of two turbulent feminists. As a sample of the women's periodical press in the early twentieth century, *The Forerunner* should be added, edited by that "militant Madonna" Charlotte Perkins Gilman.

Some may judge from this miscellaneous array of works written by women that "scribbling females" have been the major paper consumers of the world. Others, who have not merely scanned these title-pages but read these books, must conclude that from earliest times women of stature have been on hand, observing and watching, waiting and recording. Their works are fruitful of analysis. Tangential as they are to the new feminism, they have led us to today and to tomorrow.

Though not all women of stature wrote books themselves, they were frequently the source of books by others. Along with many of the women authors mentioned, other women of achievement appear in biographical anthologies compiled by early male champions of women. Boccaccio's *De Claris Mulieribus,* for example, a fifteenth-century *Who's Who* of distinguished women, was in a way the Italian forerunner and counterpart of the three-volume *Notable American Women* recently prepared under the auspices of Radcliffe College. Boccaccio's compatriots, Lodovico Domenichi, Giulio Cesare Capaccio, and Marcello Alberti followed in his footsteps, assembling for future reference the lives and accomplishments of exceptional women, arranging them sometimes alphabetically, sometimes geographically. During the seventeenth century a French poet, Pierre Le Moyne, published a *Galérie des Femmes Fortes,* a book that not only immortalized the great women of the past but raised interesting questions relating to their capabilities in government, philosophy and military life. The Germans have taken with alacrity to compiling biographical dictionaries of women. In 1707 Weppling settled for some thirty learned women from Hroswitha of Gandersheim to

Madeleine de Scudéry. Only a few years earlier, his fellow scholar Juncker included women in his learned *Schediasma Historicum,* but relegated them to an Appendix. Not so George Ballard who produced his comprehensive *Memoirs of Several Ladies of Great Britain, Who Have Been Celebrated for Their Writings or Skill in the Learned Languages Arts and Sciences.*

Other anthologists have been more selective. One Wilhelmus Nagge in 1622 stressed women of the philosophic sects, Socratic or Peripatetic, Stoic or Pythagorean, and in the same century the distinguished French critic Gilles Ménage assembled a bevy of women philosophers in his *Historia Mulierum Philosopharum.* Along with his women Platonists and Epicureans, however, he felt obliged to round out the book by including women relatives of celebrated male philosophers!

Military, if not militant women have provided fascinating subjects for a dictionary of pen portraits. My favorite happens to be *Joan-ereidos: Or, Feminine Valour; Eminently discovered in Western Women, At the Siege of Lyme,* a seventeenth-century work in which James Strong extolled the women warriors of England during the civil wars.

Most of the biographical compilations about women written by their male champions, however, are more ornamental than useful. They may be classified as "Books of Fair Ladies" in which legendary women, Biblical heroines and queens of history are featured. The beauty of woman's body and soul is usually documented with classical and Scriptural references and women are damned by praises not too faint but too generalized. From Agrippa to Tasso, from Agnelli to Dolce, the authors of these works on the nobility and excellence of women uphold woman as symbol rather than women as human beings of achievement. Their books belong in a feminist library none the less, for they mirror the attitude toward women of the approving but complacent male.

Far more interesting are the books written by men about specific women. Fighting women and praying women, learned women and thinking women, adventurers, courtesans, actresses and *femmes fa-tales*—all have sat for frontispiece portraits that introduce books heady to read and fascinating to collect. While Blanche of Castile provided a dignified study in diplomatic skill to the French historian Combault, the Duchess of Marlborough intrigued her Boswell with skills of a different sort. Women powers behind thrones have enthralled biographers through the centuries. So too have women whose adventures created *causes célèbres:* the Marquise de Fresne, whose husband sold her to a corsair; Anne Marie de Moras, a French financier's daughter who was kidnapped by a count; and one of the most famous of kidnapped women, Elizabeth Canning, whose strange case involved the bigwigs of eighteenth-century England and who is described by the non-feminist oriented *Dictionary of National Biography* as a "malefactor."

Praying women and do-gooders—the Marys and the Marthas of history—naturally found a host of analysts who have investigated the mysticism of a Madame Guyon, the character of a Countess Matilda, the conversion of a Mother Seton, the virtues of a Santa Rosa of Lima, the first American saint, or—perhaps most interesting of all— the legends of a Pope Joan. Joan, who was said to have dressed as a man, been elected Pope, and died in childbirth during a Papal procession, may have been merely a figment in a heretical mind. Like the "malefactor" Canning, Pope Joan inspired a library of books and pamphlets.

How many male biographers have been drawn to women subjects. The first vernacular biography of the Queen of the Nile was written by Giulio Landi and published in 1551 by the Venetian House of Aldus which for some strange reason saw fit to append to it an Oration on Ignorance. The actress Mademoiselle Clairon, the French Amazon Genevieve Prémoy who served as cavalry officer in the royal dragoons under the name of "Chevalier Baltazar," the early poets Christine de Pisan and Olympia Morata have all inspired pen portraits.

Of these, perhaps the woman who relates most closely to today's women is Christine de Pisan. Born in Venice around 1364, she was taken as a child to Paris where her father served as astrologer to the king, Charles V. Brought up at court, Christine was married at the age of fifteen to the royal secretary Etienne du Castel of Picardy, by whom she bore three children. Thus far her life differed scarcely at all from the lives of well-born ladies at a medieval court.

In 1380, however, the king's death deprived Christine's father of his position. He died shortly thereafter and by the end of the decade her husband was also dead. At the age of twenty-five, Christine de Pisan, without visible means, had three children, an aged mother and indigent relatives to support. She did what many women of later centuries have done in similar circumstances: she wrote for a living. Love poems to her husband's memory, ballads and rondeaux were followed by prose narratives, romances and commentaries, including an eye-witness report of Charles V and his court. Christine's fame circulated along with her manuscripts. Both Henry of Lancaster and Galeazzo Visconti Duke of Milan invited her to their courts. The lady refused.

Now her writings were beginning to center upon what might tentatively be called the feminist causes of the turn of the century. In 1399 she produced in her *Epitre au Dieu d'Amour* a defense of women; a few years later her *Dit de la Rose* described the Order of the Rose whose members were sworn to protect the honor of women. Christine's *Trésor de la Cité des Dames* and her *Livre des trois Vertus* were both designed to instruct women in all matters from the choice of clothing to the conduct of life.

Meanwhile, in France the struggle between the Orleanists and the Burgundians, allies of England, culminated on the field of Agincourt. After the disasters of civil war, Christine de Pisan retired to a convent. The silence of her last years was broken only once, and then most appropriately, by a song in praise of Joan of Arc. When she died, this medieval feminist left many manuscripts behind her. With the invention of printing they were eventually published. William Caxton printed *The Moral Proverbs of Christyne de Pise* translated by Anthony Earl of Rivers in 1478. Eleven years later, at the order of Henry VII, Caxton himself translated her *Livre des Faitz d'Armes, et de Chevalerie* and printed it as *The Fayt of Armes and of Chyvalrye*.

None of those extraordinary incunables, I am sorry to say, has ever passed through our hands. Instead, we had to content ourselves with two nineteenth-century monographs by appreciative Frenchmen on Christine de Pisan. These we sold to the twentieth-century collector Miriam Y. Holden. In Mrs. Holden's library of books by and about women, Christine de Pisan, a medieval French writer who used her literary powers to earn a living and to champion her sex, was at home.

In their books about women men have usually revealed as much about themselves as about their subjects. They have dearly loved to set guidelines for women to follow. In 1574 both the Italian Giulio Cesare Cabei and the French theologian Pierre Doré published a courtesy book for widows. Two centuries later a German publicist, Friedrich von Moser, wrote a manual on the conduct of the wives of ambassadors. Both the costume and the dowry of the Renaissance lady have been treated at length, the "Duties of the Female Sex" inquired into, and the question of whether the "corsage" or the "bosom" merits greater favor has been seriously debated.

Obviously men have long been willing and eager to educate women. Despite the condescension implicit in such teaching, some of the books in this category do belong in a feminist library. The emancipated Poulain de La Barre advocated in the 1670's an almost unlimited education for women, asserting that no studies, from geometry to Cartesianism, were beyond their comprehension. A hundred years later a book charmingly entitled *Truth Triumphant: or, Fluxions for the Ladies* accepted the hypothesis that woman could grasp scientific and mathematical problems. Its author was courageous, but not courageous enough to sign his name to the treatise which remains anonymous. Not so Count Algarotti, author of *Sir Isaac Newton's Philosophy explained for the use of the Ladies*. From Fénelon to Erasmus Darwin there have been writers galore who have offered suggestions for improving the curriculum of what was generally called female education.

While many men have debated whether or not women should be educated at all—a collection of Italian discourses on that subject was published in 1729—one anonymous writer declared he would rather live with lions and dragons than with an uneducated woman. His reasons were not altogether altruistic, however. According to *Le Caractère d'une Femme sans Education*, uneducated women were avaricious, ruined family life, dominated their husbands, and had an inordinate taste for wine.

None of these treatises may be very militant, but they paved the way for militancy. They disclosed problems, restrictions and attitudes. They hinted, if not at reform, then at the need for reform. The sixteenth and seventeenth centuries dearly loved lively disquisitions on such subjects as "What are the relative merits of man and woman?" or "Are women human?" In their pages male chauvinists had their say: Giuseppe Passi castigated tyrannical, hypocritical and ambitious women; one Dr. Pancrace upheld male superiority; *Hippolytus Redivivus* located in woman the cause of all evil. An array of gallant male champions of women, from the "Stupor Mundi" Erasmus to the Spanish humanist Vives, tutor to Princess Mary, took up the challenge as early apologists, defenders and dissectors of the virtues and even the privileges of women. In feminist dialogues and debates women were discussed, their graces outlined and their capabilities adumbrated. In 1563 one Gallic champion of the cause came up with a treatise in which he concluded that woman was actually a rational embodied soul. A later Frenchman in *La Triomphe des Femmes* (1700) castigated male chauvinism by asserting that the role of master which man assigned to himself was to be condemned. As early as 1553 Guillaume Postel in *Les Tres-Merveilleuses Victoires des Femmes du Nouveau Monde* exalted Joan of Arc as the New Eve and announced that the female sex should dominate the world. How much farther have the twentieth-century feminists advanced? Such early debates and discussions, satires and lampoons sowed the seeds of today's overtly feminist literature.

Other seeds were sown in other early works. Surely those tomes on the unhappy legal aspects of being a woman contained fuel for later incendiaries. Imbedded in *Magna Charta,* stipulated in royal edicts and statutes, elaborated in legal dissertations, the regulations stand: the restrictive laws relating to the inheritance of property and the dowry, divorce and remarriage, and, in a Medici edict, legislation prohibiting women of ill repute from riding in coaches!

It is a legal work pertaining to women that certainly marks one of the earliest appearances of the phrase "women's rights." *The Lawes Resolvtions of Womens Rights; or, The Lawes Provision for Women,* published in London in 1632, is actually a "Woman's Lawyer," a guide to women's legal status and hence to such rights as may have been accorded them. By the end of the eighteenth century *The American Spectator, or Matrimonial Preceptor* could proudly boast that "in this sequestered happy region" "the rights of women, as well as of men" are acknowledged. Moreover, the frontispiece of that volume depicts a conjugal scene at an American table where the wife is seated and the husband stands.

The rights of women were not the exclusive property of nineteenth-century suffragists or twentieth-century feminists. Even in those early books where rights were never articulated they were often implicit. Flores' story of Grisel and Mirabella which we had in a 1581 edition was really an only slightly disguised combative feminist tale vindicating women. It was translated into several languages and came to be called a "ladies' Bible." Surely Pierre Petit's Latin dissertation on the Amazons, published in Amsterdam in 1687, is nothing but a comprehensive survey of the first feminist movement. It contains fascinating accounts of the Amazons: their appearance and customs, their military expeditions, their government and education. As a matter of fact, one copy of that work was bought from us for presentation to Gloria Steinem, a transaction bringing highly inflammable coals to a feminist Newcastle.

It was, of course, not only male champions of women but women themselves who from earliest times contemplated their wrongs and their rights. In 1601 Lucrezia Marinella cited with chapter and verse the nobility of woman as opposed to the ignominy of man. Later in that century Madeleine de Scudéry presented in her *Les Femmes Illvstres* a survey of celebrated women of antiquity, though it must be admitted she published it under the name of her brother George. Madame de Pringy, the Marquise de Lambert, Miss Hatfield all cogitated the advantages and disadvantages of being a woman, woman's abilities and disabilities, and the need to extend her privileges and increase her education. In 1694 an anonymous *Serious Proposal to the Ladies, For the Advancement of their true and greatest Interest* was issued in London "By a Lover of Her Sex." In it the author, now recognized as Mary Astell, proposed a kind of female retirement home whose inmates were to go in for intensive religious, moral and mental training. While there may not be much resemblance to today's Halls of Academe in Mary Astell's monastic set-up, surely it contained the germ of the woman's college.

Once women became self-acknowledged "lovers of their sex" their cause was onward. That cause was aided and abetted by many men, among them the myriad of writers who fulminated about women's dress. Instead of describing ornaments appropriate to widows or attacking, as William Prynne did in 1628, braided curls or "Love-Lockes," some writers, like the French physician Gassaud, saw in the corset the cause of many female disorders and diseases. Here in America the phrenologist Orson Fowler crusaded against "tight lacing" in the 1840's and, with an army of dress reformers, brought us to Amelia Bloomer herself and eventually to today's free clothing.

Neither sociological nor philosophical nor legal rights had any meaning unless they were based in economic rights. Career women have concentrated less upon demanding rights than upon exercising them. Yet their biographies must be included in a feminist library for these women workers and earners changed the economic aspect of the world. Women joined the labor force early on, not only as servants (see *L'Etat De Servitude,* 1711) and as midwives (see Angélique Le Boursier du Coudray's own work, *Abregé De L'Art Des Accouche-*

ments, 1773), but as engravers (see Elizabeth Blackwell's *A Curious Herbal,* 1737) and as journalists (see Mary Manly's *New Atalantis).* In my own *We the Women,* first published in 1963 and subsequently reprinted, my purpose was to assemble a dozen nineteenth-century American women who had pioneered in entering the different sciences and arts, trades and professions. *We the Women* consists of biographies of a handful of earning, working women to whom economic emancipation meant more even than the right of suffrage. They believed with Julia Ward Howe that "the professions indeed supply the key-stone to the arch of woman's liberty." Among them is the lawyer Belva Lockwood who ran for the Presidency of the United States and who was the first woman to plead a case before the United States Supreme Court. In that book the chemist Ellen H. Richards has a chapter, a nineteenth-century ecologist who reported and analyzed the pollution in nineteenth-century water, food and air. All the women included in *We the Women* echoed Margaret Fuller's rallying cry:

We would have every arbitrary barrier thrown down. We would have every path laid open to woman as freely as to man . . . . If you ask me what offices they may fill; I reply—any. I do not care what case you put; let them be sea-captains, if you will.

Margaret Fuller published her *Woman in the Nineteenth Century* in 1845. In a way, her book was the culmination of centuries of subliminal struggle and half a century of overt struggle. By the end of the eighteenth century, the militant feminist literature of today had had its patent and obvious beginnings. Perhaps the first recognized landmark in the movement was Mary Wollstonecraft's *Vindication of the Rights of Woman,* the book in which she condemned the degradation of her sex and advocated female education on a national scale. The *Vindication* had been preceded by the author's *Thoughts on the Education of Daughters,* another provocative book that devotes a chapter to the "Unfortunate situation of females, fashionably educated, and left without a fortune." Incidentally, Mary Wollstonecraft was paid ten guineas for that book—her first—before she went on to become a governess in the Kingsborough family, then the wife of William Godwin and the author of the famous *Vindication.*

The nineteenth century is rampant with such *Vindications,* but perhaps the most world-shaking of all is the work of Margaret Fuller. Exotic American bluestocking and citizen of the world, she was a friend of woman because she was a friend of humanity. By 1845, when *Woman in the Nineteenth Century* was published, the thirty-five-year-old author had already lived several lives. Educated in Latin and Greek, French, German and Italian, philosophy and literature, Margaret Fuller was not only a powerful intellect but a dynamic, perhaps formidable personality. For friendship she had a special talent, and her friends included Emerson and Bronson Alcott, Elizabeth Peabody, the Channings. She moved in the circle of Transcendentalists but always she was unmistakably herself. Wherever she moved her influence was felt, whether she taught school or edited *The Dial,* delivered her famous Conversations on Boston's West Street or visited the community of Brook Farm. After her tour of the midwest, Margaret Fuller wrote her first original book, *Summer on the Lakes,* and following its publication Horace Greeley invited her to serve as literary critic on his *New York Tribune.*

Before she accepted the invitation, she spent some weeks in Fishkill Landing, New York, working on her second book. In July 1843, *The Dial* had carried her article, "The Great Lawsuit. Man *versus* Men. Woman *versus* Women." In Fishkill, before joining the staff of the *Tribune,* she expanded that article into a book. In so doing, the observer became the participant, calling for inward and outward freedom for women, a freedom that should be acknowledged as a right, not yielded as a concession. If Isabella had furnished to Columbus the means for voyaging to America, this land must pay back its debt to woman. Society and individual character must be regenerated together and in such reform woman must be given a share. *Woman in the Nineteenth Century,* published in 1845 by Greeley and McElrath, fulfilled its author's ambition to impel the general stream of thought and, indeed, is still fulfilling it.

After its publication Margaret Fuller plowed other fields. In her work on Greeley's *Tribune* she was an outspoken and stirring journalist. In 1846 she sailed for Europe, finding in Italy a lover—the Marchese Ossoli—and a cause: the struggle for Italian independence. Margaret Fuller never returned to her country. The barque *Elizabeth* on which she sailed home with her husband and her child foundered off Fire Island in May of 1850. Her manuscript history of Italian liberation was lost; her body was never recovered.

Margaret Fuller's colorful life and tragic death; her writings; her bold approach to woman in the nineteenth century took powerful hold of me and became the subject of my first biography. Today her book and the magnetic personality behind it seem to have renewed their power. *Woman in the Nineteenth Century* is a foundation stone not only in a feminist library but in evolving feminism.

Side by side with the work of Margaret Fuller must stand the writings of Frances Wright, the distinguished freethinker whose career was a series of experiments in reform. Her *Views of Society and Manners in America* is a philosophy of life as well as a survey of the republic. The ephemeral orations and newspaper articles of Victoria Woodhull, recently collected in *The Victoria Woodhull Reader,* enunciate radical, often revolutionary doctrine on sex and eugenics, sociology, economics and political theory. In that nineteenth-century American pamphlet entitled *The Principles of Social Freedom,* she declared:

Yes, I am a Free Lover. I have an *inalienable, constitutional,* and *natural* right to love whom I may, to love as *long* or as *short* a period as I can; to *change* that love *every day* if I please, and with *that* right neither *you* nor any *law* you can frame have *any* right to interfere.

There is no doubt that Victoria Woodhull, the first American woman stockbroker and the first woman candidate for the Presidency of the United States, gave a powerful impetus to the feminist movement during the 1870's. She claimed that most women's rights had already been granted constitutionally and needed only to be exercised. Gathered together, her theories form a microcosm of the country's most advanced thought on women and she emerges as an effective mouthpiece of reform and a colorful and collectible feminist.

How many other nineteenth-century collectible feminists suggest themselves. The early literature of suffrage alone is voluminous and the *History of Woman Suffrage* begun by Susan B. Anthony, "the Napoleon of the woman's rights movement," leads directly on to the reports of the President's Commission on the Status of Women. The Wollstonecrafts, the Wrights and the Fullers connect us with the Friedans and the Firestones. The long distance we have traveled from the *Centones* of Falconia Proba to the *Sexual Politics* of Kate Millett can be traced in our feminist library. The writings of the past *are* the bridges to the present. Early feminist books document the past but they also link us with the present and lead us to the future. A feminist library provides us with a rich source for exploration, for it forms a discipline of half the human race.

5

Public Relations

[LR]

The entire human race is involved in public relations. The term has become an integral part of American life and can be applied to the seven stages of man. The school system at all levels has its public relations man/woman as have department store, political convention, employment bureau, brokerage house and the Friendly Funeral Home which puts its best foot forward for the last man down.

The antiquarian book trade is no exception. Unfortunately the public image that has resulted in part from the trade's PR is not altogether accurate. To the romantic, the rare bookseller is an ascetic dwelling in a crenellated tower, his parchment-like fingers clutching a Coptic gospel or a fourteenth-century manuscript. To the less romantic he is a hard-driving businessman whose only interest in a book is its price.

Both portraits are, of course, utter bosh. The average rare book dealer is quite normal. Whether he dwells in the city or the country, he usually occupies a well-appointed office replete with steel files and steel shelves, electric typewriter and even a dictaphone. In the country he often enjoys a handsome house filled with books, a well-stocked bar, well-trimmed lawns, and even several grandchildren. Contrary to popular belief, city and country species are fond of animals. The Sallochs have eighteen cats, one dog, and goldfish. M.B.S. and L.R. adore their present incumbent Louisa May, the most enchanting and illiterate of dachshunds.

The bookseller member of the genus humanum, however, does enjoy a unique position. He pursues a profession which combines scholarship with commercialism. And although some members of Academe maintain an aloof attitude toward members of my profession, let me advise these haughty gents that the specialist dealer will always hold his own against any member of their ranks and possibly vanquish his professorial opponent.

It is not only with such academics that the antiquarian bookseller must maintain public relations, but with many different members of the human race who have in common one interest: a passion for books. With his clientele—university adviser, librarian and private collector—the bookseller develops his particular brand of PR.

The librarian of today is usually a relaxed, affable, understanding individual. The firm of Leona Rostenberg—Rare Books enjoys excellent relations with several of this breed who exactly understand their library's needs, lacunae and plans to develop certain holdings. I can speak with only the highest respect of Liz Niemyer, Nathaniel Puffer, Dean Larsen, Bill Cagle, Sam Hough, Ken Carpenter. All are suffused with enthusiasm. Nat spends a day with us. "Anything else?" A call from Liz pinpoints the Folger's desiderata. We cannot supply modern firsts to the Lilly Library but Bill Cagle will always find something in a catalogue which fits into its varied holdings. Bookbuying for Dean is a constant joy. A visit to his university remains an unforgettable event marked by warmth and enthusiasm. Sam Hough lives in books. When he received a copy of our Catalogue "1776" he phoned twice after checking it, once the same day and again a week later. "I found more items we must have. I took it to bed with me." In ninety degree heat Ken Carpenter scaled the shelves for economics and related texts. "Not tired, Ken?" "Nope, let me have a cold drink." More books—more gingerale!

During recent trips to the Mid- and Far West we met a few of our academic customers—the special variety which loves booksellers and does not look down the nose at their scholarship. We spent less time eating and drinking than discussing books relating to sixteenth-century diplomacy, the ambivalent role of Catherine de Medici, the Huguenot Wars, the French philosophes, the influence of Mady's Franco-American publisher Joseph Nancrede, and the twenty books issued by William Brewster at his secret Leyden Pilgrim Press.

The book fair is probably the best test of the dealer's ability to handle his own public relations. It is the magnet for librarian and private collector. The antiquarian book fair has become an annual event here and abroad. It is at the fair that the antiquarian dealer, master of a small realm ten by eight and a half feet, displays his scholarship, his salesmanship and personality. He greets old customers and welcomes new. At our booth at the 1977 New York book fair we greeted several of our old customers. The enthusiastic Aldine collector T. Kimball Brooker carried under one arm his copy of Antoine Auguste Renouard's *Annales de L'Imprimerie des Alde.* "Any Aldines?" was his immediate query.

Our faithful book friend Irving Levitas informed us that he had all the Judaica in our Fair catalogue but would like to look at the copy of the Leon *Catalogue,* the catalogue of American first editions. "Sorry, sold, Irving."

At our booth a tug of war actually took place between a stout Brooklyn lady and a young blond Dutchman. They were contesting a small book, a Hebrew grammar, *The First Gate to the Holy Tongue* by William Robertson.

"I picked it first," bellicosely declared the lady of Brooklyn.

"Madam, you took it out of my hand," firmly objected the polite Dutchman. Interjecting, we commented that we could not tear it in half. Youth yielded to age and the blond young man remarked, "My interests are many. I shall buy your *Rime e Lettere* of Veronica Gambara, a most interesting Renaissance lady."

There are—alas—some visitors who regard the book fair as merely one of the many things to do, an item listed on the calendar of events around town. This group always includes the idle, indifferent visitor who throws a hostile glance at an unfamiliar sign, picks up a sixteenth-century volume, stares contemptuously at the fine print, yawns and throws it rudely across the counter. "Not at all what I want. Don't you have anything readable—Jack London or Zane Grey?"

Our booth is inevitably selected as the rendezvous for a group of friends who have decided to meet at the fair and there make plans for drinks and dinner. Upon arrival the men arch their backs against our vitrine making all viewing impossible, while the ladies cluster together and block the entrance to the booth. Their shrill chatter drowns the mumblings of a prospective customer who futilely attempts to study the vitrine or wedge his way in.

"Your earrings are divine. Look, if we have drinks at the St. Regis we can go to that adorable little French restaurant opposite—the most marvelous mussels. Did you see the price of that *Ulysses* over there? This place is a bunch of robbers."

At this point one of the ladies has picked up a copy of our *Faerie Queene*. With a crash poor Spenser falls on his side, his back cover detached. She smiles archly at us:

"Did you know that the cover of this book is broken, Miss?"

My partner Madeleine B. Stern, habitually calm and collected, does occasionally blow her top. Perhaps a good blow is helpful for a positive no-nonsense public relations attitude. As the lady at fault picks up the front and middle of Spenser, abandoning his back cover, I hear the voice of M.B.S. exuding from a deep freeze:

"Will you move on! You are not only obstructing any possible view of the vitrine but you are also blocking the entrance to our booth."

The lady of the jet earrings snaps furiously at M.B.S.:

"Say you have a nerve. We paid to come in here and we intend to stay and look at every book. You call yourselves educated people."

And yet there are many glorious book-loving, enthusiastic individuals who spend all three and a half days at the fair. They love us and we return their affection. They arrive at the preview and remain until each unsold book is placed in its packing case at closing time. They are exhilarated by the variety of books and manuscripts and the dealers—many from overseas. They converse with all their good friends, the bookmen.

"I am so exhausted girls, my gawd, am I tired," laughs an old customer. "Let me sit down a moment with you and talk before I look at your books. Did you see the First of Hobbes in Booth 10? A beauty! You have it. Good! No, I am not buying it, but what else do you have in political theory?"

Such customers are a delight not only when we meet them at the biennial New York book fair but also at all fairs that have mushroomed throughout the country.

As chauvinistic New Yorkers, defending our woebegone city against abuse, we welcome the New York book fair for a variety of reasons. We are on home base; can collapse exhausted in our own beds and bring supplemental material on the morrow. Also we basically believe that the New York book fair is the most sophisticated in the country, attracting visitors most of whom know exactly what they wish to acquire. The cocktail crowd—an integral part of every fair—is overshadowed by serious, knowledgeable buyers.

Chauvinistic New Yorkers who join other fairs should cater to the varying interests of a great continent. It is the fault neither of Los Angeles nor of San Francisco that Leona Rostenberg—Rare Books does not specialize in Western Americana and showed poor judgment in displaying on the west coast an emblem book of 1555 and *The Life of Cosimo de' Medici* by the Younger Aldus. At Los Angeles several visitors stopped to inspect our vitrine, looked at us and our sign, Leona Rostenberg—Rare Books, New York City. Their indulgent smiles indicated that these easterners understood nothing of western culture.

"Anything you would like to see?" inquired Madeleine Stern as a bespectacled lady glanced at our show case.

"Why should I want to look at anything?" she replied walking briskly away.

Her more timorous bibliophilic sister arrived at our booth that afternoon. She smiled diffidently.

"Anything I can show you?" repeated the not quite so affable M.B.S.

"Oh I would not want to bother you ladies. But do tell me what are these old books?"

"This is an emblem book by the Italian Paul Giovio, the other a *Life of Cosimo de' Medici.*"

"Oh how nice," she returned glancing again at our sign. "Tell me ladies, how did you ever get out here?"

Emboldened by this intimate query she continued: "What an interesting name you have. It really puzzles me. Perhaps you can answer my question." She entered our booth, taking my hand, gazing fervently at me. Oh Lord, I thought, she wants me to join a mystic eastern cult.

"Tell me Miss Rostenberg, do tell me, is it the ROS-TEN-BERG or the GUT-EN-BERG Bible?????"

It is true that my maternal ancestors dwelt in Mainz and were occupied with the Old Testament and Maimonides' digest of rabbinic law. Yet it was a cosy feeling to realize that you had lived over five hundred years (and looked it) and that your family had initiated the greatest cultural invention for man. My PR had obviously improved.

Shortly before closing, a breathless young man visited our booth.

"What's this, huh?" he commanded, picking up an Aldine Lucian from our shelves.

"Lucian," I replied.

"Lucian who?"

Not waiting for an answer, he continued, "How come you have such books? Do you have James Abbey's *A Trip across the Plains* or Robinson's *California and the Gold Regions?* Let me tell you, those are books!"

There is no doubt that a healthy relationship between dealer and customer depends upon an appreciation of respective interests. Hence our experience at California book fairs can be attributed to our own lack of interest in Western Americana and the average Western customer's ignorance of our kind of book. Nonetheless, mutual understanding of the many antiquarian specialties must prevail.

When Madeleine and I visited London in 1947 for our first great venture in book buying, we were over-awed by the many shops and their variety of books. Although for several years we had studied English and foreign catalogues, personal immersion in books and meeting their owners were a gigantic experience—one remembered with poignant nostalgia. We were novices on the London anti-quarian circuit—pilgrims at a shrine. We selected books with hesitation. We were awed by the great names of the trade. At the time we did not realize that we were establishing our public relations with the English trade and they with us. One reaction to our early London visits cropped up in a review of *Old & Rare: Thirty Years in the Book Business,* in which Clifford Maggs wrote:

I find the partners first visited Maggs in August 1949. Their visits followed the same pattern so precisely, year after year, that we might all have been automata performing our prescribed motions. No words wasted, a quick greeting, and then to work combing the shelves.... After two hours or so, I would be summoned and the piles gathered together on our "Pickwick Table," the unpriced items priced (promptly accepted or rejected), and Miss Stern would sit down and record their purchases in a cashbook. When totalled up, she would ask if a cheque on account would suit us, and their annual visit would be over.

Miss Rostenberg was clearly the dynamic personality of the firm, and initially I regarded the slightly severe protective Miss Stern as an in-dispensable assistant and amanuensis. Strangely incurious about these two amusing ladies, I seldom spoke about them to colleagues, and confess that until reading their book retained the idea that Miss R was a refugee-bookseller from Germany, but I had been aware for some time that they were authors of scholarly bibliographical and biographical writings.

It is true that my "Ach Gott" in the German of my ancestors to some of Mr. Clifford's prices (to which he refers as "grumbling a little about the increase in prices") must have misled him. It is also true that after the polite salutation of "Ohayoo gozaimasù" (Good Morning) in Japan I automatically responded "Danke schön."

Although it has taken Clifford Maggs thirty years to realize that I was not born in Berlin's West End but in the infamous borough of the Bronx, we nonetheless enjoy excellent personal and trade public relations as we do with many English and continental colleagues.

It amazes me that Madeleine and I—rabid anti-Nazis—attended the Congress of the International League of Antiquarian Booksellers held in Vienna in 1954. Perhaps we sublimated our feelings in a longing for the past, pre-World War I Vienna, with its dashing hussars clad in fur-trimmed capes, its waltzes, its gaiety. I realized that after a few days there my PR was working poorly. Most Viennese dealers in my eyes wore S.S. uniforms. I felt a strong sense of guilt and unhappiness. At the Palais Auersberg, where the farewell dinner was held, I deftly changed the place cards removing those of all Germans from our table. When confronted by one of the official hostesses I brusquely replied: "I will not sit with Germans."

I saw no hussars in fur-trimmed capes waltzing with exquisite brunettes with pompadoured hair, but rather a few clumsy, aging bookmen. Toward the end of the evening a German dealer, Herr Domizlaff of Munich, was presented to us. Simultaneously he clicked his heels and kissed our hands. We returned a cool "Guten abend."

"You will be visiting Munich after the Congress?" he inquired.

"We certainly shall not."

"And why not?" he continued somewhat incredulously.

"On principle!"

Herr Domizlaff clicked his heels once again and quickly turned away.

My general behavior at Vienna evoked some criticism and a strong letter from our very good friend Winnie Myers of London, an ardent Zionist. Infuriated and embarrassed I read her note: "Why did you visit Vienna if you still detest the Germans?" I replied to Winnie but I did not admit that she was right. Since we had decided to attend the Congress we should have kept our "cool" and furthered our international PR. Her letter also informed me that of all the German antiquarian booksellers Herr Domizlaff had helped fleeing Jews the most, having concealed them in his home at great personal risk. She enumerated a list of the many antiquarians he had aided in getting out of Germany. I felt quite sheepish but at the time still considered all Germans a bad lot and strongly resented Winnie's interference.

After a lapse of some years during which our firm had expanded in many directions but still emphasized books of the Renaissance— many of them written by German humanists and printed in Germany—we reflected upon our purchases and from whom we had bought them during the last few years. Some had been obtained from American refugee dealers who periodically returned for business and personal trips to Das Vaterland. Others had been acquired from Dutch dealers who had recently attended German sales or visited German dealers. In short we were aware that much of our stock had come to us from German sources and the indirect route had been costing us a pretty penny. Nor had we been at all logical. We reassessed our attitude. Were we to impugn modern Germany for the misdeeds of her fathers? Did we not relish book buying in France, which had condemned Alfred Dreyfus and applauded all anti-Dreyfusards? Was not my darling mother a born Dreyfus, a distant cousin of the maligned captain? She had adored her visits to Paris. Had I not studied in Strasbourg, where 1,200 Jews had been burned alive on the Rue des Juifs during the thirteenth century? Had not the England we keenly loved damned the Yankees two centuries ago? In short, if we wished to persist in our exclusive practices we should remain at home, bury our heads and look for books along the sands of the Long Island shore.

I was quite unhappy the first day of our Munich visit. I saw the ghosts of young and old Jews. I gazed with revulsion at the beer hall of Hitler's "putsch." With weak knees and much hesitation we pulled the bell of the office-residence of Herr Helmuth Domizlaff. I have never conducted any conversation within an ice house. Attempting to defrost a solidly frozen Herr Domizlaff proved futile. He remained thoroughly glacial until I addressed him as Herr Doktor Domizlaff.

"I am not a *Doktor*."

"Oh, I thought all Germans were."

A tiny thaw appeared at the corner of his mouth. Despite this glacial trickle, his frozen courtesy caused violent discomfiture.

"I have no books for you now. Momentarily I await the arrival of Mr. Walsh of Harvard. If you return tomorrow, perhaps I can show you something. Guten Morgen."

We had been dismissed. Conversation between the two partners did not resume until lunch. Violently I turned to M.: "And you don't agree he's a Nazi?" Displaying her usual logic and recalling the reasons for having come to Munich, Madeleine calmed me. The following morning we returned to the premises of Mr. Helmuth Domizlaff. Apparently he had slept in an overheated bedroom during the night, since a fairly warm smile greeted our arrival.

"I have put some books on a table for you. There is a splendid collected volume of sixteenth-century tracts relating to European-Turkish political relations and military skirmishes." (Obviously not purchased by Herr Doktor Walsh of Harvard.) We examined the collection carefully. It was glorious—tracts with woodcuts depicting turbaned Turks, bloody battle scenes, janissaries with scimitars high, views of Constantinople, mosques, and in the foreground the Sea of Marmora. We were enthralled. Mr. Domizlaff reacted to our enthusiasm—suddenly the room was warm and friendly. "Oh yes, we shall buy this," we declared almost in unison. As the maid brought in morning *kaffee* my eyes directly hit the piercing glance of Helmuth Domizlaff.

"Indeed Mr. Domizlaff, I know I owe you an apology."

"It is now fourteen years since we met in Vienna and I have never forgotten what you said."

Though somewhat contrite, I launched into an offensive: "How could I have known you were a good German? In my book you were all bad. I have since discovered my error and I sincerely apologize."

Today we are very good friends and my admiration for the scholarly, high-principled Helmuth Domizlaff rivals my regard for such great bookmen as E.P. Goldschmidt, Ernest Weil and Cesare Olschki. Although we have not visited Germany in several years, I am convinced that were we to return he would again arrange for us a Bayrischer Abend as he did upon our third visit. There we met several of his friends who had been saved at the risk of his own life. Actually M.B.S. believes that Germany is the most democratic country in Europe. Although we usually agree on major issues and despite my completely defrosted Helmuth Domizlaff, I question my partner's opinion.

During our annual bookbuying trips we have seldom missed Paris. Here our PR is excellent and we are greeted with the usual "Bouquinez comme vous voulez." Although this chapter is designed primarily for ruminations upon public relations, it does bear some culinary undertones. In France, as far as we are concerned, they are very under. During an approximate thirty visits to Paris and la belle campagne we have been invited twice to lunch and once to the truly festive board of the genial Monsieur and Madame Brun of Pélissanne, Bouches des Rhônes. Here we were overwhelmed with genuine quiche, beef provençal and a divine tarte des abricots, wines and magnificent cheeses. We heeded, or attempted to heed, the perorations of the gesticulating M. Brun against Algeria, strikes and book vandals. His was the only French home where we were warmly dined at the family table and we still wonder at the French aversion to outsiders. Is it insularity or a parsimonious strain indigenous to la belle France?

For the past twenty years we have been faithful customers of an extremely knowledgeable French dealer. We not only drool over his super stock but also enjoy his discussion of books. He rejoices also in our annual cheques. On one occasion he invited us to his home for lunch. Famished, we anticipated an elegant French meal. Our host explained that Madame and he always preferred just a bite or two at noon—perhaps an egg or a tomato. Savoyards and tea topped off our sumptuous repast. Fortunately I had tucked a bar of Suchard in my pocket. It is true that in developing PR, one becomes familiar with national mores. Despite our host's restricted diet we still admire him, and for the past six or seven years he has displayed his magnanimity in quite another style. After our annual visit he accompanies us to the bus stop where, having instructed us regarding the correct route to the Rue Royale, he presents to each of us—with the air of un grand seigneur—a one-way bus ticket.

During the Spring of 1976 we visited a distinguished French antiquarian dealer. Arriving in Paris we habitually settle in our room—that is, Mady Stern usually unpacks her wardrobe placing like with like, while I throw everything into a top drawer. We presumably invigorate ourselves with some wretched French coffee, a long crusty roll and camembert; gaze with renewed ardor at

the intersection of the Rue Boissy d'Anglas and the Avenue Gabriel;
summon a cab and speed over to the Left Bank anticipating our first
annual purchase on French soil.

"Maybe we'll find a 1625 Grotius."

"And maybe we won't," I sourly reply as the taxi careens around
the magnificent Place de la Concorde. "This guy must think we are
foreigners," we shriek as he turns right across the bridge, heading for
the Pont Alexandre and Les Invalides.

"Monsieur, à gauche," we sternly advise, "à gauche, s'il vous
plaît."

He pleads misunderstanding.

Arriving at our destination, a small green-shuttered shop on a
quiet street, we are greeted by a well-informed young man who
smiles effusively and informs us that his employer will arrive during
the afternoon.

"May we look at books now?"

"Comme vous voulez, mes amies, comme toujours."

Ladder ascension represents for us the hope of the antiquarian
book prowl because we are still optimistically convinced that the
right book lurks on the highest shelf. This of course is not true.
During this particular '76 dig our young friend approached us
somewhat furtively:

"I believe this year we shall do together some vairy beeg bees-
ness." We regarded him with uncommon interest as he continued:
"We have acquired for your inspection and purchase the greatest
collection of tracts evair assembled by one firm in all of France."

We staggered. Madeleine descended from her top perch demanding: "Where is it Monsieur? Let us see it immediately."

"Ah Madame," replied M. Paul, "this all takes time for you to
view this collection merveilleuse. It consists of over 800 tracts—all
extrêmement rare—uncommon—in superb condition—presque tous
en maroquin."

We glanced slightly hysterically at one another. Even devoid of
such glowing adjectival descriptions, a collection of over 800 tracts
to become ours! We greedily envisioned this magnificent acquisition
of pamphlets, a mirror of the daily life of every sixteenth- and
seventeenth-century Frenchman.

"If you return Thursday, mes chères amies, you may inspect the
entire collection."

"Thursday is out of the question. We leave for Amsterdam."

M. Paul shrugged his shoulders. "Then we shall make it to-morrow."

"Impossible, we have appointments. How about today?"

M. Paul hesitated. "Perhaps if you come at six. M. le patron will be here then."

The day proved tediously long. We visited other dealers, wedging our way into the so-called Librairie of a stout bouquiniste who dwelt not in marble halls but within the narrow confines of two parallel stone walls—perhaps a discarded cell from the Conciergerie. He remained quite jovial and talkative as the three of us attempted to pass one another without being crushed flat against either wall. He pulled out a few dull cartularies, some faded monastic rolls and an occasional tract, chatting amiably about his mailing list of 1,200 clients who included a few dukes and pretenders to the throne of France. We sincerely hoped that he planned no reunion within the stout walls of his cubicle. In contrast we visited an elegant shop rich in incunabula and woodcut books. The proprietor displayed the French edition of *Hypnerotomachie. Discours du songe de Poliphile.* Paris 1546.

"But we are searching for the 1499 Aldine edition, Monsieur."

"You wish an Italian edition when you can have the superb French?"

We dropped in at Madame Bona's for tea which neither of us really desired. It was now 4:50. As we approached the corner of our rendezvous we paused and clasped hands. "Good luck!"

Young M. Paul was not in evidence as we nonchalantly entered the shop. The secretary, smiling, offered to take our coats and umbrella as we settled in for the "kill."

"Monsieur ici?"

"Ah oui, Mesdames."

The curtains dividing the shop parted as M. Paul entered staggering under a mountain of morocco-bound tracts. His employer came forward bowing extravagantly, pointing to the mounting piles, beaming:

"C'est extraordinaire, hein? Une collection superbe pour vous."

The table was shortly covered with a myriad of tracts in calf and morocco of varying hues—in red, blue, yellow, olive green, purple and dark brown, some emblazoned with a former owner's coat-of-arms. The rich perfume of morocco assailed us.

"I am going to die," I murmured, summoning a higher power in the bibliophilic realm to steady me, to sharpen my wits for the forthcoming discussion. More tracts arrived as a third dealer e-merged from behind the curtains, a gentleman well known to us. We shook hands. He smiled enthusiastically, envisioning his cut from this triple entente. The pervading scent of the parfum maroquin was disturbing. We picked up one or two tracts, a *Lettre* of the Queen Mother, Marie de Medici, the *Réponse* of her weak, irresolute son Louis XIII, a pamphlet regulating the cleaning of the Paris streets in 1632. Nothing much had really changed in almost three and a half centuries. The table was now a sea of calf and morocco in variegated hues.

"Merveilleux!" M. Paul and his employer exclaimed ecstatically. "We shall leave you alone while you study them and consider the purchase. Is that agreeable?"

We sat at opposite ends of the table contemplating this hoard. Mady opened two or three tracts.

"You realize that they are almost all of the seventeenth century— very few of the sixteenth."

"I know," I agreed in a small voice. "But it is a huge collection." We sat together discussing the price we would pay before we were felled by the parfum maroquin. The mumbling behind the curtained partition unnerved us. Suddenly M. Paul emerged, contemplating the table.

"Voila, 1617, 1618, 1619, 1620, 1621, 1622, 1624," he declared, patting the backsides of calf and morocco. "You are very fortunate to have the first choice of this collection."

"May we see M. le patron now?" we requested, our voices a bit tight.

"Mais oui, certainement."

M. le patron entered, holding aloft a much penciled piece of paper.

"Le prix, s'il vous plaît, Monsieur?" we demanded breathlessly.

"Ah le prix! Now I shall explain it all to you. Voilà the original price. Now we have arranged everything to your best advantage. Here we have your professional discount and from this, my friends, we have deducted a very special discount for you alone. Hence the netissimo price of this greatest collection of tracts in France is only . . . ."

The penciled slip left us speechless.

I suddenly found my voice. "Quel prix, Monsieur! They are quite common."

"But chère Madame, they are all bound in morocco and calf."

"I wish they were not," interrupted Madeleine. "They should appear as they came from the press. They are news-sheets not French classics."

M. le patron studied the piece of paper. Together with M. Paul he refigured the different columns.

"You wish to purchase the collection and I wish you to have it. I have readjusted the price at the best possible figure."

We glanced at the paper shaking our heads. Heartsick, we realized that the price had been set not for the tracts but for hundreds of yards of leather.

"No Monsieur we shall not purchase the collection."
We were not leather merchants. Besides we would rather buy a cottage in East Hampton.

"You will change your mind and return Friday," M. le patron declared, shaking our hands.

On Friday we were in Hilversum, Holland. We spent the day with our dear Hilde Rosenthal, from whom we purchased the *Works* of Benedict Spinoza bound in full red morocco. The great Dutch philosopher would have disdained this lavish binding, but unlike the authors of the tracts, he deserved it!

At this point in our European public relations we snatch the opportunity to nominate the aforementioned Hilde Rosenthal for Antiquarian Bookwoman of the Year and Past Years. When we are on the receiving end of her public relations, experiencing PR in reverse, so to speak, we bask in creature comfort. A car fetches us and drives us to her shop, where coffee awaits us. A pile of books is arranged on a table for our inspection. We are given free rein to search her almost never-ending book house. A delicious lunch relaxes us and the suggestion, "You must be tired," is ignored as we scurry back for more books, more tea, more book talk.

Similar courtesies are extended by Bob De Graaf, who picks us up for the drive to Nieuwkoop. Book talk punctuates the vista of gentle poplars, green canals and windmills in the distance. His remarkable wife Emmy has coffee ready as we talk people, books, and kids. His Renaissance shelves are searched. The children troop in. An excellent dinner follows. As we drive back the canals have darkened, the poplars become faint shadows, the book talk a bit drowsy, but rich in friendship and understanding.

Such exceptions as exist to this brand of public relations do not exist in Holland, where the kindness and generosity of the Dutch dealers metamorphose book hunting into a world of discovery and delight. Yet exceptions do exist. A French dealer on the Rue des Saints Pères, for example, once informed us in a raucous bark that we had mixed up the titles on his bottom shelf. Only recently, visiting for the first time an English dealer new to the trade, we experienced a strange variety of hostility and indifference. Our host refused to show us his Aldines "in the back" (if there were any in the back), found quoting a wearisome task, and argued vociferously about states and first issues. I reacted equally undecorously and upon later meditation wondered whether this gentleman was anti-feminist, anti-American or anti-dealer. Yet most antiquarian dealers are eager to sell their wares.

It is true that books destined for a special customer or collection may be put on ice—concealed from the prying eyes of a visiting bookman. Although the English invariably refer to a good stock as "bits and pieces," they cordially invite the visitor to "have a look." It is not uncommon to find a French dealer bent on an important appointment or just about to depart for lunch (of course without you) just at the time of your arrival. His secretary or assistant is always placed at your disposal but he cannot make prices until Monsieur returns. Of course Monsieur may not return that day. Public relations are further strained when, after an unsteady climb to the topmost shelf on a shaky ladder, a fine collection of books and tracts relating to the Guise-Valois struggle is discovered. Bringing a few books down at the risk of life and limb my partner is informed sweetly but firmly by Mademoiselle that all of these books are "on reserve."

"But what are they doing there if they are not for sale?"

"That is why they are there. Few are permitted to climb the ladder," she smiles.

The search for books never ceases despite frustration, disaster, hunger, weather, health or the lack of it. At the end of a book-buying trip with our hearts turning westward, it is always most comforting to discover on a bookseller's shelf a familiar title—one you have had and sold—and actually to find the same copy of a book that had once been yours is a poignant experience.

"Good heavens this was our book!"

"Your book?" queries the English dealer sucking his pipe.

"Just think we purchased it from Goldschmidt at least twenty years ago. Dolf Van Gendt visited us and bought it. Now it is here. Indeed, it is well traveled."

We fondle the rather unexciting *Eloge* of Galileo. The English dealer eyes us amusedly, convinced that most Americans are slightly cracked.

"Let's buy it back," Mady suggests.

The Englishman's eyes now indicate that perhaps not all Americans are so cracked. Many books—like Mistress *Folly*—are great travelers, living at times in a peaceable kingdom, but more often in an atmosphere of intolerance, brutality, blood.

When the Galileo *Eloge* reached the old house in the Bronx we placed it on the third shelf from the bottom of our case of mixed pickles. It would probably travel the high seas again, a bit more worn, certainly more aged. While we were preparing a catalogue which was to include the Galileo, I ripped open one leg. Although it is difficult to believe, this was a purely bibliographical accident. I tripped over the four-volume reprint edition of Filippo Argelati's *Biblioteca scriptorum Mediolanensium,* and the cutting edge of Volume One tore open my right leg. Result: ten stitches!

The surgeon had instructed me to keep my leg elevated and on this raw, cold wintry day, ensconced in my study, I sat swathed in a variety of sweaters, my leg resting on a chair. It all sounds rather cosy, but I might add that the oil burner was out of order and although the repair man had been summoned three times, there was no indication of his arrival. Madeleine had departed for the library. Steeped in a foul humor, I was surrounded by card trays, descriptions and an electric heater. The front doorbell rang—certainly too timidly for a repair man. Although our old housekeeper was in residence, having returned from one of her many retirement trips to Germany, the house was in the command of sweet grey-haired Lola, who never came back from market without the report of a "killer" lurking on the front lawn. Lola tiptoed into my room closing the door carefully behind her. She gripped my shoulder, whispering, "Miss Leona, there's a 'killer' in the vestibule." Absorbed in a catalogue description and a throbbing right leg, I displayed little reaction until she repeated: "I said there's a 'killer' downstairs but I kept him locked in the vestibule. Don't worry—he can't get into the house."

"A what? Who is he, Lola?"

"Go see for yourself. Just take a peek into the vestibule."

I hobbled downstairs to behold the prisoner in the vestibule—a handsomely dressed gentleman in topcoat and homburg and carrying, along with his grey gloves, a copy of our Aldine catalogue. I was convinced that no Bronx Mafia "capo"—even if descended from the

Manuzio family of Venice—would carry our catalogue with him.

As the "killer" entered the downstairs foyer, he flourished his instrument of death—our Aldine catalogue. He beheld one of its compilers dressed in worn, dirty slacks, two sweaters, part of a right leg displaying layers of bandages.

"Mlle. Rostenberg?" my assassin queried. "I am M. Jacquard of Paris." Recognition overtook me—an excellent foreign client.

"Oui, je suis Mlle. Rostenberg. Votre manteau, s'il vous plaît," I floundered. "J'ai dix sutures dans ma jambe droite et nous n'avons pas de l'huile."

My visitor looked utterly confounded. He had not come from Paris to visit a dealer who "had ten stitches in her right leg and no heat in the house."

"What is wrong with you, Miss Rostenberg?" asked M. Jacquard in impeccable English.

At this point our dear old housekeeper, who had been reading the *Staats-Zeitung* all morning, emerged.

"Ah you are the oil repair man. Guten Tag."

It was very difficult for M. Jacquard to enter my study since it was barricaded with file boxes, trays and the extra chair for my right leg.

"You must excuse everything, Monsieur. Please look at the books. They are here and outside in the foyer."

Oh where was that partner of mine??? The bell rang furiously, rocking the ladder on which my customer was balancing himself.

"It is the furnace repair man," I smiled reassuringly.

"Hey Miss R. Joe here. Whas a matter, huh? I don' mind takin' a look at her now but I'm tellin' ya I aint got time to fix her, y'understand."

"Yes Joe," I replied meekly as M. Jacquard, a specialist in early political theory, pulled down two Hotmans, a Bodin, the 1550 "Testina" Machiavelli and Rousseau's *Extrait du Projet de Paix Perpetuelle.*

"These are very significant texts. I wish to buy them."

Lola entered, elegantly remarking, "Lunch is bein' served."

I elbowed her outside and tensely inquired: "What do we have for lunch?"

"Nothin' Miss Leona, really nothin'!" Eyeing the "killer" she asked, "Is that fella stayin' for lunch?"

"Yes," I angrily replied.

"I can give ya'll a nice egg," she continued.

"Isn't there anything in this house?"

Lola's eyes displayed a mischievous gleam. "Well, there's Cocoa's turkey!"

Our old housekeeper had discovered turkey on sale and had roasted a twenty-six pound bird for our darling dachshund Cocoa, who obviously celebrated Thanksgiving daily.

"I could fix it up real nice, Miss Leona."

I presided at the table as Lola brought in the remains of Cocoa's stringy bird decked out with much parsley. This lavish course was accompanied by a half empty jar of mayonnaise streaked with ketchup. Reassuringly my customer informed me he always dined lightly at noon, although his face revealed some exquisite pain.

With grandeur I summoned Lola: "Do we have any cheese?"

"Oh sure Miss Leona, we got cheese."

Enthroned on a large platter a small nibbled piece of Philadelphia Cream Cheese slashed by incisions of butter and grape jelly arrived. M. Jacquard drank his coffee. It had been reheated from the morning. As I took a gulp of this miserable mess, a cheerful voice greeted us.

"How splendid you came to visit us, M. Jacquard. Tout va bien?" Mady entered.

"Join us for some nice coffee, pet!"

Our customer from Paris was well read in seventeenth-century courtesy manuals. He took my hand warmly as he departed: "When you visit Paris, do me the honor and permit me to take you to lunch."

A year later after we had returned from our annual bookbuying trip to Paris during which M. Jacquard had not invited us to lunch—had it been his PR or ours that had failed?—I decided to sell the old house in the Bronx. I opened negotiations with the Riverside Memorial Chapel, Inc. at the corner. The home of Old and Rare would be razed.

During the protracted proceedings the ceiling in my study gave every evidence of imminent collapse. After several severe storms large yellow water stains were apparent as well as flaking and an ominous crack. Were we to depart the house alive before a large chunk felled us, it was essential to summon the plasterer. So on a sullen wet Tuesday we awaited not only Sam Jackson the plasterer but also one of the "boys" from the Riverside Memorial Chapel, Inc. Our old housekeeper Babette was still with us barking orders from the third floor where she devoured newspapers and apples and coddled our dachshund Cocoa-Leona. She also anticipated the arrival of the Riverside Memorial Chapel "boy" since she had great empathy for funerals and cemeteries.

This time when the front door bell emitted a weak tinkle, Babette, now downstairs, called peremptorily: "Miss Leona come down. The funeral fella is here." The visitor now ushered into the downstairs foyer was not a "killer" but an elderly gentleman attired completely in black. I was a bit puzzled that a representative of the Riverside Memorial Chapel, Inc. would wear a black knee-length double-breasted tightly fitting overcoat and carry a black hat and gloves, since all he had to do was run down the hill. It is true that in every other aspect he resembled one of the older "boys" of the Chapel. I was more puzzled when my "mortician" spoke with a heavy foreign accent.

"Good day, Madame Rostenberg, I am Mr. Hendrik van Bussum of Ryswick, Holland. I have been referred to you as a dealer in Dutch books." As Babette turned away in great disappointment, my PR began to work and I enthusiastically beckoned Mr. van Bussum to follow me to my study. There Mady enthroned him in a small armchair directly under the flaking ceiling. His black double-breasted coat, which he refused to remove, soon became a whitish-grey.

"I am particularly interested in acquiring those writings of Joannes Oldendorpius which I do not already own."

We staggered a bit since the *Directory of the International League of Antiquarian Booksellers* does not list us as Oldendorpius or even as Dutch specialists.

"We do have one work by Oldendorp. Here you are Mr. Oldendorpius, I mean Mr. van Bussum," I laughed sheepishly showing him the *Consilia* of this sixteenth-century jurist. Mijnheer van Bussum smiled indifferently:

"My dear, I have two copies of the first edition of 1589 and several variants. This is much too late. I am searching for a copy of the *Commentarii inutiles* . . . ."

As our Ryswick customer idly glanced at our edition of the *Consilia* we heard a light step and the thumping of a pole. Mr. Sam Jackson did not knock but gaily entered the flaked room.

"Hi Miss R. How y'all?"

Ignoring the presence of Hendrik van Bussum ensconced in our armchair, Sam raised the window-pole and jabbed the ceiling. Plaster snowed down covering our guest. Mady and I were semi-paralyzed.

"Well Miss R., this here ceilin' sure's gonna fall—real soon now. She's bad, real bad. Boy that's some crack, ya'll got. One day real soon you and Miss S. will be sittin' here nice and cosy like that little fella in that there chair and that ceilin' she's gonna come tumblin' down, jes' tumblin' down."

Nonchalantly leaning against the window-pole, Mr. Jackson, struck with the vision of the two ladies buried under piles of plaster, engaged in wild gales of laughter. Mr. van Bussum, still faintly visible, clutched the *Consilia* of Joannes Oldendorpius.

To divert him we offered him a copy of the *Opera* of Joannes Oecolampadius whose name not only began with an "O" but was similarly euphonious.

"I collect only Oldendorpius," he reacted stonily.

It was only then that we realized his predicament. He was physically unable to extricate himself from the small armchair. As he rose it rose with him—and with the plaster on his coat. Mr. van Bussum seemed confined not only to Oldendorpius but to the chair, which we were tempted to present to him. A mighty tug released him. He grimly returned the copy of the *Consilia*, departed the study with relief and bowed a stiff farewell. Mr. van Bussum needed no memento of his visit to the Bronx.

After the final successful negotiations, not with Mijnheer Bussum of Ryswick but with the "boys" of the Riverside Memorial Chapel, Inc., we began preparations for the move from the Bronx to Manhattan. Since we assumed that after twenty-five years in business our customers would be familiar with our "calling," we circulated a removal notice that made no specific reference to it:

LEONA ROSTENBERG and MADELEINE B. STERN
NEW MAILING ADDRESS

Box 188
Gracie Station
New York, N.Y. 10028

CHANGE OF RESIDENCE

40 East 88th Street ·
New York, N.Y. 10028
Telephone: (212) 831-6628

By Appointment Only

Reaction to this seemingly innocent announcement was varied. Numerous phone calls congratulated us upon the long postponed move. In reply to one foreign voice Madeleine hesitated a bit:

"Who is it? I did not get your name."

"Ah, my name is Giuseppe Montani. You do not know me. Is Leona? Is Madalena?"

A pause.

"I received your card. You say you move. How nice."

Was Giuseppe Montani a specialist in Italian municipal history, canon law, or the thermal baths of Friuli? Madeleine was becoming interested. The Italian voice continued:

"You say 'By Appointment Only.'"

"Yes."

"Tell me, dear lady————What You Do?"

When a similar call greeted us a month later we knew our removal card was making the rounds—being passed from hot hand to hot hand at airports, bars, bus terminals, discothèques. "Old & Rare" were joining an even older profession.

If the antiquarian bookseller is to practice harmonious public relations, he certainly must retain a sense of humor. He must smile at the indecision of librarians, the caprices of private collectors and the ignorance of would-be collectors. An optimist could easily be transformed into a pessimist by the impossible United States Postal Service—not to mention the content of some mail: "Thank you for sending me the pretty little volume of poetry of Lucrezia Gonzaga. It was very moving. I am afraid, however, you did not mention a small yellow spot on the bottom of leaf e3. I therefore regret that I must return this otherwise attractive volume. However if you can send me 'on approval' the 1623 edition of the divine Michelangelo, I shall be most obliged. I promise a prompt decision. Good luck to you! Yours respectfully, Wilma Silversmith." Other mail is more positive. The word RUSH is printed in red on a library order in response to an offer submitted three months earlier. This is followed by the admonition: "This order will be cancelled within 30 days if delivery is not made within this period. Thank you."

We have saved much of our mail for use by a friend who teaches a course in social psychology at one of the CUNY branches. She will shortly receive an enlightening communiqué regarding the history of Poland. It came from a non-buyer but close reader of a recent catalogue. "In your catalogue No. 63 #75 A. M. Fredro is described as an 'Austrian author.' Please note that A. M. Fredro (ca. 1620-1679) was a Polish author. The area where he lived belonged to Poland until one hundred and twelve years after the publication of the book mentioned in your catalogue (the book was published in 1660, the area was annexed by Austria in 1772). Sincerely, R. Krystyna Dietrich." Thank you very much Ms. Dietrich! Your information and our gratitude can only help promote PR between dealer and collector.

This chapter has for the most part treated the PR between foreign colleagues and ourselves. Our American associates have been excluded. Regarding this omission and other matters, I refer again to the review of *Old & Rare: Thirty Years in the Book Business* by Clifford Maggs who wrote:

One may well wonder as to Les Silences de Mesdames Rostenberg and Stern concerning certain booksellers. Those tantalizing diaries, what stories remain to be told! One would have enjoyed some sketches of the partners' American colleagues, and it seems perhaps a little unfair that . . . their characters are not drawn for us. It is puzzling. Maybe it is professional etiquette, which however does not extend to their European colleagues.

After reading *Old & Rare* our old friend Sam Hough of the John Carter Brown Library posed a similar question: "Of course you couldn't dissect your [American] colleagues now (might you leave a manuscript somewhere not to be opened for ten years?)"

In reply to both these gentlemen let me state that we are happily following their suggestions. The "stories" that "remain to be told" have been told and our American colleagues have been "dissected" on a lengthy strip of papyrus which has been sealed and deposited with a leading antiquarian bookseller of Bibliopolis. It will be opened and read before the International League of Antiquarian Booksellers meeting there anno 2175 when the bicentennial of *Old & Rare* will be celebrated.

6

Books That Swing The Pendulum*

[MBS]

Not merely booksellers, but the books they sell have "public relations." Books have been published that have radically changed the world. Indeed, books have been written about those books. The political significance of Machiavelli and Jefferson, of Thomas Paine and Adam Smith, of Malthus and Thoreau has been analyzed and dissected time and time again. But there are other books of less stature and renown than the writings of those giants which deserve at least a chapter of consideration.

The books we have in mind—and often in stock—have rarely struck a succession of verbal blows that have immediately changed the world. Rather, they have created a climate of opinion. For five centuries they have articulated opposing views of political life, from autocracy to libertarianism, from a defense of tyranny to a support of civil liberty. The books that embody such political concepts provide neither boudoir nor closet reading. They have entered the public arena. There is no better history lesson than a study of their opposing

*This chapter is limited by and large to books on political theory. No attempt has been made to consider pendulum swingers in the sciences or other fields. For a Short Title List of the books referred to in this chapter see pages 173–199.

philosophies. Having filtered through the mind, such books have pushed the pendulum of opinion now a little to the right, now a little to the left. And so, thanks to them, the world does move.

During the sixteenth century, the political theorists who lodged for a while on our shelves seem to have been content for the most part with hanging the pendulum rather than moving it. One after another they contemplated the nature of government and its varieties: monarchy; aristocracy; republic. Platonic and Aristotelian concepts, the Greek city states, the Roman empire, the Florentine state, the Venetian republic, the papal vicariate, the Hapsburg dominions were all described and analyzed while being used as springboards for discussions of statecraft. Law and justice, war and peace, subject and chief of state, neutrality and liberty, citizenship and patriotism each had its proper niche in a succession of predictable chapters. Whether such books were written in dialogue form or as straight and sober tomes, they all appeared modeled upon the same mold and designed to achieve the same goal of universal harmony. Most of them, for some strange reason, were the work of Italians, and the vision persists of one Italian savant after another scurrying from Padua to Verona, from Florence to Rome, conferring with like-minded Italian savants, exchanging similar opinions, and returning to home base to write a treatise on the architectonics of the state. Some were secretaries of cardinals, others preceptors to ducal offspring; some served as diplomats, bishops or jurists. But all, even when they refuted one another, seemed to arrive at more or less the same conclusions. From Botero to Sansovino, from Contarini to Paruta, they elaborated their theories, developed *La Scienza Politica*, and helped suspend the pendulum that other writers would swing.

Some writers of the Renaissance and later periods specialized in one particular aspect of political theory: the nature of the ruler. To Machiavelli he was *The Prince*; to Erasmus, as well as to a host of other analysts, he was *The Christian Prince*. With a zest that at times seems all but uncontrollable, they outlined over and again the requisite temperament, discipline, authority, training, virtue and states-manship of the ruler. Again, no appreciable pendulum swing is discernible here except that in time the duties and obligations of the king were given almost equal space with his privileges and pre-rogatives. One outstanding book entitled *L'Idea del Prencipe Politico Christiano* was able to harmonize political interest with lofty prin-ciple. Written by Diego Fajardo de Saavedra, a seventeenth-century

Spanish diplomat, the *Idea* investigated the entire career of a future monarch from his deportment and relations with his subjects to his conduct with foreigners and his behavior in war and peace. Our copy was adorned with 102 emblematic engravings all representing some symbol of statecraft and kingship. The first showed Hercules slaying the serpents in his cradle. The last showed a skull with sceptre and overturned crown.

As attitudes toward sceptre and crown were formulated, the pendulum swung more noticeably. Some of the more literary monarchs enunciated and defended their own divine right. The *Declaration* in which the wisest fool in Christendom, James I of England, asserted his supremacy as head of state and his immunity to papal allegiance was translated into French in 1615, five years after a French monarch had been assassinated. Its spirit was instilled the same year into *La Grandevr De Nos Roys et De Levr Sovveraine Puissance,* where the greatness of the French crown is exalted. Earlier and later there were hosts of writers who aligned themselves on the side of the ruler, replying to reformers and would-be reformers, extolling the theory of divine right, absolving the monarch from all guilt since he was unbound by the acts of his predecessors and indeed free from all human controls. In France, Germany, England and Scotland these apologists for the crown spoke up, and their treatises lined our shelves: Jean Savaron's *De La Sovveraineté dv Roy* (1620), announces that the king has received his authority from God alone and hence is responsible neither to lay nor to ecclesiastical authority; Sir George Mackenzie's *Jus Regium: Or, The Just and Solid Foundations of Monarchy* (1684) declares that "the Lawful Successor Cannot be Debarr'd from Succeeding to the Crown"; John Nalson's *Countermine* of 1678 justifies the king's prerogatives against the attacks of dissenters. By that time, however, the pendulum had swung far enough to the left in England for the author to be arrested and summoned before Parliament to justify his attitude.

In spite of the absolutists who assailed sedition, in spite of divine right, the crown and sceptre were upon occasion overturned not only in emblematic engravings but in fact and in books. With every royal assassination, pamphlets for and against tyrannicide emerged from the press. Sometimes the pamphlets attempted to precipitate the assassination. On May 14, 1610, Henry IV, King of France, was riding in his carriage, reading a book, when a fanatical French Jesuit, Ravaillac, leaped from behind and murdered him. The scene is implanted upon my mind, for we had a contemporary relation illustrated with a woodcut depicting the fatal act. We also had much of the literature that followed, including a scholarly Latin tome on the legal principles of tyrannicide by a French jurist of Poitiers and an attack upon tyrannicide by a French Jesuit. Later, across the Channel, less than a decade after the decapitation of Charles I, an incendiary pamphlet was published that incited readers to the assassination of Oliver Cromwell! *Killing no Murder* has been called "the most famous example of the free expression of free opinion in English political literature." Ironically dedicated to Cromwell himself, it condemns the tyrant and defends tyrannicide.

For every *pro* there is a *con*, for every *con* a *pro*. From left to right to left the pendulum swings as the books roll from the press. The supporter of tyranny opposes the supporter of tyrannicide. But once the prerogatives of kingship have been questioned, the ground begins to be cleared for the people's government and its champions. In that long passage leading from endorsement of limited monarchy to the contractual theory of government and on to popular sovereignty, we have had many printed representatives. Perhaps because our own inclination would give a sinistral swing to the pendulum, we have taken enormous pleasure and pride in studying the works of those spokesmen for the people and passing them on to others. In so doing we have almost shared in the evolution of government itself.

Two sixteenth-century French political theorists have always been welcomed to our shelves. Both taught jurisprudence, one at Bourges, the other at Toulouse, and, though deeply influenced by early texts on government, they were practical men who endeavored to construct a political science that would be in harmony with sixteenth-century fact. François Hotman, author of the *Francogallia*, and Jean Bodin, author of the *République*, have been called proponents of limited monarchy. In the early 1570's, when the weak and fanatical Charles IX occupied the French throne and the St. Bartholomew's Day Massacre was perpetrated, Hotman, followed by Bodin, advanced the unusual idea that the monarchy was limited by the people and their right to election, referendum and deposition. In theory at least it was the people who delegated power to the ruler; the king was merely their agent. Out of such a concept the so-called contractual theory of government was quick to evolve, a theory that would eventually lead to the development of constitutions and the division of powers.

Probably the first to articulate the idea of government as a contract between ruler and ruled was an advocate at the court of the Bourbon King Henry IV. Using a pseudonym, Philippe de Mornay, Seigneur Du Plessis wrote a treatise entitled *Vindiciae contra Tyrannos* (1579), translated into French as *De La Pvissance Légitime Dv Prince Svr le Pevple, et du peuple sur le Prince.* There he stipulated that, while the king did indeed possess certain rights, the people did too, and among those rights was the right of rebellion. Government was a contract between ruler and subjects, and if the prince breached the contract his subjects were absolved from obedience. If all this sounds remarkably familiar to readers who have never heard of the Seigneur Du Plessis, it may be because phrases from the American Declaration of Independence are ringing in their ears.

Between 1579, when Du Plessis wrote the first Latin edition of his work, and 1776, when the Declaration was signed, the contractual theory of government was elaborated and extended. A seventeenth-century Dutch magistrate, Joannes Althusius, championed Du Plessis, enlarging the applications of the theory. In England, Algernon Sidney in *Discourses Concerning Government* upheld the natural compact idea, finding place for the authority of Parliament as well as for a hereditary nobility. On several counts of treason, including his view of the king's subjection to Parliament, the author was condemned to death, dying in the Tower in 1683.

A century later, back in France, the theories proliferated as would the severed heads. During the trial of the English monarch Charles I, John Milton had enunciated in his *Tenure of Kings and Magistrates* (1649) the principle that the relationship of subject to ruler is a voluntary one, abrogated at will. In 1789, at the outset of the French Revolution, a French version of Milton's work appeared: *Théorie de la Royauté, d'après la Doctrine de Milton*—a reminder less of a precedent for tyrannicide than of a pattern for government by contract. The leading eighteenth-century French theorist was doubtless Jean-Jacques Rousseau, the citizen of Geneva who in his *Du Contract Social—Social Compact*—based all government upon the consent of the governed. Upon that concept the American Constitution would stand. Among the many editions of Rousseau's work which we have had, a late issue of 1797 was among the most interesting and the most ironical, for it bore upon its title-page a portrait of Napoleon Bonaparte and it was dedicated by its publisher to Citizen Bonaparte! Between 1762 when the Citizen of Geneva wrote his *Contract*

Social and 1797 when an edition of it was dedicated to Citizen Bonaparte, the pendulum had done some violent swinging. Much of that swinging had been effected by the *philosophes* who rallied round the Rousseauean concept of the *Social Compact*, adding ideas on the division of powers and the limitation of power, the state of society and the state of nature.

Some writers went a step—or a pendulum swing—beyond the contractual theory of government to insist that government, whose purpose is the welfare of the people, resides exclusively in the people. As early as 1576 the Swiss reformer Théodore de Bèze announced that the power of supreme law was the people's—the Third Estate's—and that the monarch's will was superseded by that law. This, in essence, is popular sovereignty, of which we have seen glimpses from time to time and from nation to nation. Antony Ascham, English parliamentarian ambassador to Madrid (where he was murdered in 1650) wrote in his pseudonymous *The Original & End of Civil Power* a strong revolutionary statement of government of the people, by the people, for the people. The eminent German jurist Samuel Pufendorf gave a systematic form to the study of that natural law which became familiar to Americans as "the Laws of Nature and of Nature's God." As early as 1574, one French writer, René Choppin, cogitating the role of the peasant in the manorial system, announced that the peasant had not only duties but rights and privileges. Two centuries later another Frenchman, Rabaut de St. Etienne, a fiery member of the French National Assembly, exalted the Third Estate and condemned the usurpation of its rights by the nobility.

With the Third Estate in the ascendancy, on paper at least, civil liberty and eventually civil disobedience were on their way. Over much of the world, popular sovereignty was becoming part of the political climate. The pendulum was swinging left of center. Long before the words *Liberty, Equality* and *Fraternity* had been united into a rallying cry, they had been demanded in print. During almost every reign in England voices could be heard of those crying in a wilderness or orating on a platform. Those whose words were committed to print can still be heard: the political writer in the service of Oliver Cromwell who in his *Jus Populi* (1644) called for the political rights of subjects; the anonymous author of a pamphlet issued in 1659 just prior to the Restoration, who stipulated that the rotation of elected representatives was an integral part of civil liberty; that great pamphleteering man of the people Daniel Defoe who, reviewing the reign of King William, powerfully defended English liberties. It was in England—two hundred years before Thoreau's *Civil Disobedience* —that an anonymous treatise awkwardly entitled *An Exercitation concerning Usurped Powers* concluded that it was not only unethical but unlawful to give allegiance to any usurped power.

Probably it was Rousseau who most fervently adumbrated the natural equality that should be the heritage of man. The Academicians of Dijon had set the theme of inequality among men as the subject for a *Discourse*, and in his response Jean-Jacques painted a glowing picture of a primitive society where inequalities had been non-existent, advanced the theory of the injustice of property, and supported the doctrine of the original, natural equality of man. Our copy of the first edition of his *Discours sur l'Origine et les Fondemens de l'Inégalité parmi les Hommes* bore upon its title-page the appropriate cartouche of Liberty.

In Rousseau's path strode the Comte de Mirabeau with his challenge to autocracy and his denunciation of arbitrary and tyrannical intrusions upon civil liberty. The thoughts of both those political philosophers filtered across the seas either in imported or reprinted editions. As for the Marquis de Condorcet, an English translation of his work on the *Progress of the Human Mind* was published in Philadelphia in 1796. There the author endorsed not only man's civil liberty but woman's too—the perfect equality of the sexes, the highest possibilities for human attainment. Our edition, published for the French émigrés who had settled in Philadelphia, eventually reached a larger audience. To us it embodied the connections between two worlds and the contagion of free thought.

In the oppression of tyranny men looked toward liberty. Similarly, in the long nightmare of war men dreamed of peace. The blood-stained corridors of history are paved with declarations of war and treatises on military strategy, relations of furious conflicts and eye-witness accounts of battles and retreats. From time to time across those corridors there pass the diplomats and negotiators, the arbitrators and internationalists. The pendulum, swung one way by the war-mongers, has its direction changed by the peace-lovers. The earliest proponent of peace to cross our bibliopolic threshold was a Carthusian monk named Ambrosius Alantsee. His *Tractatus . . . Fedus Christianu*[*m*] came to us in a 1504 edition. In it the idealistic author saw fraternity as the basis of national and international understanding and called for peaceful co-existence among the Christian nations of the world.

Another century brought forth the illustrious Dutch jurist Hugo Grotius, the "miracle of Holland," whose great work *On War and Peace* formed the basis of international law. By 1925, when the tercentenary of its publication was celebrated, this monumental treatise had been republished forty-six times and appeared in twenty-nine different translations. While the greatest collection of Grotius is suitably owned by the Palace of Peace in The Hague, copies of *On War and Peace* have reached all corners of the world, including, as we shall see, the Borough of Brooklyn.

Hugo Grotius began life as a child prodigy, writing Latin verse at the age of nine, matriculating in Leyden University at eleven, and at sixteen publishing an edition of an encyclopedic work by Martianus Capella. Having set up as a barrister in The Hague, the young Grotius handled a case that early stirred his interest in the subject of the lawfulness of war. A captain of the Dutch East India Company had captured a Portuguese galleon in the Straits of Malacca. The question arose: Could a private company like the Dutch East India Company take prizes at sea? In his defense of the captain, the lawyer Grotius presented the novel doctrine that the ocean is free to all nations. In addition he wrote a treatise entitled *De Jure Praedae* which remained in manuscript until 1868 but which contained a chapter on the "Mare Liberum" and in many ways was a precursor to *On War and Peace*.

Grotius was involved not only in legal affairs but in theological and political controversies. After the coup d'état of Prince Maurice of Nassau against the liberties of Utrecht and Holland, Grotius, a Remonstrant, was arrested, tried, and condemned to life imprisonment. In June 1619 the learned barrister was confined in the fortress of Louvenstein where, despite the harshness of his sentence, he was allowed not only the companionship of his wife but the use of books. Once read, those books were sent out of the fortress along with the prisoner's dirty linen in a book chest. An omnivorous reader, Grotius must have made use of a great number of book chests and in time the chests were passed from Louvenstein unopened by the warders. Less than two years after his imprisonment, Hugo Grotius made his famous escape by hiding in a book chest. Disguised as a mason, he was conveyed across the border and eventually arrived in Paris.

There the exile wrote down his thoughts on men in society who, he claimed, are "bound together by a natural law which makes promises binding," a belief which forms the basis of the "doctrine of the original contract." The *De Ivre Belli ac Pacis Libri Tres,* regarded as the groundwork for the modern science of the law of nations, was first published in Paris in 1625. The author received two hundred copies, giving some away, selling others at a crown apiece. Copies were sent by the publisher to the Frankfurt Book Fair. One copy of the first edition somehow found its way, centuries later, to the Borough of Brooklyn, far across those seas that Grotius had first announced were free. There we saw it, in the back office of a bookseller-publisher-collector who specialized in books on the law. And there we bought it, a remarkably large, fine copy of this landmark in internationalism. A short time later we sold our prize to the Newberry Library, but in between the buying and the selling we watched Mijnheer Grotius give a powerful swing to the pendulum.

Others followed who wrote on internationalism, among them Henry IV's great prime minister Maximilien de Bethune, the Duc de Sully, whose *Memoires*, printed at his own private press, included the first draft of his "Grand Dessein," a plan for the unification of the states of Europe into a federation of hereditary monarchies. Samuel Pufendorf who taught the law of nations at Heidelberg had his own views of internationalism. He was represented on our shelves by a study of international law in which he regarded man as a social being whose conduct must be conditioned by community life.

The eighteenth century with its wars and revolutions was also a seedbed for peace plans. In France the distinguished Abbé Saint-Pierre projected a scheme for perpetual peace and outlined an ideal government of sovereign states led by well trained students of political science. His compatriot Ange Goudar was not quite so ambitious. In his *La Paix de L'Europe . . . ou Projet de Pacification Générale*, he called not for perpetual peace but merely for a twenty-year international armistice. The ideals and the plans varied with the planners. The French publicist Mably, analyzing the methods of arriving at international accord, stressed the role of treaties and ambassadors, alliances and the balance of power. Rousseau, commenting upon Saint-Pierre's project, suggested a code of international law that would be controlled by a Congress of Nations.

By the nineteenth century, though there was still no Congress of Nations, there were at least Congresses for Peace. The Brussels Peace Congress of 1848 opened with delegates from seven nations and adopted a resolution recommending that Great Britain and the United States lead the world in disarmament. Its proceedings found a place on our shelves. So too did the proceedings of the Paris Peace Congress of the following year. Then, before 840 delegates, Victor Hugo declared that in the future the cannon would become a museum piece for the world would be united into a federation of sovereign states. Across the seas, the American Peace Society had been formed in 1828. Its *Prize Essays* were concerned with international government and law, arbitration and the establishment of a Congress of Nations to adjust international disputes. As president of the American Peace Congress, the abolitionist judge William Jay published a pamphlet that became a landmark in the development of internationalism. *War and Peace: the Evils of the First, and a Plan for Preserving the Last* demanded an international tribunal for the arbitration of all disputes. Like many idealistic political thinkers, William Jay believed that war could be eliminated by the growth of public opinion against it. In the shaping of that public opinion, he and many who preceded and followed him, had a hand.

Perhaps no writers have swung the pendulum of public opinion with greater zeal than those who couched their ideas not in sober political treatises but in satires and utopias. The abhorrent nature of tyranny was never more graphically painted than in a satirical drama of 1748 entitled *Le Congres des Betes* in which, at the conclusion of the War of the Austrian Succession, the nations are personified as animals—fox and leopard, boar and monkey—while a sardonic folding plate depicts the four-footed monarchs of Europe in unholy conclave.

If a satirical cloak or allegorical disguise sets free a vitriolic pen, an imaginary country is perhaps best adapted to serve as background for an ideal commonwealth. Sir Thomas More first named utopia Utopia; Thomas Campanella called it City of the Sun and Francis Bacon dubbed it New Atlantis. Whatever they were called, these never-never lands were usually governed in peace and international harmony. In 1793, in the midst of the French Revolution, a journalist, Beffroy de Reigny, using the pseudonym of "Cousin Jacques," envisioned a lunary empire where liberty and equality were the order of the day, where the rights of man were exercised, where slavery and all arbitrary distinctions were outlawed by a utopian constitution. The setting of another later utopia was not quite so remote. In *L'An 5865*, the French writer Mettais transferred his ideal commonwealth not to the moon but to Africa!

Unlike many purely imaginary utopias, James Harrington's *Oceana* (1656) was modeled upon an actual republic. Moreover, both the author and his manuscript were involved in such cloak-and-dagger adventures that they repay more than a casual glance. Described as a man with "quick-hot fiery hazell eie and thick moist curled hair," Harrington was certainly his own man. Having studied at Oxford, he traveled to Rome where, it was reported, he refused to kiss the Pope's toe, a dereliction he later explained to King Charles I by stating that after kissing the king's hand he could not possibly kiss any prince's foot.

Despite his republican principles Harrington was definitely attracted to the ill-fated Stuart monarch. He may have been briefly imprisoned for refusing to take an oath against helping Charles to escape, and it was said that he was among the entourage who accompanied the king to the scaffold. There is no doubt that he preferred Charles' kingship to Cromwell's autocracy, and in the *Oceana* the republic he describes resembles a moderate aristocracy. There, Harrington, Cromwell's "subtle defamer," attempts to prove that a true commonwealth is possible in England. His model commonwealth is based upon the Venetian Republic which the author had visited and admired. In Oceana (England) power depends upon the balance of property. Laws are proposed by a senate, voted upon by the people, and executed by a magistracy. The elaborate system of rotation and balloting which Harrington developed is said to have played a role in the introduction of the ballot in the nineteenth century.

Before publication, the manuscript had an eventful history. Seized by Cromwell, it was later restored to the author by Cromwell's daughter Mrs. Claypoole. In her history of publishing in England between 1551 and 1700, Leona recounts the episode delightfully: "Shortly after its theft, the harassed author sought the intercession of Elizabeth Claypoole, Cromwell's daughter, . . . Harrington visited the residence of Mrs. Claypoole where he fondled her small daughter declaring dramatically that his own child had been stolen. The lady's consternation was immediate to which the author declared 'his child' was 'the issue of his brain.' It had been misrepresented to Mrs. Claypoole's father and taken out of the press by his order. Assured that the work contained nothing prejudicial to the regime of her Lord father, Mrs. Claypoole . . . 'had [his] Book speedily restor'd to him.'"

Despite the author's protestations, the book—ironically dedicated to the Lord Protector—was indeed prejudicial to Cromwell's regime. Once published in 1656 by the Fifth Monarchist Livewell Chapman, it was attacked from all sides. After Cromwell's death, Harrington established a club, the Rota, for the discussion of his political schemes. Having hidden for a while in disguise in the home of John Milton's friend and publisher William Dugard, the author of *Oceana* was in 1661 committed to the Tower for endeavoring to change the form of government. Subsequently released, Harrington died in 1677 and was buried next to Walter Raleigh. Unlike Raleigh, Harrington never visited the New World, but his "child," "the issue of his brain" did. *Oceana* is said to have influenced the American colonists and so the book gave a strong swing to the political pendulum.

The influence of most of the books on political theory and practice that have crossed our paths is difficult to trace with any degree of accuracy. In one way or another they probably did introduce an idea or spread a concept, prepare the ground for change, alter the political climate. Their effect was gradual and undramatic. There have been other books, however, whose influence can be traced since they have noticeably swayed opinion or led to action. They are not necessarily greater or more important than the books whose effectiveness cannot be firmly assessed. Their impact is simply more demonstrable. For better or for worse, they have been instruments of action, created by the pen that is indeed mightier than the sword.

Such a pen was wielded at times by rulers themselves. From our shelves Henry VIII of England has thundered his *Assertion of the Seven Sacraments* in opposition to Martin Luther. His book, which we had in a Latin edition of 1523, attacked the Reformer and proclaimed His Majesty Defender of the Faith. This was a manifesto by means of which a monarch changed not merely the sequence of his wives but the course of English faith. The course of English history was changed again by *An Act* of 1649 *Declaring and Constituting the People of England to be a Commonwealth and Free-State*. This folio broadside was adorned with the device of the English Commonwealth which it ushered in under the Protectorate of Oliver Cromwell. A decade or so later, after Cromwell's death, the pendulum swung back with a powerful royalist manifesto—the famous *Declaration of Breda*—issued by the exiled Charles II in which he stipulated the terms by which he would accept the crown. His *Declaration*, which came to us in a first printing, was issued in April 1660. The next month Charles was pronounced king and Restoration followed Commonwealth.

Much of the history of France was triggered by printed instruments that have rested for a time upon our shelves. In the long and often tedious annals that mark the struggle between church and state we have had *Concordats* or *Pragmatic Sanctions* that defined, regulated and limited the power of the Pope in French dominions. Of still more impelling influence was the great *Edict of Nantes* promulgated by Henry IV at the end of the sixteenth century. By its terms French Protestants or Huguenots were granted not only freedom of religion but freedom to hold political office and enjoy a voice in the government. We never had the *Edict* in first issue, but we have had much of the related legislation as well as a detailed and enthusiastic account of the services at Notre Dame on June 21, 1598 that celebrated its signing. Upon that joyous occasion the Archbishop of Glasgow and ambassadors from Florence and Venice joined the dignitaries of France to hear the choir of Notre Dame peal forth a thanksgiving echoed in the hearts of the French populace.

Almost a century later the pendulum swung back again as a different monarch, Louis XIV, issued another *Edict* formally revoking the *Edict of Nantes*. By terms of the *Revocation*, the liberal policy of Henry IV was reversed and Huguenots, denied freedom of worship and excluded from public office, left France for more receptive shores. Like those who would flee the Nazi terror two hundred fifty years later, they enriched the countries of their adoption—Holland, England, and even America. Besides the *Revocation*, we collected dozens of related *Decrees* that elaborated upon it; we found legislation that denied Huguenots the right to enter the homes of Catholic nobles or retain Catholic domestics, and which refused them not only the services of Catholic physicians but the right of burial in certain areas. As it swung the pendulum, the *Revocation of the Edict of Nantes* pushed much of the human race as far back as the *Edict of Nantes* had carried it forward.

The theorists, like the monarchs, forged their instruments of action. It was the seventeenth-century Bishop of Salisbury, Gilbert Burnet, whose pen brought the Established Church to the side of William of Orange at a critical time when a native-born king deserted England and a foreign potentate defended it. It was the great French sceptic of the eighteenth century, Voltaire, who directly triggered legislative action with his *Treatise on Religious Toleration*.

He had been moved to write this work on persecution and intolerance because of the so-called Calas Affair. Jean Calas, a Protestant merchant of Toulouse, had six children. One of them, Louis, had converted to Catholicism. Another, Antoine, was found hanged in his father's warehouse in the autumn of 1761. A rumor, completely unfounded in fact, spread among Catholics to the effect that Antoine, a suicide, had been murdered by his family to prevent him from converting too. The fraternity of White Penitents buried Antoine as a martyr. In a day when the accused was allowed neither counsel nor permission to confront those who testified against him, when secret trials were commonplace and four hundred different legal systems prevailed in France, the Calas family was condemned to the rack for the murder of their son. The family appealed to the Toulouse parlement which in its mercy selected the father for torture and death. On March 9, 1762, the sentence was carried out. Jean Calas was broken alive on the wheel and burned to death.

This was the case which engaged the attention of the aging sceptic of Ferney who converted it into a cause. Setting aside his literary projects, Voltaire laid the matter before the Council of State at Versailles with the purpose of forcing the admission that Calas had been unjustly condemned. He held that

. . . it is only necessary for five or six *philosophes* to understand in order to upset the Colossus. There is no question of stopping our lackeys going to Mass; it is a question of snatching fathers of families from the tyranny of impostors and inspiring them with the spirit of tolerance.

Voltaire labored to spread that "spirit of tolerance" and to achieve a fairer method of trial. Among his labors was his *Treatise on Religious Toleration* in which the author considered the historical and philosophical aspects of the Calas Affair, persecution and the laws of nature and society, the abuses of intolerance and superstition, universal toleration. Its publication led to the improvement of the legal position of French Protestants and eventually king and Council of State annuled the proceedings of the parlement of Toulouse and declared Jean Calas innocent.

When we catalogued our copy of the first English edition, we captioned it "A Book that Led to Action." In it Voltaire, who had supreme faith in human reason, had spread both reason and humanity abroad. A book prompted by a judicial murder had served as catalyst to "upset the Colossus."

The pamphlet literature of the American and French Revolutions is punctuated with such catalysts, swinging the pendulum now right, now left, leading to action or reaction. After the anti-American *Taxation no Tyranny* exploded from the English press in 1775, *A Defence of the Resolutions and Address of the American Congress* replied to it, announcing that resistance to usurpation was honorable self-defense and that the greatest treason was that of the government against the community. During the French Revolution a flood of pamphlets enunciating assent or dissent helped destroy the monarchy and enforce the rights of man, helped spread the Terror and lead to the dictatorship of Bonaparte.

The written word has activated monarchy and revolution, dictatorship and parliamentarianism, anarchy and communism. While we hesitate to go far beyond the eighteenth century in the stock we accumulate, from time to time we do venture into more modern times, and so Proudhon has visited us with his affirmation of political anarchy and the abolition of property; Karl Marx's *Capital* in the first English edition of 1887 has analyzed for us the economic structure of society and the labor theory of value. Indeed, Bakunin's *Dieu Et L'Etat*, in which the Russian revolutionary demanded the total abolition of the state, fulminated on our shelves. Posthumously published at the expense of a comrade, that treatise became the spokesman for Russian nihilism. Next to our copy of Bakunin we placed the plans for the Soviet and socialist revolution outlined by Lenin in *Die Naechsten Aufgaben Der Sowjet-Macht* of 1918.

Our bookcases devoted to political theory suggest indeed that nations and their governments may be shaped by the printed word. Surely opinion is so shaped. We have come a long way from those Italian Renaissance tomes that objectively cogitated the varied forms which *La Scienza Politica* might assume. Or have we? Down the centuries and across the countries of the world, the pendulum has swung to right, to left. Humanity has taken one step forward, another step backward. All that can be said with any degree of certainty is that we do not stand still and that such steps as we do take are often determined by those who write books.

7

Perils & Pitfalls
At Home & Abroad

[LR]

A movie audience of a bygone era sat enraptured before a silent film entitled "The Perils of Pauline." These two Paulines—Madeleine and Leona—are well aware of a variety of perils lurking in the antiquarian book trade, which is incorrectly regarded as a serene, sedentary profession. These hazards are emotional and physical, suffered by the armchair bookman as well as his more venturesome colleague stalking books abroad.

Emotional frustrations are often more disturbing than physical perils. Consider the reaction of the dealer to the listing of the first edition of Adam Smith's *Wealth of Nations* (1776) at £90 in a catalogue which has been sent surface mail from Hobart, Tasmania. The dealer, after some mild collapse, has three choices. He may phone, cable, or send an airmail letter form. He decides to cable the Tasmanian antiquarian Angus Crawford-Smith. The Western Union operator insists that the slightly hysterical American supply her with the Hobart area code. Tense, the dealer replies he is unaware of the Hobart area code. A few minutes later the operator reports in an authoritative voice:

"Take down the area code for Hobart, South Dakota."

"But, Miss, I clearly said Hobart, Tasmania."

"You will require an overseas operator."

After later communication with an even more authoritative individual the semi-prostrate dealer is informed that all cable lines will be tied up for a minimum of seven hours. One valium and a large Scotch prove ineffective. An airmail letter sent in desperation to Mr. Angus Crawford-Smith, Hobart, Tasmania, is returned after four weeks for insufficient postage. When an English dealer a year later offers a copy of Adam Smith, *The Wealth of Nations* (London 1776) at £ 2,900, his American colleague downs two martinis and violently tears the offer to shreds.

Attendance at an auction induces certain emotional and cerebral reactions. The behavior pattern of dealers at auctions is, therefore, quite interesting. A colleague may choose an unobtrusive seat in the rear and attempt to attract the auctioneer's attention with a slight wink, the rubbing of the chin, positioning a stubby pencil at a 90-degree angle, removing spectacles, or keeping the mouth agape. Another member of the trade chooses to sit up front where he strives to fixate the auctioneer with a mad grin. Occasionally he grins too long and unwittingly buys items 70 through 91.

Tension at auctions is understandable. If a dealer arrives with a legal-size sheet covered with bids, his blood pressure can become dangerously high. On the other hand, boredom may also envelop the dealer who arrives at the rooms with bids on numbers 27 and 301. Obsessed with restlessness he rereads the catalogue twice or thrice, finding numbers 88 and 207 fairly interesting. Failing to read the detailed description of each item, he acquires both books. They are dogs. No. 88 lacks two leaves and No. 207 is water-stained through-out, the back cover detached, and, according to Brunet, "une édition peu distinguée." An auction customer must have nerves of steel and remain calm within a mantle of self-discipline.

Probably the greatest emotional hazard encountered by the anti-quarian bookman is the insufferable service of the United States Postal Service. An invoice from Sotheby Parke-Bernet at 77th Street and Madison Avenue may take eleven days to reach us at 88th Street and Madison Avenue. It is true that if it has been dispatched during a June heat wave, the invoice may need to cool off in Alaska or perhaps drop in at the home office, 34-35 New Bond Street, London W1A 2AA.

The rudeness and ignorance of the average postal clerk discourage a mail order business:

"Package too big. Bring it back, ya follow?"

"It's according to specification."

"Try Window Four."

"There is nobody at Window Four."

"So whadda ya want from me? He's out to lunch. Ya think he got nothin' to do like you?"

Affiliated to some extent with the United States Postal Service is the United States Customs. Most European shippers are sufficiently careful not to submit their American customers to the ordeal of clearing books through customs. In *Old & Rare* I discussed my role as customs lady for the late Herbert Reichner. In retrospect my hours spent at Bowling Green were idyllic in comparison with a recent visit to the smart headquarters of the United States Customs Service, now located in the World Trade Center at the tip of Manhattan.

The bus trip to the World Trade Center consumed nearly as much time as a trip on the Concorde to London. Upon arrival at our destination we queried a guard about the location of the United States Customs.

"Over there, ya follow me," he replied, pointing his finger in the air. Instructions from a second guard were more detailed:

"Ya see that there corridor, follow it right down to the end, y'understand. Then go left. Y'll see a door, open it, go through and ask."

At Room Six, United States Customs, an official stamped our notice twice, once in red and once in black.

"Thank you very much," we smiled gaily.

He stared glumly. "I ain't done nothin'. Go upstairs and get ya forms. Ya better hurry. They close soon for lunch."

A middle-aged blond proved our saviour. "Go to the end of the line dearie. Others ahead of you. Have we ever filled out forms for you before? Because if we did we are not allowed to do it again. Read the sign."

Our blond filled out a lengthy dossier.

"How come girls like you don't have a broker, huh? Let me tell you this is just the beginning. You're in the book business. What kind of books?" she continued suspiciously. "Please sign in four places and when you've signed ya gotta post a bond. You follow me. Go to Building Two and see the bondsman. Now if I'm not here when you finish with him come back at three."

"But we wish the books today!"

"Honey, that ain't got nothing to do with me."

The bond was posted (not to be repaid by Uncle Sam since, as our efficient blond had informed us, we are in a privileged position to be able to import merchandise from abroad).

"You girls don't realize your privilege. Not everybody has the privilege to import. This country grants you that special privilege, y'understand?" The dossier eventually returned to us suggests that antiquarian dealers should engage in paper trade.

"Nice meeting you girls. Now all you have to do is get to the Customs Division of the G.P.O. at 33rd Street. Be sure to use the right entrance."

Our reception at G.P.O. was somewhat conspiratorial. "Which one of you ladies wants to come in and inspect the package?" We both volunteered.

"Only one of yuz can sign the papers."

Once in the large package room, a postal clerk opened a cabinet and, winking at me, brought forth a small box.

"Here yuz is. But ya gotta sign. Not yet. Mr. A. over there is fillin' out the forms."

"Sign here, Miss. Just sign your signature."

The package weighed not more than two pounds and bore £ 22 postage. Sent airmail at our request, it had aroused the curiosity of the United States Customs officers who had found in it neither heroin nor nuclear secrets.

"Nice seein' ya goils. Come again."

In conclusion, I wish all my dear colleagues the best of luck in all cables to Hobart, Tasmania, auction chills and fever, negotiations with the United States mails and the mystique of the United States Customs.

If such emotional hazards do not deter the beginner in the antiquarian book trade, he must beware of other dangers. Reading a single-spaced mimeographed list printed on both sides of the page (with offset throughout) may imperil his vision to such an extent that he is forced to sport a tin cup. Falling, or almost falling from a swaying fourteen-foot ladder is a harrowing experience. Is it not a challenge to cross a narrow high parapet dividing two book-lined rooms of a Liège antiquarian when you are wearing spike heels? Is it antiquarian fulfillment to be crushed under an avalanche of books cascading down from a top shelf, your watch crystal smashed, the blood of an injured wrist blending with red morocco? Is the stomach not in conflict with the soul when your Japanese host offers you hot sake followed by three courses of raw fish which are arranged most attractively in flower designs? Are Gallic W.C.'s romantic, or would you not prefer an American "john" to two cold holes on the cobbled Rue de Tournon, the Rue Saint-André-des-Arts, the Rue Jacob, and all the damp Rues of La Belle France?

Lack of familiarity with the German calendar may upset a fast-paced buying trip and imperil a long planned schedule with a rapid succession of holidays when practically all shops are closed: Gründonnerstag, Karfreitag, Ostermontag. And later on you might as well remain in bed during Muttertag.

The hazards of travel in the pursuit of books are manifold. The chances of tumbling into the Grand Canal are favorable if you happen to be scanning the title-page of a sixteenth-century octavo purchased on the Calle della Mondola in Venice. Attempting to reach the premises of Luigi Gonelli & Figli on the Via Ricasoli opposite the Florentine Duomo, we were almost crushed into the stout wall of a sixteenth-century building when a motor scooter zoomed past. These are minor Italian hazards. What of Italian train service? Has it attempted to match the United States Postal Service in incompetence and non-service?

Since we had experienced the waywardness of Italian trains on other occasions we decided to purchase in advance two tickets at the New York office of Italian Railways for the 'rapido' which departed Florence for Milan at 8 A.M. We were informed that this was a crack train known for its punctuality and excellent service. It was essential to arrive at Milan on time to permit us to get to the airport to enplane for Amsterdam. We congratulated ourselves on our perspicacity and envisioned no difficulty whatsoever. The agent at the New York office of Italian Railways had not known or had neglected to inform us that this particular Sunday would inaugurate daylight-saving time in Italy.

It was now a bright Sunday, the first day of Italian daylight saving. We arrived at the station well in advance of our 'crack' train. Here we were greeted effusively by a porter who immediately transferred our four pieces of luggage on to a rack strolling away with his cargo.

"What in the world is he doing on the track marked 'Roma'?" I queried, somewhat concerned.

"Stop fussing."

We glanced at our watches. Our porter seemed extremely content as he wheeled the luggage up and down smiling at us as if we had transferred to him for safekeeping four small children. Now and then like a nanny he patted their backsides reassuringly.

A train marked 'Milano' roared into the station. "How will we ever get the luggage over here?" I shrieked, at the same time attempting to climb the high steps.

The conductor warned me away. "Reservato! Studenti! Proibito!"

The children waved and laughed, reaching out to the station vendor crying "Gelati, gelati, gelati." A whistle shrieked. "Addio!" The Milan train bounded out of the station. We stood aghast. It was now 9:15. I mildly suggested to M.B.S. that she consult the station-master about the arrival of our 'rapido' for Milan. It was now more than an hour late. Arriving at his office we read "Fermate." In reply to several frenzied questions a policeman replied: "Domenica—e tarde."

At 9:20 A.M. we were fully convinced that our 'rapido' was lost somewhere in the Tuscan hills. An explanation was finally wrung from the station-master, who had now completed his breakfast, that since it was the first day of daylight saving the matter had become complicated.

"We have no direct information from Rome but it is quite possible that they have forgotten to dispatch this excellent train."

We summoned "nanny" to bring "the children" across the track. At this point one of the two lunch boxes provided by the hotel for the train trip slipped from my arm. There was an immediate explosion of one of the large bottles of carbonated water. Bomb threat or another Arno flood?

"We must leave," Madeleine stated imperiously. "I shall not remain in Florence another moment. We shall take a taxi to Milan."

"You're either Croesus or crazy," I replied.

"We are leaving. We have to get to Milan. We must make the Amsterdam plane with all our appointments lined up for tomorrow."

"Quanto a Milano?" my partner asked the first taxi driver. He eyed our American coats, suits and the "four children" piled high on the luggage rack.

"A Milano, Signorina? E molto distante." He gestured impressively. "Un grande viaggio, Signorina. Capisce?" We nodded. "Allora, 100,000 lire."—over $ 150.00. All our profits were to be dissolved into a taxi ride to Milan. At this point "nanny's" eyes darted to us and the luggage rack as he calculated his tip. A young cab driver stepped forward promising us a smooth drive to Milan at almost half the price. We hopped into his rather worn cab, "nanny" placing the "children" in the trunk and up front. We were off.

Our taxi driver introduced himself as Ruggiero humming and singing, turning to us:

"May I stop and telephone my sister to inform her of my good fortune—una buona fortuna?"

"Si Signor, felicemente."

Upon Ruggiero's return a few minutes later we began our steady trek northward hitting the autostrada surmounted at intervals by the overhanging Ristorante Pavesi. We sat back in our car inspecting the two lunch boxes, the one a bit forlorn, the other intact. We nibbled at a chicken sandwich and drank sparingly of the one bottle of water, behaving somewhat as if we were heading for the Numidian desert. A hissing sound from the front of the car interrupted our conversation. I turned to Signorina Stern.

"What is that sound? Do you recognize it?"

"Fortunately, no!"

The hissing increased; Ruggiero stopped the car, opened the hood, looked in. He reached for a hammer and banged the radiator shortly turning around and smiling at us:

"Niente. Va bene."

We continued for another half hour during which a persistent knock took the place of the hissing. Once again Ruggiero stopped the car, opened the hood and looked in. As he reached for the hammer I joined him, ignoring Signorina Stern's objections:

"You don't even drive. What are you doing?"

This time as Ruggiero hammered he looked a bit glum.

Mady inquired, "E pericoloso, Ruggiero?"

Giving his radiator a vicious blow he turned to Madeleine:

"In twenty minutes I will know whether the situation is dangerous." The taxi crawled, heaved, sighed and came to an absolute standstill. The location of its demise was just off the autostrada directly in front of a latrine which stood in close proximity to a small picnic ground, where several families were enjoying pasta, wine, thick chunks of meat stewed in garlic. Several gentlemen on their way to or from the latrine surrounded the car all talking and advising together. We had hopped out.

"E pericoloso, Ruggiero?"

"Adesso e molto pericoloso!"

The picnickers pointed in the direction of a town. Ruggiero hopefully departed for a mechanic or another car while we studied our watches.

"Una emergenza," we wailed to the curious crowd of women and children who stared and giggled.

While we awaited Ruggiero's return, we should have composed a brief text for the forthcoming edition of the Red Cross *Manual* or the *Booksellers Travel Emergency Guide*. My friend, M.B.S., authoress, was not in an inspired mood. A picnicker informed us proudly that we were not far from the famosissima citta di Parma.

"Meravigliosa!"

Within half an hour a car, a driver and Ruggiero drew up at the picnic grounds. The driver helped transfer "the children" from the front and trunk of the cab. We arranged the financial settlement with our second driver to Ruggiero's satisfaction. He clasped our hands sadly: "Buona fortuna, signore." The picnickers waved "addio" as we sped toward Milan arriving at the airport a split second ahead of schedule. Over our bourbons we contemplated the perils of the chase.

It was a particularly lovely Spring—that of 1968—when again we returned to Paris. The chestnuts were in bloom and all of Paris was en fête. It is true that we had read of some student rumblings and demonstrations but was not student discord in vogue? We mentioned the unrest to the handsome M. Claude of the Crillon management, who laughed off our concern.

"Mesdames, je m'étonne. The students are pranksters. C'est amusant, n'est-ce pas?"

It was not quite so amusing the following day when our Paris taxi having reached the Left Bank began to limp, crawl and stop altogether as it approached the Rue des Saints Pères. Its progress had been impeded by some student agitators who were engaged in hurling chunks of pavement across the street. The driver advised us to descend. "C'est très désagréable, les scélerats." Trained as an historian, I could only recall that the early insurgents of the French Revolution had carried pitchforks—some urban artisans had also hurled rocks. As aliens in the Terror of 1968 we scuttled close to the store fronts suddenly espying 30 Rue des Saints Pères, the librairie of M. André Deruelle, specialist in archaeology, erudition, heraldry and French regionalism. We had not visited the shop for many years since we had found the books extremely dull and the proprietor extremely cantankerous. It had almost proved impossible to examine the books since they were guarded by a succession of surly assistants who begrudgingly pulled out volumes one at a time. Yet sanctuary within M. Deruelle's shop now appeared extremely attractive.

M. Deruelle eyed us with some confusion not recalling our names.

"Votre nom, s'il vous plaît."

After consulting several files with the assistance of a dour blue-smocked assistant he returned.

"Je me rappelle."

We scanned the titles of several volumes: *La paroisse de l'Eglise Saint-Pierre de Caen* of G. Huard, *Ausone et les commencements du Christianisme en Gaule* by P. Martino, and Colonel de Coynart's fascinating study, *La Guerre à Dijon* 1870–1871.

"Let's get out of here. Better to join the students."

Actually the university crowd had wearied of too much muscular activity and had retreated to the Café des deux Magots where we joined them.

The following morning as we started off on our rounds, we were stopped by M. Claude whose voice reflected some slight concern.

"You will of course have no difficulty in finding a taxi here, but you may have some trouble getting back."

As the days followed the long crisp loaves of bread became fewer. During a stroll in the Tuileries Gardens we stood aghast at the sight of the statuary defaced by red paint and daubed with graffiti. No bus schedule existed any longer and if perchance a bus arrived at all there was no assurance it would take you to your destination. The driver sailed headlong at his whim taking his passengers to the Gare St. Lazare, the Porte Orléans, the Opéra. Headed for the Boul' Mich we were deposited at the Etoile. Shortly all forms of transportation ceased; the têtes de taxis, like the bus stops, were deserted. The newspapers ceased their dire predictions since they had ceased printing. Plumbers, street cleaners, electricians, toll keepers, all hailed la Grève Nationale—a general strike!

Would the antiquarian booksellers also strike? What difference did it make? We could never get to their shops. *A pied??* How long could we traverse the beautiful boulevards and narrow streets of Paris *à pied?* M. Claude strove to calm our fears and threat of departure. We had no idea how to depart although we did have a Sunday booking from Orly to Munich—our first visit to Das Vaterland. Jehovah's revenge!

"My dears, this will all pass soon. The French are extremely rational. Have no concern. All will be normal within twenty-four hours. Enjoy your lunch."

We sat in our room and craned our necks to glimpse the Place de la Concorde.

"The guillotine was placed out there," I declared airily.

"How will we get to Orly?" Mady mused. Sitting upright she turned to me: "I wonder what Emil is doing. He'll know the answer. After all he is half-French."

We had bumped into our colleague Emil Offenbacher on the Rue de l'Echaudé during our early buying in Paris. Emil had just come over and adored everything French: its books, its people, its shop windows, its shoes and of course its wine and food. But then Emil had lived in Paris for several years. Having departed Germany in the wake of the Nazi holocaust, he had set up in Paris as an antiquarian bookseller—M. Emile Offenbacher. An excellent bookman, he pursued neo-latin verse, early science, alchemy and technology. He had absorbed much of the impeccable taste of the French bibliophile, and moving to Kew Gardens, Long Island after the war, he had continued to specialize in his chosen fields. We had often discussed French mores with him and a knowing smile betrayed his familiarity with the reasons for Gallic frugality and insularity.

As I continued to penetrate the ghost of the guillotine, the phone rang. It was our French friend Emile.

"How are you making out? There is really nothing to worry about especially since you plan to leave Sunday morning. Orly of course will be in order. Friends of mine have been coming and leaving. I am not at all worried. I have money in the bank here—really no concern. This is a passing thing. I will try to get over and see you—if not, bon voyage."

M. Claude had secured for us a private car which was to take us to Orly Sunday morning for a flight to safe, democratic Munich. His farewell as always most cordial sounded slightly ominous: "A bientôt, Mesdemoiselles. If you have any difficulty at Orly rest assured that your room at the Crillon always awaits you."

Upon our arrival at the airport no porter greeted us. With the help of the driver we pushed our luggage through the gates. The airport was jammed with passengers running in every direction, children crying, the loudspeaker blaring: "The flight to Madrid has been cancelled. Attention please, Flights 745, 335 and 201 have been detained."

We rushed to Lufthansa. The attendant shrugged: "We have no information about the Munich flight. It may or it may not leave. Remain here." After half an hour had passed Mady suggested that I approach this gentle Mädchen in Uniform since my German was so fluent. Das Mädchen who was manicuring her nails murmured a monosyllabic reply: "Wait."

As we sat on our luggage meditating upon the joys of bookbuying the loudspeaker reverberated through the airport:

"The last flight from Orly is now about to depart. Will all passengers for Moscow, Flight 33 go directly to gate eleven. Let me repeat. The Moscow Flight will leave from gate eleven. This is the last flight to depart Orly. The airport will be closed."

We rushed back to Lufthansa. The attendant was applying lipstick.

"Do you have any idea when the Munich flight will leave if the airport reopens?"

"Perhaps Tuesday. Auf Wiedersehen!" she remarked adjusting her shoulder strap bag.

As we pushed our luggage out of the airport lobby we collided with a frantic American family who had just alighted from a chauffeur-driven car. We hailed the driver. "C'est fini, hein?" he inquired as we sped toward Paris. We received a charming welcome not only from M. Claude but from his assistants, the concierge and the little pages. "Your room awaits you comme toujours. How nice to have you back."

When we recounted our experience to the cashier of "Angelina" on the Rue de Rivoli, she shook her head announcing to a single waitress: "Pas de jambon demain."

After "lunch" we telephoned the Francophile Emile. The timbre of his voice was slightly altered.

"I hear there are some difficulties in the city but they will pass. A demain."

It was about 10 A.M. "demain," when Emil Offenbacher of Kew Gardens telephoned us: "Do you know the banks are closed? Things seem to be a bit serious. I shall be right over." The small lobby of the

Crillon presented a miniature Orly. The guests were rushing back and forth. Mady had already requested the concierge to book us two flights to Munich via Brussels that day.

"Would you please tell me how we get to Brussels—à pied?" Undaunted, Mady had returned to our room to pack. Eager to serve in a desperate cause I stated: "I shall see what I can do." Entering the hotel's telephone room I heard wild sobbing. The operator had thrown herself over her machine.

"Etes-vous malade, Madame?"

"C'est impossible. Ça ne marche pas," she sobbed pointing to the silent instrument of her profession. Louder she wailed: "Ça ne marche pas." Above her sobbing I heard a page call my name.

"What is it?" Had the U.S. fleet come to our rescue?

"Mlle. Stern vous cherche."

Madeleine was hysterical when we were reunited in our room.

"Oh my God, where have you been? The management said you had gone for a walk in the rain."

"In the rain—but it's not raining. They're all crazy."

We returned to the lobby. As we conferred, in strode Emil Offenbacher looking very determined, very American.

"What are your plans? Whatever you do count me in."

At this juncture, deus ex machina, M. Claude, walked toward us beckoning three antiquarian booksellers to a quiet corner.

"I can arrange for a car to take you to Brussels." Our saviour continued, "It will be expensive."

Emil promptly agreed to share expenses. We were to pick him up at his Left Bank hotel for which he immediately departed—à pied.

M. Choppin, the driver of the hearse engaged by M. Claude, was aristocratic and supercilious. He cared little for our non-Vuitton luggage, and when we emphatically stated that we must pick up a friend on the Left Bank, he refused.

"This will prove impossible. We shall be detained well over an hour. The crowds are impassable."

We remained adamant.

En route to the Left Bank the car was detained at the Pont Caroussel for well over an hour since all moving conveyances attempted to depart Paris: autos and trucks, baby carriages and go-carts, barrows and tractors, skates and three-wheelers colliding and entangling with one another, their owners gesticulating, imprecating, smiling and laughing. Friendships were formed. Women entered men's cars. We expected the momentary birth of a new French citizen. Vive la République!

M. Choppin stopped the hearse before Emil's hotel. Opposite were the headquarters of the French Communist Party. Its defenders shrieked and hooted: "A bas le capitalisme!" The car plunged ahead. Once on the autoroute, we whizzed ahead past deserted toll booths —out of France—on to Belgium. Emil was in high spirits. "I had planned to visit Brussels. How nicely it has worked out." We were less enthusiastic. We had not planned a visit to Brussels but to Munich. Had Sabena reserved our bookings made in mad confusion by the Crillon concierge?

"You will get to Munich," Emil reassured us. "Give my warm regards to Domizlaff."

Sabena had saved two seats on the 5:45 flight for Munich. We buckled our seat belts contemplating the irony of our situation. We were seeking a haven in Germany!

Though Munich proved an attractive enough refuge, London has been the city we have always loved the most. We were familiar with its past and happy in its present. It was during the last year of our old friend, Irving Davis, that Italianate Englishman who had relinquished his earlier dwellings and moved to a small, crooked house in Hampstead. We visited him on an exceedingly chilly April morning. His shelves still displayed some unusual books. A small electric heater exuded the only warmth in his book room. We both coveted it, Mady informing me that nobody had ever expired from spontaneous chillblains.

"I cannot even hold the books. I am so chilled."

Sucking his omnipresent pipe Davis watched us, smiling a bit, his jacket open, his tie askew: "Mind you, why don't you take the heater and place it closer to the shelves, but have a care."

Utterly absorbed in an eighteenth-century volume relating to heating and ventilation, I began to feel uncomfortably hot. I noticed my partner sniffing the pages which related to the heating of a French château.

"Rather warm in here," mumbled Davis. "I say, Miss Rostenberg, are you by any chance on fire???"

Having straddled the heater I looked at my grey flannel skirt which now bore an ugly spreading brown stain.

"Have a care," continued Davis. "It's jolly warm now. I'll open a window or two. Perhaps we could do with some tea. Your skirt seems a bit damaged. Rather reminds me of a nasty binding I once had. I believe the copy had once belonged to Cardinal . . . ''

I switched the front of my skirt to the back and plumped down on a small chair. Was it that seat or mine that had become a block of ice? The tea was also cold. We never saw old Davis again and as for my skirt, the saleslady at Harrod's informed me that I might try rubbing the scorched area with a half-crown!

Charred and frozen, chipped and damaged, like Pauline we have survived the perils and pitfalls of the chase. What is more, we are looking forward to our next installment.

8

Curiouser & Curiouser*

[MBS]

The books we bag are sometimes more curious than the chase. Long before *Alice in Wonderland*, actually in 1607, an Italian physician and jurist wrote a learned Latin treatise consisting of five books entitled *De Cvriosa Doctrina*. This chapter borrows from Alice and her Italian forebear insofar as it is about the curiosities that have passed through our hands. Obviously what is curious to some may be commonplace to others and we have no desire to go so far out on the limb of language as to give our definition of *curious*. One or two examples may suffice to encourage readers to stay on to the end of the chapter. We think it curious for a French author to write on the one hand an éloge of "Nothing" which he dedicated to "No one," and, on the other, an éloge of "Something" which he dedicated to "Someone." Actually, "Nothing" has been a very popular subject among scholars of the past and it may not be an exaggeration to observe that it still is. "Something" is another thing altogether.

To start, then, with what our Frenchman, Monsieur Louis Coquelet, might call "Nothing"—the book that is not a book. Our first candidate among the curious is the non-book, the "book" that may

---

*For a Short Title List of books referred to in this chapter see pages 173–199.

be an ephemeral bit of paper or an alphabet, a panorama or a peepshow. If we think of the book only in conventional terms, then this non-book is "Nothing." But in that intriguing, far-out area of the curious to which you are now cordially invited, the non-book is definitely "Something." Here is our éloge to it.

By this time readers are aware of the attitude of Leona Rostenberg—Rare Books toward the ephemeral. While we do not go so far as to hold that the throwaway of today is the treasure of tomorrow, we do have a healthy regard for the seemingly insignificant, evanescent brochure, tract or broadside. We have delivered paeans to it in *Old & Rare*, and those who survive or skip to the last chapter of the present opus will note that respect for the ephemeral is a major article in the Rostenberg antiquarian credo.

A collection of Italian *bande* of the sixteenth century or of French edicts of the seventeenth or of American Revolutionary pamphlets of the eighteenth is invested with historical importance and stature. Less imposing but no less interesting are those *individual* decrees that throw light upon the goings-on of an earlier time, especially the curious goings-on.

In the public squares of Florence, for example, during the sixteenth century, the playing of cards or marbles, checkers or quoits was prohibited and malefactors who persisted in such levities were fined ten scudi. We have this bit of curious information thanks to the Italian *bande* or decrees issued by the Medicis. Littering the streets was another transgression of the Renaissance immortalized in other decrees. As for the public houses of Tuscany, wandering players, tightrope walkers and odd characters were—alas—denied the right of performance there. At more or less the same time in France, sovereigns were issuing statutes forbidding the sporting of silk hose and taffeta doublets, lace collars and gold braid trimmings.

Economists can find learned reasons for all such prohibitions; historians of costume must note that what was forbidden must have been desirable; sociologists will perceive interesting connections between tightrope walkers and Renaissance pubs. As for us, we study our old decrees with their woodcuts of Medici or Valois arms, and value them as curiosities that are also mirrors of the past.

In a way those early royal decrees were forms of advertising, ways of making known regulations about snuffboxes or the use of rags in papermaking. By the nineteenth century, industry had whole-heartedly subscribed to the brochure method of advertising, and pamphlets and fliers covered the country and filled wastepaper baskets.

One that was saved from the latter fate was issued in 1845 by the American Ice Company. The Company had introduced their ice into Scotland and published a pamphlet explaining the ice trade along with—in good Yankee style—the newest drinks in which ice might be introduced. The brochure was illustrated with cuts of instruments used in cutting ice as well as a refrigerator and an American water cooler. We pinned this ephemeral oddity on our screen at a book fair and promptly sold it to a colleague with an interest in technology and a taste for the curious.

During the eighteenth and nineteenth centuries, authors and publishers adopted similar ways of advertising or rather announcing their intentions to the public. These *Proposals*, as they were called, were sometimes published in periodicals, sometimes as separate brochures, and their prime purpose was to attract subscribers. Two of those uncommon ephemera that passed through our hands concerned the great Cham, Dr. Samuel Johnson: his own *Proposals* for printing by subscription in 1742 the first two volumes of the Harleian Library and, years later, *Proposals* for printing a supplement to Dr. Johnson's *Dictionary*. This ambitious project was undertaken by the Bishop of London, Jonathan Boucher, who had been an intimate friend of George Washington prior to the Revolution and who worked on this unusual project for fourteen years.

Since man proposes but God disposes, not all *Proposals* for printing by subscription materialize. Sometimes those that do not are more interesting than those that do. That Franco-American publisher Joseph Nancrede, whose papers were the object of some literary sleuthing, launched a major enterprise with *Proposals* for a complete system of universal geography. In fact, he issued a preliminary circular and two pamphlets to publicize the work, tapped scholars and libraries for information and actually went abroad to obtain maps for it. But in the end the venture was given up. The author of the proposed geography, "Balloon" Tytler, was drowned "in a fit of intoxication" and the publisher abandoned not only his scheme but his trade and his adopted country. In a way, therefore, those *Proposals for Publishing, by Subscription, A New System of Geography* remain a surviving reminder of an American publishing project of magnitude. Aware of the danger of proposing anything, I still propose the collecting of *Proposals* for lovers of the curious.

Almanacs and alphabets are also collectible non-books. Among the former we had once a Latin astronomical almanac for the year

1544 called *Ephemerides Cvm Praedictionibvs*, replete with indispensable data for astronomers, navigators and believers in horoscopes. Of alphabets we have had a variety, some consisting merely of an engraved folding plate or panorama, others printed on one folio sheet or some sixteen folding sheets. We have had so-called "artificial" alphabets and pictorial alphabets for the use of the deaf. We have had a charming military alphabet depicting drummer and lancer, general, Zouave and even a lady *cantinière*. An *Alphabet des Cris de Paris* of the mid-nineteenth century consisted of ten folding sections illustrating the letters of the alphabet with Parisian street vendors and criers—sellers of strawberries and nosegays, watercress, newspapers, engravings, almanacs—a kind of ephemeral tribute to the ephemeral. Perhaps the most curious alphabet we have had was an *Alphabet Grotesque* in which "A" stood for "Actor," "N" for "Negro," "S" for "Sorcerer," and so on with other so-called grotesqueries.

The letter "P" in my own alphabet of the curious stands for Panoramas, Playing Cards and Peepshows—non-books all of them, but certainly fascinating to the bibliophile. Because we could not part with it, we kept in stock for twenty years a late seventeenth-century Peepshow in seven panels by Engelbrecht, animating the story of Christ Scourged in the Temple. We displayed it finally at a California book fair where it was snatched by a European dealer.

As for Panoramas, we have had a dozen or more of these nineteenth-century tributes to great events published in the form of large folding compartmental plates often in color. Our panoramas have depicted the action of Waterloo and, in a foldout twenty feet long, the coronation procession of Queen Victoria showing the line of march from Buckingham Palace to Westminster Abbey. George Augustus Henry Sala, the English journalist, created several unusual panoramas. One he entitled *Grand Processions against Papal Aggression,* a colored panorama attacking Catholic influence in England. Another, drawn almost in comic strip style, was called *The House That Paxton Built*—an allusion to Sir Joseph Paxton, architect of the Great Industrial Exhibition of 1850. Sala's panorama was a tribute to every phase of that Exhibition from the peers and dandies who visited it to the food provided by Soyer. America's contribution he saw, alas, as the planter's armchair made of "ebony," supported on slavery.

Through such curious non-books the "reader" can glimpse authenticities of the past. Playing cards seem remote indeed from history until one comes upon the four sets of playing cards etched by the great Florentine engraver Stefano della Bella for the use of the young king Louis XIV of France. What a history lesson their faces give us! Louis was only seven years old, and Cardinal Mazarin, who ruled for him, took a dim view of over-educating the young monarch. Among the few "books" permitted him was the non-book that contained four sets of playing cards from which the boy could learn about the kings of France and the queens of history.

Royal decrees and statutes, almanacs and alphabets, publishing proposals and peepshows, panoramas and playing cards do not look like proper books though their appeal is certainly to the bookish. There are other oddities among books that look like books and indeed are books. A perfectly sober volume *On the Loss of Teeth and Loose Teeth; and on the Best Means of Restoring Them*, published in London in 1861 by "Mr. Howard, Surgeon Dentist to His Grace the Archbishop of Canterbury," makes a useful addition to any dental library. To us it is a curiosity because it happens to contain one of those fascinating "metamorphic" plates that depict, by means of a flap, the dramatic story of "before" and "after." Mr. Howard's book is adorned with such a plate honoring a plate, for it shows a mouth before and after the introduction of an artificial set of teeth.

Another of our candidates for the curious is the book that is not what it seems. *Poems and Sonnets. By Percy Bysshe Shelley. Edited by Charles Alfred Seymour. Member of the Phila. Hist. Soc.*, and apparently published in Philadelphia in 1887, is not at all what it purports to be. Instead it is one of the extremely successful forgeries of that artist in "forging ahead," Thomas James Wise, who not only adopted the pseudonym of Charles Alfred Seymour to "portray the gradual development of Shelley's genius," but who actually had the book printed, not in Philadelphia, but in London by Clay and Sons as one of thirty copies on English handmade paper. Shelley's *Poems and Sonnets*, designed by Wise for the not-so-wise, has become a truly curious collector's item. Its curiosity increases when one realizes that there are forgeries of the forgeries!

There are also books that began, so to speak, as paperweights. Some years ago, Bloomingdale's department store on Manhattan's 59th Street devoted a counter to "curious" Italian imports. My eye was caught by a paperweight that depicted the engraved title-page of an Italian book which I had never seen, and—even then in the snare of the curious—I bought it. It reposed for several years on my desk where I could look down at the title-page in Italian marble: *La Gigantea Et La Nanea Insieme Con La Gverra De Mostri.* Florence 1612. A few years later my partner and I were sauntering through that most improbable of Italian cities, Venice. Near the great Piazza San Marco, where all the world takes lukewarm tea or tepid fizzes, was a bookstore that specialized in maps of Venice torn from (hopefully) incomplete atlases for over-enthusiastic tourists. As we passed its window we stood transfixed, for there in all its original charm was displayed *La Gigantea Et La Nanea Insieme Con La Gverra De Mostri.* Florence 1612. It is displayed there no longer. Now it stands atop a cabinet to which its predecessor, the marble paperweight, has also been elevated. Why these seventeenth-century burlesque and satiric poems describing the wars of giants and dwarfs against the gods should have provided the model for a twentieth-century paper-weight I have no idea. It is curious, is it not?

Strange as the shapes which books or non-books may assume, stranger still are their subjects. Surely there is nothing known to the mind of man that has not been written about. Whatever is within the ken of human experience or imagination eventually finds its way into print. As a result, there is a plethora of material for this chapter. Again, some may regard our "curious" subjects as perfectly straight-forward and commonplace. But *chacun à son gout* and *chacun à son* concept regarding the curious.

To zoologists and veterinarians, the animal books that have stalked our shelves would probably be regarded as sober and useful tomes. To us they seem curious. But then we are just booksellers. Without reference to any of the chimerical beasts that adorn the pages of medieval bestiaries, we have bought and sold treatises in Latin, Italian and French, published in the sixteenth, seventeenth and eighteenth centuries, that describe and analyze, satirize and immor-talize a variety of real but unlikely animals. One of our favorites is a book on the nobility, excellence and antiquity of the ass in which an Italian poet Banchieri informs us that there is a society—the "Com-pagnia delli Briganti della Bastina"—which pays homage to that animal. Should any reader wish to join it, the author provides full details of the membership, entrance requirements and benefits, along with anecdotes of the cult of the ass. His book is adorned with nine large woodcuts depicting the members in costume and, as far as the ass is concerned, we would describe this as exhaustive if not exhausting coverage.

At least two books on the elephant have enriched our stock, one on its history and its use as a religious, literary and theatrical symbol; another on more or less the same subjects but anthropomorphosed, the title being *Les Mémoires de L'Eléphant, Ecrits sous sa Dictée, Et traduits de l'Indien par un Suisse*, which certainly internationalizes the beast with ivory tusks and long memories.

From time to time we have had illustrated volumes on the hyena and its genitals, the albatross and the tarantula. A learned sixteenth-century German provided us with an erudite treatise on the whale's spermaceti while a seventeenth-century Italian poet added to our stock a poem on the rearing and abuse of silkworms. The "Battle of the Pigs" has been a popular subject for literary wits, but perhaps the most instructive of all our animal books was the one in which Hieronymus Rorarius set out to prove that beasts are more reasonable than men. To us he does indeed prove the truth of that old German expression: *Gott, wie gross ist Dein Tiergarten!**

If the animal world supplied man with topics for curious books, how many more curiosities has he garnered from the human world. Our very habitations have given rise to architectural curiosities among books. One, published in 1776, described architectural innovations for use in the West Indies with plans and elevations designed to combat earthquakes and storms, tropical rains and intense heat. Less functional perhaps but no less unusual was our nineteenth-century manual on the famous Thames Tunnel and the architecture of that structure under the Thames. An account of an early experiment in solar heating—a hothouse that would operate by the sun's heat alone, a guidebook to the stained glass windows in a church at Gouda, a richly illustrated volume on *Floor-Decorations of Various Kinds* have all passed through our hands and in passing reminded us of the infinite variety of the printed word. Our nomination of most curious among our architectural curiosities, however, is an early nineteenth-century book on an architectural game—a so-called Chinese enigma consisting of geometric figures arranged to form architectural patterns. Perhaps this was an early forerunner of the erector set. Certainly it suggested a charming way in which to construct a castle in Spain.

*Oh Lord, how big is your zoo!

We have bought and sold as many curious books about man's clothing—his personal architecture, so to speak—as about his external architecture. The costume of the French Revolution suggested to Jean François Barailon a fascinating *Projet* including a chart describing the colors, materials and styles of collars and sleeves, buttons and linings, robes and culottes. Dandies inspired James Bisset to pen a delightful book entitled *Dandyism Displayed, or the Follies of the Ton*. His comments on male and female dandies among actors and hairdressers, cooks and tailors, pawnbrokers and salesmen are all elucidating, but most telling to us are his remarks on bookseller dandies:

> If either of you has entered the trade for mere amusement and immense profit, make it your constant endeavour to be continually idle . . . . When absolutely obliged to serve in the damnable shop, . . . look excessively sagacious.

"Painting, patching and powdering," otherwise known as the cosmetic arts, have of course injected vitriol into the ink of a variety of fulminators. One of the most violent was the Bishop of Worcester, John Gauden, who in 1662 wrote *A Discourse of Artificial Beauty . . . Between Two Ladies* in which he condemned painting the face as a badge of vanity and a mark of pride. Everything about his *Discourse* is straightlaced—except the binding, which is loose.

Details of costume have called forth as many books as cosmetics. We have had *An Illustrated History of The Hat* by the famous American hatter John Genin, whose shop adjoined Barnum's Museum in New York. Noted for his early use of novel advertising methods, he became famous by purchasing for $225 the first seats (sold at auction) for Jenny Lind's concert. The Swedish Nightingale herself would have profited from Genin's charming booklet with its illustrations of chapeaux and headgear from earliest times. A neat companion piece to this volume was *The Book of the Feet* by the patent elastic bootmaker to the Queen. His illustrated history of boots and shoes, with hints to lastmakers and remedies for corns, rounds out such oddities from head to toe.

For good measure we mention yet another clothing curiosity, a book in which the French physician Clairian considers the medical aspects of clothing, the relations of clothing and climate, the effects of clothing upon the body organs and illness. For some unexplained reason he gives special attention to trousers, particularly those worn on the eve of the French Empire—a fact which, to our mind, elevates his *Recherches* to the realms of the curiouser.

Medicine and science have both yielded considerable grist for the mill of the curious. The great German educator and reformer Melanchthon wrote a report on the incidence of "Dantzen und Springen" disease near Schweinitz, known to us as St. Vitus Dance. A most peculiar case history of a young man who swallowed a knife which was extracted through an artificial stomach aperture was described by a German physician in the mid seventeenth century. One wonders if his nineteenth-century confrere William Beaumont was aware of the operation. Another more or less medical curiosity appeared in the unusual guise of a children's book. The well-known New York firm of juvenile publishers, Samuel Wood & Sons, issued in 1815 a little volume in stiff brown wrappers entitled *The Life of That Wonderful and extraordinarily heavy man, Daniel Lambert, from his Birth to the Moment of his Dissolution; with an Account of Men noted for their Corpulency, and other interesting matter.*

"Other interesting matter" was garnered by early writers from the facts and fancies of science. The use of snow, ice and cold water provided the seventeenth-century physician Pierre Barra with considerable liquid food for thought long before hydropathy became a rage and a reform. The technology of street lamps preoccupied one of our eighteenth-century French authors, Dominique François Bourgeois, who won a prize for illuminating the streets of Paris. An undated treatise cogitated the intriguing question of when precisely a new century begins. The author was puzzled as to whether the new cycle would begin in 1700 or in 1701. We were puzzled not only by his mathematics but by the date of his dissertation.

Numbers and numerology lead many authors of curiosities by the nose. As a branch of the occult, the mystic significance of certain numbers has fascinated us too. Why we have had so many books on various aspects of the occult sciences I do not know. Perhaps it is because Leona's Mr. Thorndike, as he revolves in his grave, is sending powerful vibes in our direction.

In 1565 an Italian philosopher, Jacopo Aconzio, who abandoned Catholicism for Protestantism and fled to England, wrote a learned treatise entitled *Stratagematvm Satanae*—the Stratagems of Satan. The book was dedicated to his protectress Queen Elizabeth who was familiar with many of those stratagems. Among the false doctrines singled out by Signor Aconzio were demonology and divination. Demons and witches have attracted the attention of so many writers that any attempt to cover the subject would lead us in the unhallowed paths of Mr. Thorndike. Our own shelves devoted to the subject seem to have been filled principally by Germans and Italians. The former have been characteristically concerned with the classes and orders of demons and familiar spirits, the latter with musings about the relations between demons and witches. Such questions as whether witches can shed tears or for how long the devil is bound in hell have resulted in the consumption of quantities of paper.

The powers of demons in the human body and soul have been considered at such length that one demonic effect must surely have been writer's cramp. The early Byzantine Psellus discoursed with great erudition on the subject, while a seventeenth-century French writer, Perréaud, cited the case history of a demon's activity in his own home in the year 1612. Such case histories naturally—or unnaturally—lead us on to the heavy, sometimes tragic, often tragicomic literature of sorcery. In 1574 Lambert Daneau, counselor of the Parlement of Paris, assembled the cases of sorcery which had been heard by the Parlement. The heights or depths of sorcery in Europe were probably reached in the seventeenth century with the famous Loudun affair of Urbain Grandier which inspired not only a host of contemporary writers but a latter-day demonologist, Aldous Huxley. The sorcery theme has, incidentally, been an extremely popular one in the theater, the English stage witch having cavorted through a variety of productions including one by the Bard of Avon.

From possession by sorcery to exorcism by the church the distance is short. Our early writers on exorcism did not profit so much as twentieth-century exploiters of the subject, but they certainly cleared the ground for their followers. Hieronymus Mengus, Maximilian ab Eynatten, and a host of learned men have written compendia and manuals on the exorcism of malign spirits. They have treated every phase of the subject from the associates and satellites of exorcised spirits on to the fine points of ejecting demons from butter and milk, winds and serpents, the home and marriage.

Unnatural magic should not be confused with the natural variety although both have resulted in a plethora of reading matter. The strange activities of sorcerers and poltergeists are not always as amusing as those of the natural magicians who rely upon divining rods and automatic writing, optical illusions and spontaneous combustion, as well as rabbits and long sleeves. One of the most delightful of our books on white magic was Sir David Brewster's *Letters on Natural Magic. Addressed to Sir Walter Scott* which contained metamorphic plates showing changes in facial reactions.

Apparitions conceivably may concern followers of both white and black magic. Similarly, predictions, divinations and auguries may attract astronomers and mathematicians as well as astrologers and demonologists. The Germans have been especially drawn to what are called *Practica*, annual predictions of the state of the harvest, wars, and even pulmonary disorders arising from the conjunction of Mars and Saturn. An Italian astrologer charmingly named Rizza Casa determined the years favorable for women and marriage as well as the planetary influences upon religious and political events in France, Italy and the Ottoman Empire and on the fate of Mary of Scotland. Another, less charmingly named Nausea, specialized in predictions for the Holy Roman Empire. We had once a delightfully illustrated astrological calendar, *Tesoro di Scienze* of 1564, consisting of verses and woodcuts on the twelve months of the year with a list of the "good" days according to the moon. A seventeenth-century French guide included a monthly calendar of horoscopes indicating whether wife or husband would be first to die. A sixteenth-century German scholar, Rantzau, obligingly compiled a detailed bibliography of past and contemporary astrologers, literally opening the gates of heaven to the Thorndikean scholar.

Other methods of predicting the future have generated a variety of curious books. Horoscopes have been projected by the so-called science of metoposcopy or astrological physiognomy. The distinguished Italian Renaissance physician Girolamo Cardano claimed to be able to draw horoscopes from facial lines since the furrows on the forehead were influenced by the planets. His work on metoposcopy was enriched with hundreds of fine woodcuts depicting those furrows. Divination from entrails and lot-casting, prodigies and portents; forecasting by numbers and ciphers; even augurific sneezes, jumpings and tremors have engaged the attention of early erudite authors from Augustinus Niphus to Caspar Peucer, from Jacques Gohorry to Henry de Montagu.

At what point in all these occult sciences do we see a glimmer of that more modern occult science known as psychiatry? Is it in treatises on hypochondria? Or the studies of the passions? Is it in a work such as the *De Viribvs Imaginationis* in which the seventeenth-century Belgian physician Fyens discusses the connection between the devil and a morbid imagination? Or is it in the books on that provocative subject, the powder of sympathy?

One of the most famous of those was written by the English diplomat Sir Kenelm Digby, who analyzed the secret nostrum which even at a distance could promote the healing of wounds. Indeed the case history he described concerned the use of the powder to heal his celebrated compatriot James Howell. The so-called magnetic cure of wounds led to almost as much literary debate as the question of whether women were human. The use of magnetism to cure a sick child in Rio de Janeiro was the subject of a remarkable book by the nineteenth-century Danish poet Harro Harring, who came to America and was a friend of Margaret Fuller. The work, which is illustrated with a daguerreotype of the child in trance, suggests relationships between magnetism and psychology.

One of our most curious books—not on magnetism but certainly on a subject of psychological interest—was called *Narciso Al Fonte* by Ippolito Falcone. This strange work, published in 1675, applied the fable of Narcissus to all humanity, picturing statesmen and soldiers, musicians and painters, physicians and courtiers, merchants, theologians and kings gazing at their reflections in the fountain of self-knowledge. Perhaps this book should be regarded as a sociological item, perhaps as a philosophical tome. Or rather, with its interesting treatment of the theme of narcissism, it might be considered an unusual forerunner of psychiatry.

Far more curious books have been written about dreams and their interpretation than about narcissism and self-knowledge. *Inter* a great many *alia*, we have had a seventeenth-century French treatise on the dreams that precede illness and an eighteenth-century Latin dissertation on the relation of dreams to the physical condition of the dreamer and even the state of the mind in sleep. By 1841, we find the young American physician Nathan Allen writing his graduation thesis on the *Connection of Mental Philosophy with Medicine*. Allen was influenced somewhat by phrenology, which admits him to the realm of the curious, though Sigmund Freud would not have found him curious at all.

On the other hand, Freud would most assuredly have regarded as unusual the testamentary directions of the eminent English book collector, bookseller and bookbinder, James Edwards. Mr. Edwards stipulated that his coffin be made out of the shelves of his library. To expedite the matter, in 1815, a year before his demise, he put his books up at auction. The collection included the famous Bedford Book of Hours, the Fust and Schoeffer Bible, and Luther's copy of his translation of the Bible. We could boast none of those treasures, though we did have *A Catalogue of The Valuable Library of James Edwards, Esq.*, in which the prices fetched were marked in red ink.

Bibliomania in its many aspects has expressed itself in a number of curious books. Among those that have delighted us has been a *Bibliothèqve Imaginaire* of 1615—a "library" of imaginary satires and fictitious titles reflecting the political confusion of the seventeenth century, not to mention the riotous imagination of the anonymous compiler. Then, at the mid-eighteenth century, there was *A Catalogue of Curious but Prohibited Books* that included among the delectables "The Art of not Thinking," "Modern Nobility. (Newest Edition, very cheap)," "Germany the true Sinking-Fund," and "The Works of a Celebrated Foreign Lady, Stitch'd, or in Sheets." We have had bibliographies of lost books, notably the *Livres Perdus* prepared by the distinguished Gustave Brunet from the papers of Joseph-Marie Quérard, known as "A Martyr to Bibliography." My own modest attempt to reconstruct the library of Sherlock Holmes—*Sherlock Holmes: Rare-Book Collector, A Study in Book Detection*—may, it is hoped, figure among the curiosities of some twenty-fifth-century bibliomaniac.

Almost everything relating to books has been the subject of some curiosity. As far as paper is concerned, there has been the *Historical Account* of Matthias Koops, "Printed on Paper Manufactured of Straw Alone," with an appendix printed on paper made from wood. There has been the delightful *Papyro-Plastics* on the art of modelling in paper, illustrated with cut-out paper figures of windmill and house, stove, boat, and even inkstand. Ink and its immortality inspired the Florentine poet Ciampoli to a sonnet sequence in 1626, while the quill pen and its achievements moved Michael Fendius to the production of three hundred distichs. Of printing curiosities we mention only one: Breitkopf's invention for printing maps with movable type by a method known as typometry. His work on the subject, *Über den Druck der geographischen Charten*, includes a colored folding map which is "one of the curiosities of printing."

How many strange subjects have materialized into "curiosities of printing." We have had a treatise on vagrants written under a pseudonym and another on ruffians written by a jovial priest of Lucca, Tommaso Buoni, under an anagram of his name, Buoso Tomani. Jean Chassanion used his own name when he penned a study of giants, their history and their remains. The argot of the poor has been interpreted; the literature of the street has been assembled—the latter in a comprehensive bibliography that lists four hundred thirty-five items emerging from the Siege of Paris and the Commune, including a menu of rats and cats. Authors have inquired into sleeping and waking; laughter, especially the laughter of Democritus, has attracted a bevy of poets and philosophers.

Democritus laughed at human frailties, and those frailties and addictions have sent writers to their inkstands. Card playing and dice shooting have been the subjects of learned treatises as well as of ephemeral edicts; entire libraries have been built around the subject of tobacco—pro and con. As for drugs, we have had a fascinating survey of *The Opium Trade* by the aforementioned Nathan Allen as well as the only comprehensive account of hashish in the United States prior to the twentieth century. *The Hasheesh Eater* by Fitz Hugh Ludlow, who became addicted before he entered college, was published in New York in 1857. The author's personal narrative of his experiments with the drug provides a vicarious trip for armchair travelers.

Boredom gave Frederick the Great a topic in his *Dissertation Sur L'Ennui*; applause was investigated by a seventeenth-century Italian archeologist, Ferrarius, who cogitated applause by hand and drum, cymbal and song. The dawn has been celebrated, not only intermittently as by Homer, but exhaustively as by Matthias Witlich in his *Avrora Carmine* of 1565. Treatises have been written on enigmas; first-person narratives have been spun with a coin for hero and at least one dialogue has been published in which an animated lamp tells the author of its successive transmigrations.

To the pen surely nothing is alien. If the printed word conveys the best that has been thought and said in the world, it conveys the most curious too. Non-books and novelties, books on strange subjects from symbolic cabbages to imaginary kings enhance the library of the collector and give to the bibliomaniac conversation pieces to last a lifetime.

9

A Tantalizing Trio:
Books We Should Have Had

[MBS]

There never was a better conversation piece than that fascinating copy of Erasmus' *Praise of Folly* whose picaresque romance has been traced by my partner. The book eluded us in the end because, lacking faith and acumen, we never deserved to possess it. Three other books have eluded us too, though to them we could claim—and still claim—a proprietary right. There may be no justice in bibliophily, but there are certainly tales to tell.

One of the three was a book unknown even to its author, a book whose very existence was my discovery. The second was a book common enough to be found on many dusty shelves, yet altogether neglected, until I hit upon the unusual interest of its illustrations and the remarkable concatenation of people involved in its production. The third was a book I myself had written—a unique copy illustrated by a great artist. Surely to those three books I had more than a proprietary interest. Yet the divine right of bibliophiles has proved no more substantial than the divine right of monarchs, and those books have never been mine.

The first of my tantalizing trio is a collection of animal stories for children entitled *Will's Wonder Book*, written by Louisa May Alcott and published anonymously in Boston by Horace B. Fuller in 1870. This is the book of whose publication its illustrious author was unaware although it survived rejection, loss, and, in a manner of speaking, piracy.

If Louisa Alcott herself did not know that her animal tales had been published as a book, how did her biographer, coming so late upon the scene, deduce its existence? Like many discoveries, this was a serendipitous stumble.

As a biographer of Louisa May Alcott I naturally researched in depth her early days when she edited a juvenile monthly published by Horace B. Fuller of Boston—*Merry's Museum*—and, like many editors, found she had to write as much as she edited. One of the stories she contributed to the periodical was a serial entitled "Will's Wonder-Book." In the bibliographer's retentive but grasshopper mind, the title stuck.

A few years later Louisa's biographer was engrossed in a book on American publishers and, as she leafed through the pages of that indispensable directory of books, *The American Catalogue*, her eye— and her heart—stopped at the listing of an anonymous book published in 1870 by Horace B. Fuller of Boston. Its title was *Will's Wonder Book*, the title familiar to her as an Alcott serial in a magazine for children. Could the two be the same? If so, here was a previously unknown juvenile by the author of *Little Women*, a book unknown not only to Alcott biographers and bibliographers but to Alcott herself.

With the customary palpitations I examined the one recorded copy of the book, which was in the Library of Congress, and compared it with the serial that had run in *Merry's*. The two were identical.

I had indeed discovered a "new" book by an old and well loved author. But, as with most discoveries, the "find" did not end the research but rather renewed it. Why did Louisa Alcott never know that *Will's Wonder Book* had appeared between boards in 1870? Why had it eluded her many faithful chroniclers? The history of this charming little book, only one copy of which was known to me, had to be investigated. Compulsive bibliomania had set in.

Three possible beginnings suggested themselves: research could start with the story, with the publisher, or with the author. The story itself had appeared first as an eight-part serial in *Merry's Museum* between April and November 1868 when the author was working also on *Little Women*. The installments or chapters had been devoted to the wonder book of nature and in the facts they revealed about bees and ants, spiders and butterflies, squirrels and moles, the author's indebtedness to her Concord neighbor Henry David Thoreau was apparent. The book charmed but did not elucidate the mystery.

As for the publisher, Horace B. Fuller had worked in the firm of Walker, Wise and Company of Boston before taking over *Merry's Museum* and in all his endeavors had demonstrated a deep interest in children's literature. This was information but it led no further on.

In her 1867 journal Louisa had written:

> F. asked me to be the editor of "Merry's Museum." Said I'd try. . . . Agreed with F. to be editor for $500 a year. . . . On the strength of this engagement went to Boston, took a room—No. 6 Hayward Place—furnished it, and set up housekeeping for myself.

And there Louisa Alcott had apparently written, among a variety of poems and stories for *Merry's Museum*, her series of animal tales for children. Or had she?

Had she not rather, laboring under the constant demand for material, dredged up a story she had already written and polished it up for *Merry's*? A study of her journal seemed to indicate that this may well have been the case. In August 1864 Louisa had written:

> Wrote another fairy tale, "Jamie's Wonder Book," and sent the "Christmas Stories" to W. & W., with some lovely illustrations by Miss Greene. They liked the book very much, and said they would consult about publishing it, though their hands were full.

Those few sentences were brimful of clues to the researcher who knew that "W. & W." referred to Walker, Wise and Company for which firm Horace Fuller had worked, and that "Miss Greene" was the artist who provided the cover design when he refurbished *Merry's Museum*. As for the title, *Jamie's Wonder Book* might easily have been metamorphosed into *Will's Wonder Book*. The pieces of the puzzle were beginning to take shape.

As it turned out, Louisa's *Wonder Book* had as strange a history

when it belonged to "Jamie" as when it was later assigned to "Will."
Rejected by Walker, Wise, it was apparently offered to Ticknor and
Fields who promptly lost the manuscript. In June 1867 Howard
Ticknor wrote to the author:

> Will you kindly . . . see if you have anywhere a letter from me or from
> F[ields] proposing terms for the unlucky juvenile the MS. of [which] is
> playing hide and seek so aggravatingly with us? . . . I wish to effect a sort of
> settlement,—prospectively, for I am sure that that material will turn up.
> Also let me know how much you paid Miss Greene for drawings.

The *Wonder Book*, rejected by Walker, Wise and lost by Ticknor
and Fields, had not yet completed its sad odyssey. A letter written in
1874 by the now famous Louisa Alcott reveals that the incredible had
taken place—the manuscript had been lost a second time:

> Eight or nine years ago H. Ticknor accepted the Ms. & was to bring it out
> as a Christmas book. . . . But . . . I was told that the Ms. was lost. So I
> rewrote it & waited a year or two longer, when . . . the doomed Ms. again
> vanished illustrations & all. . . . I did not try the book again but at intervals
> sent several of the tales to various magazines & papers, for I considered them
> mine. . . .

Louisa Alcott, who had serialized the tales in *Merry's Museum*,
considered them hers. But Horace B. Fuller, who had published them
in *Merry's Museum*, also considered them his. In November 1870, in
time for the Christmas trade, after the author had severed her
relations with the periodical and when she was traveling in Rome,
Horace B. Fuller had without authorization published *Will's Wonder
Book* between boards. Moreover, he had published it anonymously as
the second volume in a series, with the result that its authorship
remained untraced until, in the serendipitous bibliographical moment that has already been ticked off, it was discovered by the
present writer.

My discovery was announced in an article entitled "Louisa's
Wonder Book: A Newly Discovered Alcott Juvenile," which appeared
in *American Literature* in November 1954. Immediately the *Antiquarian
Bookman* relayed the information to collectors and emblazoned upon
its front cover a reproduction of the binding of *Will's Wonder Book*. In
a subsequent issue some bibliophilic wit advertised among his wants a
copy of *Will's Wonder Book*.

In 1954 only one recorded copy—that in the Library of Congress which I had examined—was traced. Today I know of three other copies. A Boston bookseller obviously unmindful of the wit and wisdom in the *Antiquarian Bookman*, not to mention *American Literature*, listed a copy of the *Wonder Book* at $5 or $10. Promptly deluged by orders from better informed collectors, he declined selling. Harvard gently advised the dealer that the book would be purchased, but at a fitting price. Apprised of the quality of the pearl he had almost cast, the Boston bookseller magnanimously gave *Will's Wonder Book* to Harvard. In due time another copy reached C. Waller Barrett and is now in the Alderman Library of the University of Virginia. The fourth copy was purchased from a Vermont dealer, at a fitting price, by the Clarke Historical Library of Central Michigan University and that copy, edited by the discoverer, was reproduced in 1975 as *Louisa's Wonder Book—An Unknown Alcott Juvenile.*

That unknown juvenile—unknown no longer—is still among the rarest of children's books. Yet if four copies have survived, surely there must be a fifth reposing on some shelf, hidden in some attic, its green or purplish cloth covers fading under the dust of time. To this copy I stake my claim. Louisa's unlucky juvenile, her doomed manuscript, has become a *Wonder Book* indeed, unknown to its creator, unowned by its discoverer. If there is a paradise reserved for bibliophiles, I shall hope at last for a presentation copy from the author.

Item Two of my elusive trio bears a lengthy and awesome title: *Rationale of Crime, and its Appropriate Treatment; Being a Treatise on Criminal Jurisprudence Considered in Relation to Cerebral Organization.* Published by Appleton of New York in 1846, this was the American edition of a treatise by an English phrenologist Marmaduke B. Sampson. Between its uninviting covers there was gold which glittered only for me.

In the course of researching my *Heads & Headlines: The Phrenological Fowlers*, I had examined the *Rationale of Crime* in the reading room of the New York Public Library. I noted that it upheld the most advanced views on criminals and crime, that it was profusely and graphically illustrated with heads of criminals, and that it had been edited by a feminist reformer, Eliza Farnham. The gold surfaced when I read her "Introductory Preface" in which she acknowledged her debt:

to the officers of the Penitentiary on Blackwell's Island for their politeness in furnishing me with facilities for taking the daguerreotypes, and to ... Mr. Brady, to whose indefatigable patience with a class of the most difficult of all sitters, is due the advantage of a very accurate set of daguerreotypes.

The *Rationale of Crime* had apparently been illustrated from daguerreotypes made by none other than the great Mathew Brady and, having appeared in this country in 1846 when he was only twenty-three years old, must represent some of his earliest work. In this penological-phrenological tome I had struck a bonanza. And so I had to dig deeper.

Details of Daguerre's process reached this country in 1839. Two years later young Brady arrived in New York and in 1844, when he was twenty-one, he set up his Daguerrian gallery in an "unpretentious studio" across from Barnum's Museum. Why should he have produced some of his earliest daguerreotypes for such a book as the *Rationale of Crime?*

The query and its answer plunged me headlong into the seething reforms of the 1840's and introduced me to a group of extraordinary devotees. Among the reforms of a reforming age that saw effective panaceas in brown bread and cold water as well as in abolition and women's rights, phrenology—a "science" of the mind—promised to improve the mental faculties and lead man, under the guidance of skillful practitioners, to perfection. Phrenologists were naturally opposed to the gallows as well as to the horrors of the penitentiary and were inclined to view crime not as a sin but as a curable disease. America's most popular phrenologists, Fowlers and Wells, had an office not far from Brady's studio and there seemed little doubt that the young artist had dropped in from time to time to examine the display of skulls and busts if not to sit for an examination.

In 1844, the year that Brady opened his studio, the forthright pioneer who was to edit the *Rationale of Crime* was appointed matron of the women's prison at Sing Sing. There Eliza Farnham proceeded to introduce a variety of reforms based in part upon her phrenological view of crime. She had already been "phrenologized" by Lorenzo Fowler and although in time she would be dismissed from her post and branded an infidel and "woman of ill fame," she continued to endorse the "science" of mind that professed to answer the Sphinx's question, "What is man?"

This was the woman who in 1846 introduced to the American

-epublic a book on the phrenological reform of crime by the English phrenologist Marmaduke B. Sampson. The English edition lacked notes and illustrations. Eliza Farnham determined to supply both—copiously. In order to do so she picked an assemblage of brains encased in fine phrenological skulls. In the selection of cases for illustration she sought the counsel of Lorenzo Fowler of Fowlers and Wells. To produce outline drawings of the heads of prisoners she hit upon the future engineer Edward Serrell who first measured those heads at Sing Sing "from the bump of amativeness to the tip of the nose." To make the engravings she chose Tudor Horton who, with his brother John S. Horton, conducted business on the same street where the Fowlers plied their phrenological trade. Finally, and most interestingly, she invited young Mathew Brady to take the daguerreotypes.

Either because of his own growing reputation or his proximity to the Fowler firm, Brady had obviously become known to Eliza Farnham. Now, participating in the work of a group of dedicated reformers—the production of an American edition of a book on penology—he journeyed with the editor to Blackwell's Island and to the Long Island Farm School. His sitters included ten criminals on Blackwell's Island, five men and five women, most of them imprisoned for grand or petit larceny. His camera was turned upon representatives of various ethnic groups, among them an Indian half-breed and two blacks, an Irish vagrant and a German woman. To supplement the work at Blackwell's Island, Brady journeyed with his equipment to the Long Island Farm School where he made eight additional daguerreotypes of boy inmates.

When it appeared in 1846, the American edition of Sampson's treatise naturally excited sympathy from such journals as Greeley's *Tribune* and the *American Phrenological Journal*. From other papers it aroused a vitriolic antagonism all but impossible to understand today. Branded as being aptly suited to an age of "quackery, infidelity and humbug," it was classed with:

the catch-penny pamphlets on *Phrenology* by which scheming speculators on public credulity are constantly working to replenish their purses. We are sorry to see it published, though we have no great apprehension that it will be very widely read.

Not a single reviewer mentioned Brady's daguerreotypes.

Eliza Farnham left Sing Sing in 1848 for other fields. The Civil War, dividing the nation, sat for its portrait before Mathew Brady's camera. The "science" of phrenology degenerated into a pseudoscience and the science of penology took two steps backward and one step forward. The *Rationale of Crime* gathered dust.

More than one hundred twenty-five years after its publication, it was my happy lot to shake off that dust. As I pored over the engravings based upon the Brady daguerreotypes in the Appendix of the *Rationale of Crime*, the book came alive for me. I knew how it had been created and why and who, among this world's minor reformers, had created it. Especially I knew that it contained what were in all likelihood engravings made from Mathew Brady's earliest daguerreotypes for book illustration. In an account of the *Rationale of Crime* prepared for the Library of Congress *Quarterly Journal*, I announced my find.

That Library's copy of the book bears a most unlikely ownership inscription, for it belonged to New York City's future mayor A. Oakey Hall, "the Elegant Oakey" who would send thousands to prison before going on to become Boss Tweed's henchman. While I would rejoice to place any copy of the *Rationale of Crime* upon my own bookshelf, the copy I secretly hope for is the one that must have been presented by the editor Eliza Farnham to the daguerreotypist Mathew Brady in appreciation of his "indefatigable patience" and in anticipation of his future work.

Tantalizers One and Two I have at least examined, albeit in library copies. Tantalizer Three I have never even seen. This is especially ironical because the book in question is *Purple Passage: The Life of Mrs. Frank Leslie* (1953), of which I happen to be the author. The irony applies of course to a particular and quite extraordinary copy.

Mrs. Leslie, a nineteenth-century American grande dame who played a variety of roles in coruscating style—journalist and salon leader, publisher of the mammoth House of Leslie and fascinating Edwardian courtesan—had preoccupied me for some time. I had relished tracing the highs and lows of her career and sleuthing the ups and downs of her private life. Both aspects of her history were rewarding, for while Mrs. Leslie wore a blue stocking on one leg she sported a scarlet one on the other. In addition to her extramarital conquests, some of which centered in high places, she boasted four husbands. The last if not the best was Oscar Wilde's brother, William Charles Kingsbury Wilde.

Some years after my *Mrs. Leslie* had made her bow, in 1960, I read another kind of "intimate memoir" entitled *Portrait of Max* by the well-known playwright S. N. Behrman. As a biographer I was fascinated by this evocation of a personality, this portrait of Max Beerbohm, caricaturist and novelist, talker, listener and wit, who had known Shaw, Kipling, Yeats, Bennett and of course Oscar and Willie Wilde. I was well on in the book, reading of a conversation that had taken place in 1955, when S. N. Behrman visited Max in Rapallo. Then, starting on page 289, the following paragraph rose up and hit me:

I [S. N. Behrman] had lent Max a book about Mrs. Frank Leslie, the widow of an American nineteenth-century newspaper tycoon. Mrs. Leslie had married Willie Wilde, and for this reason I thought the biography might interest Max. He had the book on the tea table next to his chair. He picked up the book and a pencil and, on the inside of the back cover, rapidly sketched Oscar and Willie for me. These are probably the last drawings Max ever did, though he did not regard them as drawings. "Scratches," he called them, and yet they are quite remarkable, too. You see that the two men are brothers, all right: Willie, flabby and amiable, hoping for the best, and doomed; Oscar, grinning in Hades, ghastly, and doomed. After giving me the now illustrated book, as a kind of thanks for lending it to him, Max went on talking about Willie Wilde, who, I found, interested him more than Oscar did.

"A book about Mrs. Frank Leslie . . . . the now illustrated book." Even though my name had nowhere been mentioned, this book was mine, certainly my *Mrs. Leslie*—that copy, extra-illustrated by Max Beerbohm, must become mine. I had a double proprietary interest in it as author and as dealer in rare books; and in that lovely old house in the Bronx where Leona and I then carried on our business I picked up my pen and dashed off a note to S. N. Behrman, asking if I might not purchase his glorious copy.

Behrman, whatever his failings, was a prompt correspondent. His reply was brief, to the point, firm but charming:

I am pleased to hear from the author of Purple Passage. I enjoyed it very much and so did Max, and we talked about it quite a bit. In fact, it led to Max's talking about Willie Wilde.

If you were a rich woman which you can't be because you are a writer, I might consider selling this copy to you. But, I couldn't bear to let it go unless I got a lot of money for it. I intend to leave it to the Houghton Library when

I die. The sketches of Oscar and Willie are full page and they're probably the last drawings Max ever did.

Having at the same time whetted my appetite and damped my spirits—as only an experienced playwright could do—S. N. Behrman concluded his letter. At this point I reminded myself that Behrman was not only a playwright but the author of *Duveen* and his association with that flamboyant personality may have exalted his sense of the copy's value. I had no doubt that it was my Bronx address that had given him a diminished view of my monetary resources. I did not pursue the subject, but tucked Behrman's letter inside my copy of *Portrait of Max* and turned to other matters.

Twelve years passed, in the course of which Leona Rostenberg—Rare Books flourished. I published a few more books, and my partner and I moved from the rambling Bronx mansion to a more fashionable address, 40 East 88th Street. In 1972—a year that marked the centenary of Max Beerbohm's birth—one of the libraries which we represent at auction gave us a commission bid for Item 19 at the Parke-Bernet Sale of February 1:

[BEERBOHM, Sir MAX]. Behrman, S.N. [wrote *Portrait of Max*]. *A group* of 4 T.LL.s., 4 pp. 4to, with envelopes, N.Y. & Rapallo, 1955-62, to Arthur B. Spingarn. Two of the letters concern Beerbohm.

An unkind fate seemed to hang about our relations with Beerbohm and we lost the lot of letters to another dealer. But the juxtaposition of the names Beerbohm and Behrman put me in mind of that extra-illustrated copy of *Purple Passage* which I had sought in vain a dozen years before. We walked back home from the Galleries along Madison Avenue to 40 East 88th Street and immediately I ferreted out my copy of Behrman's book to see if I still had his letter about the Beerbohm drawings in *Purple Passage*. There it was, still inside my *Portrait of Max*. But this time I noticed something about that letter that had escaped my attention when it had been sent to me twelve years before: Behrman's home address. I looked at it now unbelievingly. It was 40 East 88th Street—the same as ours.

Although I am not generally superstitious, this did indeed seem like a portent. At all events, I was driven to the typewriter to share my discovery with Mr. Behrman. In the interim he had moved again but was living nearby at an address mentioned in *Who's Who*. I was writing, I informed him, simply because I could not resist writing. I reminded him of my initial interest in his copy of *Purple Passage* and of his reply. I went on to tell him of my subsequent move to *his* address and of our unsuccessful bid for his letters at the Parke-Bernet. Then I repeated my query of a dozen years before: was that copy of *Purple Passage* still available and on the market?

Almost immediately I received the following reply:

I am glad that you did not resist writing me. When I saw that your letter was from the author of *Purple Passage* my heart leaped; I thought that you might shed light on a mystery which has bedeviled me for years: that is the total disappearance of *Purple Passage* in the endpapers of which Max Beerbohm had drawn two marvelous caricatures of Oscar and Willie Wilde. I see him now sitting in front of his little fireplace and drawing them as you or I might write a postcard. I showed the book to Mr. Shawn, the editor of the New Yorker, and he said: "These are probably the last caricatures he ever did."

Well, the book disappeared. I could find no trace of it. The deal with the Houghton Library never materialized. The head of the Houghton, whose name at the moment I can't remember, died, and that ended my relationship with it. At the same time I moved from your present residence and I lost track of many of my possessions. I thought for a long time that Mr. Shawn had taken the book with him, and he thought he might have also. He searched, but could find no trace of it in his office. It is really an awful loss to me and I feel dreadfully sorry that at least I did not send it to you so that you could have seen those two marvelous caricatures. I must surely have written you that Max enjoyed your book very much, as he was a friend of both Oscar and Willie.

Time had transposed the "inside of the back cover" to the "endpapers," had altered an intended bequest to a "deal," had relegated the great Houghton librarian, William A. Jackson, to anonymity, and—worst of all—effected the disappearance of a copy I had never seen. It was time for me to exercise one of the prime tenets in the Rostenberg Credo: sleuthing.

Behrman, it occurred to me, had concentrated his attention altogether upon the *New Yorker* which had serialized his book before it appeared under the Random House imprint. I reminded him of this obvious fact and suggested he try to trace the copy through Random House, for those "two marvelous caricatures" had been reprinted by them in their edition of *Portrait of Max*. By return mail I received the following expression of joy:

Your letter which arrived yesterday threatens to bring PURPLE PASSAGE back to me. I can't believe it, but it is so. In your letter you mentioned that the two caricatures from your book were printed in the Random House edition of MAX. I simply did not know it. I never looked at the book carefully. After working on MAX for six years and even harder with Mr. Shawn on the seven chapters as they appeared, I had had enough of the project for the time being. When I read your letter I asked . . . my secretary, to look up the MAX book and see if they were there. They were! I then asked her to call Random House. She fortunately got hold of a secretary who had worked on the MAX book and she said she would look. She called back an hour later and said she had found it. . . . [My secretary] is going to pick it up.

When this book arrives I will at once telephone you. . . .

My thanks and affectionate greetings.

This effusion, with its insight into Behrmanesque bibliophily, was followed not by a telephone call but by a lengthy silence which I at last broke with a little doggerel requesting

Dear Mr. Behrman, S.N.
Let me hear from you once again.

I did hear once again, not from Mr. Behrman but from his secretary who informed me that the extra-illustrated copy of *Purple Passage* had indeed been found and was reposing in a Random House safe. As soon as she was able to fetch it she would do so and give me a ring.

That was several years ago. As Max Beerbohm had followed to the grave Oscar and Willie Wilde and Mrs. Frank Leslie, so S. N. Behrman followed Sir Max. The widow Behrman in due course called upon my esteemed colleague Howard Woolmer to appraise the library of the defunct playwright—to which, thanks to my own assiduity, the extra-illustrated copy of *Purple Passage* had been restored. Warning me that he had no idea how the library would be disposed of, warning me also that the copy had been considerably dampstained, Howard kindly gave me the opportunity to bid on "my" book. This I did extravagantly, not at all in the style of the writer who could not possibly be "a rich woman." Nonetheless, the widow Behrman was apparently unimpressed. My offer was vouchsafed no comment.

Besides the dampstain which, I have been assured, did not affect the caricatures, this unusual association copy has another fault. In addition to Sir Max's profiles of Oscar and Willie Wilde, should it not bear also a portrait of Behrman? In a sense perhaps it does.

Kenneth Clark, writing of Max Beerbohm, described him as resembling "a precious pink Christmas present that had just been unpacked, so that some of the cotton wool still clung to its surface." Some day this cliffhanger could be metamorphosed into a Christmas fairy tale and the Beerbohm-Behrman copy of *Purple Passage: The Life of Mrs. Frank Leslie* might come home to roost.

Yet this is a most unlikely outcome. The possibility of my tantalizing trio ever being united on a special shelf in the treasure room of my library is remote indeed. I must keep reminding myself that the joy lies in the discovery, not the possession. Even so, bibliophilic justice would appear to be as elusive as my three wayward books.

10

Catalogues & Collections

CATALOGUES

[LR]

There is never anything elusive about a dealer's catalogue. If it is a good one it will be its maker's earthly representative and hopefully remembered. A catalogue is a dealer's showcase. In it he displays his wares; parades his knowledge; offers his expertise. His first catalogue is extremely significant. He has made his public début before a critical group of connoisseurs. This, his first catalogue, occasionally becomes his hallmark, stamping him as a specialist in Western Americana, medieval arts and letters, or modern firsts.

Book catalogues have existed since the days of the German printers Sweynheym and Pannartz at Rome, who around 1470 issued a listing of their publications. In 1498, in a folio broadside, the greatest publisher of all time, Aldus Manutius, cited his Greek texts: "Haec sunt graecorum uoluminum nomina, quae in Thermis Aldi Romani Venetiis impressa sunt."* Since the establishment of his firm

*These are the titles of the Greek books which have been published in the Venetian office of Aldus [Manutius] Romanus.

in 1494, Aldus had published twenty-seven books of which thirteen were in Greek. His list does not include his Latin publications since it was obviously designed to attract a specific clientele—Greek scholars gathered in Venice and Renaissance collectors of Greek books. The Aldine broadside is a prime example of catalogue specialization, setting a noble precedent. A wise antiquarian bookseller will specialize, since he realizes the province of rare books is infinite in its variety.

A general catalogue of miscellaneous books is confusing and exhausting. A dealer on the prowl will usually scan such a catalogue searching for a sleeper which occasionally emerges. A catalogue lacking a unifying theme might include: no. 1 Austen, *Novels and Letters*. 1911-1912; no. 89. Molière, *Oeuvres*. 1824; no. 91. Montesquieu, *L'Esprit*. 1748; no. 120. *Royal Adultery*. 1821; no. 145. *Zanzibar, Its Climate and Topography*. 1915. There is a sleeper in this potpourri, the rare first edition of Montesquieu's *L'Esprit*, which demands an immediate telephone call or cable. Response: "This book has already been ordered seven times." Otherwise the reader is bored by this miscellany of books and even suffocated at the end by the climate of far-off Zanzibar.

As we wrote in *Old & Rare*: "The concerns and problems associated with the production and publication of any catalogue are not completely dissimilar to the rearing and delivery of a child. There are however two differences. The period of gestation is longer. Secondly the child [is] completely literate at birth." Actually, in some cases, the period of gestation is even longer. Perhaps Mady Stern and I are Proboscidea . . . .

A catalogue is planned at the precise moment when an idea strikes. Inspiration may come at various places and from a variety of sources. Weary of gazing upon Alpine scenery during a lengthy walk around the Brienzer See in 1948, we began to discuss rare books and conceived the grandiose plan for our *Book-Notes* which consisted of a series of semi-monthly lists devoted to all aspects of the sixteenth and seventeenth centuries. After witnessing a spectacular display at the Pierpont Morgan Library we issued a catalogue entitled *Books With Illustrations*. It was no threat to the Morgan Library which however did order one item. Since we had drooled over Florence upon several visits it is not at all surprising that we published seven catalogues on *The Renaissance*. Actually one catalogue inspires another. Our catalogue *La Belle France* inspired us to circulate specialized

catalogues on *Italy* and *England*. Although we are essentially specialists in books printed between 1500 and 1750, the approaching
American Bicentennial aroused in us a heady patriotism and a
thorough inspection of our bookshelves. Not only much of our
material relating to the French "philosophes," but even a book on the
contractual theory of government published in 1573—Hotman's
Francogallia—fitted in with the spirit of '76. Here were bridges from
Valois and Bourbon France to Colonial America! Our catalogue *1776*
was the result.

The antiquarian dealer occasionally relies upon ingenuity rather
than a specific stock to honor a particular event. As specialists in
books of the Renaissance we certainly wished to celebrate the four
hundredth anniversary of the birth of Shakespeare, April 1564. It was
not essential to search our stock since we knew that we owned
neither a single Folio, a Quarto or even a promptbook which might
have been used by Master Will at the Globe Theatre. But we did
have many books which had been printed during his lifetime. Hence
we conceived the idea of a catalogue which would span the poet's
years. Our catalogue *Books Published During Shakespeare's Lifetime 1564-
1616* reflects the imagination and scholarship of my estimable partner. Texts relating to a variety of events and subjects were selected,
and captioned with an appropriate quotation from one of the plays or
sonnets. Lodovico Dolce's *Vita Di Carlo Qvinto Imp.* (1567) bears a line
from *Hamlet*: "There's such divinity doth hedge a king," while the
funeral oration upon the death of Ferdinand of Gonzaga is captioned
"Good-night, sweet prince," *Hamlet*. "Do you not remember . . . a
Venetian, a scholar and a soldier," *Merchant of Venice*, aptly introduces the collector to Pietro Marcello's *History of the Venetian Doges*
(1574).

In planning a catalogue the dealer reassesses his stock, and books
which have appeared in earlier catalogues can often be readapted.
The dealer is no magician when he pours old wine into new bottles.
He simply recognizes the many facets of a single work. The first
edition of Michelangelo's *Rime* (1623) once presented in an art
catalogue, certainly fits ideally into a list of Renaissance texts or in a
catalogue of belles-lettres. Michelangelo's early contemporary Bal-
dassare Castiglione, who wrote the basic book *On the Courtier*,
appeared as item 1 in our *Aldine Catalogue*. It would have been equally
appropriate in *One Hundred Books Relating to the Art of the Gentleman* or
in lists on military science, education, or hunting. The first edition of

Tom Paine's *Common Sense* is a suitable book for a catalogue on English history, the Bicentennial or political theory. Books are chameleons changing colors and coats, puppets dangled artfully by imaginative masters.

In an attempt to round out a catalogue whether it be our Catalogue 24, *Political Theory/ Economics/ Historical Ephemera*, Catalogue 27, *The Renaissance World*, Catalogue 31, *Literature*, Catalogue 38, *The Reformation*, Catalogue 40, *France & Italy*, or *1776*, we, like other antiquarian dealers, travel abroad, attend auctions and read countless other catalogues of our colleagues. During the perils of the chase we have often found books pertinent for a forthcoming catalogue or others to be put on ice for future lists. How felicitous was our discovery of the "American Magna Carta" embodied in the *Constitutions des Treize Etats-Unis de l'Amérique* (Philadelphia and Paris 1783) which we picked up at a French dealer's in the Spring before we issued *1776*. It is the first French edition of the Constitutions of the thirteen original States translated by La Rochefoucauld at Franklin's suggestion.

Upon arrival every book must be carefully collated—in layman's parlance, checked for completeness. It is not uncommon for dealers to overlook this chore where "small" items are concerned. Yet there can be no assumption that if a Boccaccio (Florence 1516) is purchased from an eminent dealer it must be a perfect copy. I recall with utter distaste the purchase of an Aldine 1513 Pindar from a so-called giant American antiquarian bookseller. Delighted to have the volume, we collated it immediately and to our horror discovered that two signatures were wanting. Furious, we returned the book. The owner's reply is memorable and, alas, a *caveat emptor*: "Now isn't that just too bad, two signatures are lacking in a small $450.00 book!" Fortunately, only a microscopic segment of the profession is of this mettle.

The cataloguing of a book varies with the dealer's personality. There are nonetheless fundamentals for the bibliographical citation of any antiquarian text. Books may be arranged alphabetically, according to subject matter, or chronologically, the latter arrangement quite ideal for subjects like political theory and economics. Unfortunately this method can drive a library checker to suicide or immediate resignation of his post.

The last and first names of the author must be given accurately. Of course if the name be John Smith, it would be advisable to accompany "Smith" with appropriate identification: John Smith of Badgeworth; John Smith, Captain; John Smith, Clockmaker; John Smith of Colchester; Dr. John Smith; John Smith of Montague Close; John Smith of Queens, Cambridge; John Smith of Sandwich; John Smith of Smenton; John Smith of Virginia; John Smith of Walworth; and John Smith, the writer on taxation—and there are perhaps another one hundred John Smiths all of whom have written on another one hundred subjects and demand identification. And so, having established the correct John Smith who wrote on *Sea Grammar, Stereometrie* or *Horological Disquisitions*, the cataloguer considers the title. Here the dealer who lacks basic knowledge of foreign languages and Latin begins to fumble. He has alas already cited one of the two hundred John Smiths in the genitive, perhaps hoping to enhance his appearance as "Smithii, Joanni." It does old John Smith little service to appear in the genitive when he deserves the nominative.

An accurate, intelligent transcription of any title, especially a lengthy one, is essential. It is totally unnecessary to record entire titles of eight and a half lines, and if the text, dear colleague, is in Russian, remain assured that your reader will skip that entry. A contributor to one of the co-operative catalogues of the Middle Atlantic Chapter of the ABAA copied the title of a book, consuming almost an entire page. Occasionally when the text is in German and the cataloguer is unfamiliar with this impossible language, he selects a few odd words presenting a title: *Gefressen ist*. It probably is most appropriate since this particular work should have been devoured by rodents three centuries ago. In the case of sesquipedalian German titles, cataloguers should be sure to tag the verb that plays hide and seek with various other parts of speech. As for inconsequential words in an extremely lengthy title, dots should be substituted for them.

The imprint may pose as many problems as author and title. A book issued at Leyden or Lyons, both of which translate into Latin as *Lugdunum*, can become a stumbling block. Both cities were popular printing centers and hence many seventeenth-century texts emerge with the imprint "Lugdunum" which is often transcribed by the unwary as Londini, Luton, or why not Luton Hoo? I do not wish to appear prissy or supercilious, but may I suggest that Latin glossaries do exist as well as grammars which would prove immeasurably helpful in the identification of names, imprint and date given in Roman numerals. Some books have apparently been printed in 1386 or even in 1986. Both must be fantastically rare. Having once discussed a Pilgrim Press book issued at Leyden by the Elder Brewster in 1617, I was questioned by a specialist in modern firsts whether I really meant that it had been issued at Brewster, New York. What a book!

The description of the contents of a rare book can be redundant and lengthy or over brief. The Austrian-born Herbert Reichner, my one and only employer, was rightfully proud of his command of English but over-used it not only in shouting at me but in his catalogue descriptions. His account of the *Nuremberg Chronicle* occupies almost an entire page in his Catalogue One. Mr. Reichner states that the source of this very well-known and fairly common folio was "the *Supplementum Chronicarum* of Frater Jacobus Philippus Foresti of Bergamo. The publication was promoted by two Nuremberg patricians, Sebald Schreyer and his brother-in-law, Sebastian Kammermeister, and printed by the celebrated Anton Koberger." The text continues: "The contract between the promoters of the Chronicle and the illustrators had been concluded on December 29, 1491." Actually, scarcely a reader is concerned with Herr Sebald Schreyer or his brother-in-law Herr Kammermeister unless he be descended from these illustrious gentlemen, nor is he vitally interested in the signing of the contract. The significance of the *Nuremberg Chronicle* depends upon its splendid plates and its completeness. On the other hand, a description of a book can be far too brief. A catalogue lists no. 185, Adam Smith, *The Wealth of Nations*, London 1776. This milestone is appraised by an uptight dealer: "Nice book!" The work is a classic in economics and certainly deserves a generous portion of whipped cream.

There is also a tendency to cite a variety of sources either to bolster the importance of the book or the scholarship of the owner. Pertinent references must be given. If Brunet is used for a 1515 edition of Erasmus, *Moriae Encomium*, it is redundant to refer to Graesse, nor is it essential to list all the modern lives of Desiderius Erasmus. On the other hand, the specific Erasmian bibliography by Vander Haeghen must be cited. In the same way, for Harvey's *Anatomical Exercises*, two indispensable citations would be the Harvey bibliography by Keynes and Donald Wing's *STC*.

The dealer must assume full responsibility for the condition of a book and state the incontrovertible truths. "Some staining" is scarcely sufficient for a text with huge blobs of ink and discoloration covering pages 72 to 116. "Covers somewhat loose" is a euphemism for the condition of front and back covers which fall into your hands when the volume is unpacked. "A fair copy" may turn out to be a book which has remained at the bottom of a well for three centuries or a text so crisp and beautiful that the recipient indulges in mad rapture.

Such qualifying terms as "Rare," "Extremely Rare" and "Rarissimo" are abused expressions. It is extremely difficult to establish the rarity of certain items. A sermon preached in Boston 1774 may indeed be uncommon. It was so dull and insipid that all parishioners rapidly disposed of their copies. On the other hand, another sermon, similarly disposed of and issued the same year, may be extremely rare and significant since it refers to the internal policy of the Massachusetts Bay Colony. The word "old" should not be confused with the word "rare." Age in itself does not entitle a book to a high price. The Aldine Press issued between 1546 and 1565 five editions of Cicero's *De philosophia*. I cannot say that any one of those editions is "rare," although the layman might demand for it the purchase price of a small Long Island cottage. Not only does "rare" emerge on many pages of all dealers' catalogues (ours included) but a more dangerous term: "no copy located in USA." There may be four copies on various dealers' shelves. It is true that the item may be so rare that it has not been included in any standard bibliography, but it may also be so insignificant that it has been purposely neglected. The words "Not in" should be carefully employed and not sprinkled about at random.

An antiquarian bookseller's catalogue is something very special. It may represent a course in American history, Italian letters or medieval art. It may acquaint the reader with the modern firsts of 1920 and those of 1977. Yet too many catalogues issued too frequently may "dull the fine edge of seldom pleasure." In our experience, two or three catalogues a year suffice. How often can the rare bookseller produce a handsome, healthy child endowed with vitality and an original brain? If his child is a bore, dull-lidded, heavy and pallid, don't let him roam—dispatch him to the circular file.

Catalogues are extremely expensive to produce. A printed catalogue takes a healthy slice from the dealer's revenue. With the introduction of all forms of reproductive processes, a variety of catalogues is circulated from the handsomely printed quarto profuse with illustrations to the wretched sheet typed on both sides single-space reproduced possibly on the very first mimeograph machine. It is a smear of illegibility covered with type on both sides of greyish blotched paper. There is the happy medium. Above all, a catalogue must be legible and neat, printed in a type which will cause neither blindness nor acute astigmatism. It is to be read by addicts all afflicted with a common malady, "cataloguitis." This long suffering group devours catalogues and lists at home and at office, upright or recumbent, in the subway or on the bus, in the light and in the dark, in the garden or on the "john." These incurables frequent book fairs where they clear the table of all available printed matter as well as cigarette lighters, ash trays, pencils, erasers and rubber bands. Occasionally one or two may buy a book. How beatific a dealer or customer is when a catalogue of his specialty arrives, and how sadly changed he becomes upon ascertaining that item 104 has been sold.

However, *caveat* catalogue compiler! Once your brain-child has been born, is between wrappers and has been begrudgingly accepted by the United States Postal Service, do not remain in your office fixated to the ringing of the phone. Take a trip around the world, or if you can't afford that luxury leave the city for a few weeks. The phone will perhaps ring bright and early several times. Your special librarians call and the third of these ladies or gentlemen orders seven items, three of which are sold. That flurry is followed by two days of utter silence when partner accusingly stares at partner. Finally the menacing stillness is broken.

"Oh Miss R. I have been recommended to you by Cynthia Logston."

"Cynthia?"

"Cynthia Logston, her late husband received a catalogue from you about ten years ago. My name is Phyllis Fitts."

"Hmmmm, hmmm."

"She tells me you buy the most interesting books."

"Hmm, hmmm."

"I have a set of 14 volumes all of which were dedicated to Queen Anne—imagine—dedicated to Queen Anne. She was an English . . . . "

"Hmm, hmmm."

"Are you there, Miss Rostenberg?"

"Hmm, hmmm."

"A beautiful set. They are the sermons of the Bishop of Peterborough. I also have a marvelous very early *History of Earth Tremors*, Edinburgh 1912."

[Nothing like my tremor, Miss Fitts].

"Sorry, we do not buy sermons or tremors."

Silence follows another three days when the mail responses begin to trickle in. The envelope of a former faithful customer is opened: "Kindly remove my name from your mailing list. I now collect mourning rings." Duplicate and triplicate orders for the same old item pile up. Just let me interject: "Dear beginner, don't be discouraged. You will eventually find a duplicate copy and you can always have the phone removed."

We have long been confronted by some absurd criticism: "Tell me girls, how come if you really like all these books as you say you do, how is it that you can sell them?" Let me assure the book buying world that the majority of our colleagues sustain themselves from the revenue of their profession—their books—which are to be found in the catalogues they compile and circulate—their showcase to the world.

COLLECTIONS

[MBS]

A collection equals more than the sum of its parts. This defiance of the laws of mathematics naturally exhilarates the collector and exalts the collection. I am thinking, when I use the word *collector*, of both dealer and private individual, and I am thinking, when I use the word *collection*, not of matchcovers or campaign buttons about which I know nothing, but of books. Indeed the word *collection*, though derived from the Latin word for combine or unite, closely suggests another Latin word that means read.

Be that as it may, a collection of books is not simply a combination of any heterogeneous books but of books that in some one way are connected with each other. In this respect it differs from the so-called collections of books in the catalogues Leona has described, where books are also brought together in combination but not in inter-connection.

It is the connection—the unifying basis—that gives meaning to a genuine collection of books. Perhaps the dealer may glance around at his shelves and note with satisfaction that he has really amassed quite a number of books on ornithology or witchcraft, on the French Revolution or the Spanish Inquisition, on goldmining or pottery, on cabbages or kings. He may then decide to extricate those books from their non-germane companions, place them in splendid isolation in a separate case, and, starting with such a nucleus, proceed to scout for more kindred volumes. Or perhaps a dealer may wake up one bright morning with the *idea* for a collection of books about space travel or inoculation or courts of love. If he starts with the idea and not with the books, then of course his scouting must proceed immediately on a grand scale. In either case, the dealer has made the first step in building up a collection of books on a thematic basis. As will soon become apparent, however, he has made only the first step.

There are other possible first steps, for there are many other unifying bases for book collections. Instead of a theme as a connecting link, an author may be used. Extraordinary collections have been assembled of books by and about Francis Bacon and William Shakespeare, Sir Walter Scott and George Eliot, Ernest Hemingway and James Joyce. Where the fancy takes the collector, there he flies, and if he treasures Louisa May Alcott he will not build up the works of Gertrude Stein.

A third unifying basis for a collection is neither theme nor author but genre: French novels or Italian sonnets, Scandinavian plays or American sermons. Still another is format: miniature books for some, atlas folios for others. Truly the world of books can appeal to every taste. Yet another connecting link is publisher: books published by Aldus Manutius and his family in sixteenth-century Venice or by Mathew Carey in eighteenth- and nineteenth-century Philadelphia. Bindings may become the unifying idea of a collection; so too may editions, such as first American editions. There are unifying bases everywhere. Once the basis has been established, it serves as a catalyst. The collector has found his "connection."

But, as we mentioned early on, he has just begun. The unifying basis of a collection must be crafted to reality for it may be too broad a base upon which to build or it may be too narrow. The theme of witchcraft if conscientiously carried out would probably lead the collector to self-immolation. He would find himself inundated with auguries and demonologies from the time of ancient Greece through merry old England to the time of the Salem delusions and beyond.

His subject would eventually have to be cut down to size, or to the realms of possibility, limited to witchcraft in a particular place or at a particular time or in a particular manifestation. On the other hand, if he limits his theme too narrowly he may end up with a so-called collection long before he has satisfied his urge to collect. A collection of books on needlepoint would prove an exciting venture, but a collection of books on the tent stitch might prove somewhat frustrating to assemble.

Similarly, a genre collection of books on poetry would be so extensive as to be unmanageable. Limit the genre to the poetry of American women and you have an absorbing and feasible project. Limit it to French rondeaux of the 1560's and you have narrowed the interest along with the possibilities. In the same way, if the imprints of a particular publisher form the basis of a collection, the publisher chosen should neither be one whose output consists of thousands of titles nor one whose productions were extremely limited.

In short, after a unifying base has been selected it must be assessed for attainability. Some beautiful connecting themes are simply impossible to apply to a collection of books. Who, for example, would not wish to assemble in one bookcase the first work that issued from the press of each state or future state of the union? But unless the collector has found a unique copy of *The Freeman's Oath* which issued from the Widow Glover's press in Cambridge, Massachusetts, in 1638, he might as well abandon that otherwise intriguing idea. Of course if he is one of the few owners of a *Bay Psalm Book* of 1640 he might substitute that for *The Freeman's Oath* and go on with the collection. Such caviar, however, is not for the general.

Admittedly, few collections are ever complete. Indeed it has been said that perfection, which the dictionary defines as the state of being complete so that nothing requisite is wanting, is actually a form of death. Yet the collector should be able, within the scope of his lifetime and the dictates of his pocketbook, to *aim* at completeness.

The concept of completeness will vary with the collector and collection. Some collectors will stick closely and rigidly to their theme or genre or author or publisher. Others, gifted perhaps with more imagination, will want to flesh out their collections with related background material that brings the whole to life. Such collectors will see connections where more intractable bibliophiles will not. In a collection relating to the Medici family, for example, they will include the books and pamphlets that trace not only the political fortunes of Florence, but the literary and artistic, the scientific and intellectual achievements that developed under Medici patronage. Such a collection would find room not only for obvious Medici edicts and histories, but for the less obvious: for guidebooks of Florence; for the writings of such Italian humanists as Filelfo, Ficino, Pico della Mirandola—for the many authors, scientists and artists in whose work the Medicis and their city are reflected.

The builder of a collection needs more than imagination; he needs patience, especially if he is a bookseller. No collection was ever assembled overnight, and it requires the utmost self-discipline for a dealer to place "on ice"—out of the way of eager customers—the books he is adding, one by one, to the collection he has conceived. As brick after brick is added to a building, book after book is added to the hidden bookcase in the sanctum sanctorum. Several years may pass before the collection nears completion. That is the way with booksellers' dreams.

As a matter of fact, the Medicis of Florence formed the unifying theme of a collection developed by Leona Rostenberg—Rare Books. In the course of our business, Leona and I have built up several collections, a few of which have been briefly mentioned in *Old & Rare*. The connecting link of all our collections has been a theme, a genre or a publisher. Combining theme and genre have been our *One Hundred Years Of France 1547-1652 A Documentary History* and *The French Revolution*, both consisting of pamphlets through which the dramatic history of France was traced. Other thematic pegs upon which we have hung collections have included, in addition to the Medicis, the Holy Roman Empire and the French philosophes. Obviously such themes have reflected Leona's ever deepening interest in the subject of her early choice, history and its cultural aspects, and the collections formed along those lines have made the annals of Europe come alive for me too. Sometimes we have developed genre collections such as French novels, Italian plays, Utopian romances.

Our most important collections, however, have been those whose unifying base was a publisher. Early in our firm's history we developed a collection of Elzeviers, that is, of books published in Holland by the House of Elzevier between 1621, after Isaac Elzevier was appointed printer to the University of Leyden, and 1740, when the Elzevier successor Adrien Moetjens catalogued an extensive auction sale. Having purchased at a twentieth-century auction sale— Freeman's in Philadelphia—the Elzevier stock catalogue of 1674, we tried to reanimate it by acquiring a representative selection of the works listed therein, from the little pocket "Republics" of the various states of Europe to the firm's reprints of Bacon, Buchanan and Descartes. The result was a modest assemblage of 165 items which we believed mirrored much of seventeenth-century European history as revealed in the imprints of one major publishing house.

Our most grandiose effort in the formation of collections has been directed to another, earlier, and far greater publishing house: the Aldine Press of Venice. In the course of several years, keeping our treasures "on ice," we were able to build up a collection of some two hundred fifty Aldines. They included many of the more significant scholarly productions of a house that flourished between 1494 when Aldus Manutius issued his first book and 1597 when Aldus' grandson, Aldus Manutius the Younger, died. Our 1502 Dante in pocket format; our first edition of the complete works of Plato; the 1513 Caesar with captions penned in Aldus' own hand; our magnificent copy of Castiglione's *Courtier*—all bore witness not only to the unrivalled work of the Aldine family, but to the searching mind of man during the century of the High Renaissance. Not everyone is privileged to recapture the first fine careless rapture. We were among the bibliopolic elect for, having developed one Aldine collection in the 1960's, we were able to develop another in the 1970's. Needless to say, we look forward eagerly to the Aldines of the 1980's.

All the collections we have assembled have been catalogued either in print or on the typewriter. The problems and methods of cataloguing in general, which Leona has so expertly discussed, are no different from the problems and methods of cataloguing collections. The arrangement of a collection catalogue, however, does deserve a word or two. A collection of Aldines, for example, might, like any catalogue, be arranged chronologically, alphabetically by author, or by subject. We chose to catalogue our first Aldine collection by subject, believing that such an arrangement would immediately demonstrate the varied ventures and interests of the great Venetian publishing house. The Aldine imprints ranged in subject from Courtesy and Drama to History and Literature, from Medicine and Philosophy to Science and Theology, and under such headings we grouped them.

A brief foreword outlined our purpose and mentioned the highlights of the collection, making what has been grandiloquently styled THE PRESENTATION. Both catalogue and collection were fleshed out with sections of books published by Aldine associates and imitators as well as contemporary books by and about the Aldine family. An Aldine chronology, a list of sources consulted, one index of authors and titles and another of editors and translators rounded out our catalogue which we dedicated to "those who rejoice in the achievements of the Aldine Press and its legacy to the mind of man." As for the individual descriptions, it is impossible for us today to distinguish the work of either partrer. Suffice it to say they are all by Dr. Leona R. Stern or Miss Madeleine S. Rostenberg—names, by the way, which occasionally appear on our incoming correspondence.

In all our thoughts on collections we have not yet come to grips with three nitty-gritty problems:

1) How many items should there be in a collection? When should the dealer call a halt to refrigerating his treasures and transfer them to the open market? As I have said, there is really no such thing as completeness or perfection. Yet, since man's reach should exceed his grasp, he should aim *toward* completeness. On the other hand, it is often advisable for a dealer to establish only the nucleus of a collection so that the purchaser may have the extreme pleasure of expanding it himself. Then, having relinquished one collection, the dealer can turn to another.

2) How should the collection be priced? It is our custom to price each item individually as in any catalogue or price list. We then total the individual prices. I began by stating that a collection is equal to more than the sum of its parts. On that basis, the dealer should add ten percent or more to the sum of those individual prices. Instead, Leona Rostenberg—Rare Books sometimes deducts ten per cent to make a lot price. Booksellers have imagination, patience and ingenuity. Obviously they are wanting in logic.

3) How is a collection sold? Just as he sells an individual book, a dealer may offer his collection to one specific customer, to his entire mailing list, or to any part thereof. Our first Aldine collection was catalogued and the catalogue circulated generally before an en bloc purchase was consummated. Our second Aldine collection was geared to a particular purchaser. When we catalogued one of our earlier collections, *One Hundred Years Of France*, we were far from confident of the outcome and hence wary if not hesitant in our offer. We ended our catalogue preface with the suggestion that the purchase of the collection "as a unit is advised. Inquiries will be welcomed." We had three eager purchasers for that collection.

A collection is to a dealer what a book is to a writer or a work of art to a painter. To be merely the middleman in the transfer of an already formed collection, moving it from a seller to a buyer, brings little satisfaction except to the pocketbook. The dealer might just as well be selling a barrel of fish. But the dealer who conceives a collection and gathers it together over a period of time knows a special, a creative gratification. It may be a grandiose collection such as the great thematic and author libraries assembled by and for an Arents, a Streeter, a Wilson or a Barrett; it may be a lesser collection. Whatever its scope or nature, when it is ready for offer the dealer who has assembled it pauses for a moment, as we have paused, and beholds with joy what *he* has wrought—a structure built of vellum and calfback that houses the human spirit.

11

An Antiquarian Bookseller's Credo*

[LR]

Since any credo is subjective, implying a belief in religion, philosophy, pantheism, or—in this case—the principles of the antiquarian book trade, I realize that my tenets—a baker's dozen—may differ from those of my colleagues. From the vantage point of a rare bookdealer who for over three decades has survived the vagaries of her profession, I now indite my particular credo:

I. MOTIVATION. A career in rare books may depend upon several factors: birthright—membership in a bookselling dynasty; metamorphosis from collector to dealer, or from librarian to dealer, or from a variety of professions to that of dealer. The metamorphosis may take place for any number of reasons: The young librarian may find preoccupation with the Dewey Decimal System too limiting; the lawyer may be bored by his briefs and cases; the merchant may seek escape from the frustrations of his trade. On the other hand, there may be no metamorphosis at all but a direct and daring plunge into books. The desire to work in an ivory retreat located in either rural or urban setting; the need to work at one's own pace; the association with "the

---

*A variant version of this chapter was delivered as the first lecture in the Lilly Library Lecture Series October 1975, and was published as *An Antiquarian's Credo* by Indiana University Libraries in 1976.

best that has been thought and said in the world"—all these may lure an individual into the field of rare books. In every case, however, it is an intense predilection for old and rare that motivates the individual to the profession.

II. EDUCATION. The successful dealer is ever ready to learn from his books and manuscripts, his colleagues, his customers. But his knowledge of books is basically moulded by his own academic training. Today's indulgence in educational whims limits the intellectual horizon. Unreceptive to formal education, a capriciously educated bookman remains unaware of much of the antiquarian trove. He finds himself restricted to miscellaneous English books or the cult of modern firsts. His reaction to a display of incunabula or Aldines is thwarted by his own scholarly limitations.

Admittedly, language proficiency is a harsh discipline which a permissive education rejects since the student's emotional equipment may be endangered by rigorous study. Yet the rewards from a knowledge of any foreign language are not to be lightly dismissed. Latin, Italian, German and French texts of the Renaissance have for us become heady wine; together we have relished the satire of Erasmus, the pragmatism of Machiavelli, the lucid prose of Montaigne. Language facility has permitted many dealers to travel widely in the great expanse of books and helped them mine its gold.

It is true that some of the keenest dealers and collectors have never enjoyed a formal education. Their books and their colleagues have been their mentors. John Ratcliffe, the eighteenth-century Southwark chandler who purchased the copy of *Folly* from the butcher Phineas Trott, never attended any of the great English universities. Yet his collection boasted fifty Caxtons and the sale of his library lasted nine days. Some of the bibliophilic titans of the 1920's and earlier days went to work after grade school as office boys and Wall Street runners. It must be remembered, however, that such self-taught bookmen of the "log cabin" school of collecting are the exceptions that prove the rule: There is no doubt whatsoever that a sound academic education sharpens and disciplines the mind, whets the curiosity, expands the horizon, and extends the range of collecting interests.

III. APPRENTICESHIP. No one—not even a university graduate with several degrees—should enter the world of old books without some practical training. Like the medical graduate who assumes an internship, the future bookman should seek an apprenticeship with a specialist dealer. He must become acquainted with case histories, the anatomy of the book and its significance. The apprentice observes the various phases of antiquarian activity: buying; collating; cataloguing; selling; customer idiosyncrasies; values; needs and specialties of other dealers; auction mores.

Every apprentice endures drudgery not dissimilar to that of memorizing the German past subjunctive. During my "Five Years in Siberia"—my bondage with the late Herbert Reichner—I was occupied for long periods in transposing the catalogue descriptions of several topflight dealers to three-by-five index cards, and for months scarcely lifted my head from the pages of Sotheran's *Bibliotheca Mathematica*. It was only when I came up for air that I realized I had become acquainted with the names and texts of many of the illustrious in science. I recall picking up all the catalogues which my slaver Herbert Reichner discarded. They became my future *cartes de visite* not only to unfamiliar titles but more so to their compilers, many of them the reigning illustrissimi of the antiquarian world.

The aura of books, the heady scent of print and leather, must exert a profound influence upon the apprentice who knows that eventually he will become the master with his own reference library, bright and trim, his shelves gleaming in calf, morocco and boards.

An apprenticeship hones the wit, develops specialized interests, and instructs in business techniques. The future antiquarian not only absorbs bibliophilic jargon, but learns to treasure and describe the book as an artifact—a physical entity apart from the significance of its text. After such an apprenticeship he emerges prepared to join the ranks of Old and Rare.

IV. SPECIALIZATION. Every bookseller should seek a specialty. He cannot embrace all disciplines and in his choice of a specialty should follow the interests aroused by his education and training. Having studied in the field of the Renaissance, I chose to specialize in its books and tracts. My partner, a graduate in English literature, turned towards belles-lettres. A lover of fine prints will doubtless become a specialist in art and graphics, whereas one who knows trees and flowers may become a specialist in horticulture and landscape gardening.

V. PATIENCE AND FORBEARANCE. Let no potential antiquarian dealer believe that each day is punctuated by an exciting find, a host of extravagant customers or the conversation of brilliant scholars. Unless the dealer has an open shop he may spend many silent hours uninterrupted by idle browsers. Such periods are constructive, allowing ample time for reading lists, preparation of a catalogue and the myriad details of the profession. A catalogue, as previously stated, is the dealer's showcase, requiring much contemplation and an uninterrupted stretch of time. Preparing a catalogue for the press demands accuracy, patience and concentration upon proofreading.

These periods are occasionally interrupted by frustrating incidents, requests and visits that call for even more patience than the preparation of a catalogue:

Frustration A: The Visit of a Friendly Librarian Who Has Just Been Passing Through. After wasting an entire morning mulling over twenty-seven items and selecting three, he advises the dealer:

"Just send a brief quote on these three. Nice copies. Of course there is always the chance that the old university might have them, but one thing is sure—you can count o.i promptness. Great to have seen you girls. Bye now."

Two seconds later he returns:

"Gosh, I am sorry. Left the old bumbershoot. Say, while I have you, we have been looking for the Lenin 1919 edition of . . . . Just forgot the title. We want it in Russian. Quote, will you? Bye now."

The prompt decision from the "old university" arrives five weeks later:

Regret we have Hobbes and Locke in better editions. We would like the Treaty on approval. Thanks so much for having shown me your splendid collection. I shall be in the city some time next spring and of course will drop in.

Cordially,
F. Middleton Kean

Frustration B: The "Darling" Non-Customer

During the proofreading of a small section on the classics, we look at our watches since a young woman has made an appointment for 10:15 A.M. It is after two when the bell rings.

"Oh, my dears, how thrilling your bookcases are! I must bring Robert David to see all these darling books. Let me tell you exactly what I want. I am looking for a little book for the sweetest old lady who adores French books. Nothing too old of course, and nothing too new. May I look at these fascinating shelves? What a divine hobby you have!"

After this "darling" customer has misplaced all the "darling" books on the "darling" shelves, she clasps our hands. "I just must tell Robert David about your wonderful books. The selection will be up to him. He knows so much. What a joy this has been. Thank you so much. I shall never forget this visit."

Frustration C: Futile Phone Calls

Upon our return from the Post Office our telephone service informs us of two calls. "One was from a man—I think it was a man—the other from an elderly woman. I could tell she was elderly because of her tired voice."

"Their names, please. Any message?"

"Oh, they wouldn't leave their names. The old lady just didn't say anything."

A phone call at noon introduces us to a loud, shrill female voice:

"Have you anything on the Maya-Quiche?"

Naturally, my thoughts turn to Dumas' Patisserie.

"We have a monograph on the Temple of Palenque."

"I did not ask for specific titles. I am primarily interested in the Zoltil group. How can a monograph on Palenque be of any help?"

VI. PERCEPTION. No person should attempt antiquarian bookselling unless he be endowed with that sixth sense, almost immediate perception of the significance of a text—that old *Fingerspitzen Gefühl* which we discussed in *Old & Rare*. Without this bibliophilic e.s.p., take up merchandising or ranching. This ability to assess the importance of a book is one of the major qualifications in the pursuit of Old and Rare.

VII. IMAGINATION. A single book can be many things to different dealers. Exercise of the imagination may transpose what appears to be a dull book into an exciting one. I do admit that a certain dealer went slightly overboard when he catalogued the 1502 edition of the *Tragedia septem* of Sophocles as a Freudian text. We had always regarded this Aldine octavo as a fine example of Greek typography or as a milestone in the history of drama. But was the dealer really wrong in his ascription? Sophocles certainly introduced the Oedipus theme . . . .

It is true that once we had a Renaissance work discussing the Garden of Eden. It was sold as a geological text. It is far better to jog the imagination than to become a slave to those tedious lists and manufactured guideposts: "The Hundred Timeliest Texts," "The Sixty Greatest Smallest Books," "The Fifty Books on Flycatching."

VIII. SLEUTHING. The search for books, the hunt is probably the most exciting aspect of the trade. Do not hesitate to scale bibliophilic peaks or explore dank caverns. It is quite probable that there is little gold left in "them thar" attics or basements, but . . . who knows? *Leaves of Grass* may lurk in a dusty corner or a *Divine Comedy* emerge from a damp foreign depot. The old adage that one man's meat is another man's poison applies to the antiquarian book trade. The "poison" of little interest to one dealer may be most appropriate for another's specialty. Cartwright's *Prince of Peace*, almost meaningless to a Dutch dealer, was of enormous interest to us since it concerned the American Revolution and Indians (see pp. 34–35).

Despite the pettiness of the French, the rigors of primitive plumbing, the frozen cardboard meals served on the plane, the thrill of exploration beckons the sleuth.

IX. RESPECT FOR THE EPHEMERAL. The tract, the seemingly unimpressive pamphlet should not be denigrated in favor of the stout, lordly folio. Very often the tract is a contemporary eye-witness report of an event, a battle, a murder, or the troth of lovers. In a talk delivered at the Lilly Library in October 1975, I alluded to "individual tracts of such magnitude that they have changed the world. . . . one of the most stupendous is a *Letter* written in Spanish to Luis de Santangel by a Genoese sailor, Christopher Columbus, describing a venture to the unknown isles of the Indies." There are pamphlets of every nature and of every nation. "*An Agreement of the Free People of England* by John Lilburne formulates the ultra-democratic social ideology of the extreme Leveller against authority of any kind. In a tract published an approximate 250 years later, not the authority of the individual but that of the state, the supreme being, is hailed. *What Is To Be Done?* by Vladimir Ilyitch Lenin appeared . . . in 1902. Here the great Russian advocates the necessity of a monolithic party prepared to assume dictatorial power." It is a pamphlet. Tracts have often been neglected because of their insignificant appearance. Often there is more gold to be mined in a sixteen-page pamphlet than in a seven hundred sixteen-page folio.

X. RESEARCH. A book may be researched from many points of view. It may be significant for author or imprint, binding or provenance. What was the importance of our Ames, *Rescriptio* (1617)? It was a Leyden imprint, but not an ordinary one. True, it had been issued at Leyden but it had been printed by none other than the Elder William Brewster who manned the secret underground Pilgrim Press—the very Brewster who was to accompany the Pilgrims on the "Mayflower" to the New World. We discovered through research that Ames' book was the very first of only twenty printed by Brewster and one of the three to bear his name in the imprint.

We owned at one time an incomplete set of the 1658 edition of the *Works* of Paracelsus, having acquired only Volume One. Why was this one volume so meaningful? Simply because it bore on the flyleaf a presentation inscription to Robert Browning from his father. The complete set had been in the elder Browning's library and had provided the source for young Browning's first important poem, *Paracelsus*. Upon its completion, the father, recognizing his son's great promise, presented him with the set.

An antiquarian book may be highlighted from several points of view, but every work demands careful research and none, whether it be a twentieth-century pamphlet or the 1480 edition of the *Sententia* of St. Thomas Aquinas, should be victimized by a lazy researcher.

XI. VALUE. An antiquarian dealer who knows "the price of everything and the value of nothing" misses out in the end. A book— "the pretious life-blood of a master spirit"—should never be regarded as a mere dollar symbol or a "hedge against inflation."

XII. TRADE ASSOCIATION MEMBERSHIP. It is a privilege to be a member of the Antiquarian Booksellers Association of America, Inc. The Association was formed in 1948

to engage in study and research for the purpose of furthering friendly relations and a co-operative spirit among persons engaged in dealing in and selling books and other printed matter in general . . . to uphold the status of the antiquarian book trade and maintain its high professional standards.

Sixteen antiquarian dealers signed the Certificate of Incorporation; eight survive. They, their colleagues and their successors strive to continue the ideals of the Association. Let every member of the ABAA serve his guild to the best of his ability.

XIII. JOYS OF THE TRADE. My credo has brought these two Paulines, Madeleine and Leona, continued delight in the pursuit of their profession. They have specialized in the fields of their interest; applied the tools of research to their books; gained fresh insight into those tracts and texts which have passed through their hands.

Other dealers may have other credos. Ours has brought us a summa of joy in the endless world of books.

HIC LIBER SCRIPTUS EST—HAMPTONE ORIENTALE—
MXCLXXVII

SHORT TITLE LISTS

Short Title Lists*

A NEW FOUND LAND:
AMERICA IN STRANGE PLACES*

1. [Berkeley, George]. *A Miscellany, containing several Tracts on Various Subjects.* Dublin: Faulkener, 1752. (p. 37)

2. [Boeckler, Johann Heinrich]. *Bibliographia Historico-Politico-Philologica Curiosa.* Germanopolis [Frankfurt] 1677. (p. 37)

3. Bonardo, Giovanni Maria. *La Minera Del Mondo.* Venice: Zoppini, 1585. (pp. 35, 36)

4. Bosso, Fabrizio. *In Fvnere Philippi II . . . Hispaniarvm Regis Oratio.* Pavia: Bartoli, [1598]. (p. 29)

5. Bottoni, Domenico. *Pyrologia Topographica Id Est. De Igne Dissertatio.* Naples: Parrino & Mutio, 1692. (p. 36)

6. *Brevis Assertio Et Apologia Acclamationis . . . Portugalliae Regis Ioannis Inter veros Lusitaniae Regis nomine Quarti.* N.p. ca. 1655. (p. 30)

7. Britaine, William de. *The Dvtch Vsvrpation: or, a Brief Vievv of the Behaviour of the States-General of the United Provinces Towards the Kings of Great Britain.* London: Edwain, 1672. (p. 32)

8. *Candid Enquiry into the Present Ruined State of the French Monarchy, A.* London: Almon, 1770. (p. 37)

9. *Capitoli Delle Paci Conchiuse Tra' Le Potenze Aleate, e Quelle Di Francia, E Spagna A Utrecht li ll Aprile 1713.* Turin: Màrone, [1713]. (p. 33)

---

*Editions cited are not necessarily the earliest. They are those that have actually passed through our hands. For our comments about them see the pages indicated.

10. Carew, Bampfylde Moore. *The Life and Adventures of Mr. Bampfylde-Moore Carew, commonly called The King of the Beggars*. London: Millar, 1782. (p. 34)

11. *Carnaval, Le, de la Barbarie et Le Temple des Yvrognes, Par M. de M.****. Fez 1765. (pp. 36–37)

12. [Cartwright, Edmund]. *The Prince of Peace, and Other Poems*. London: Murray, 1779. (pp. 34–35)

13. *Catalogue, A, of the Damages for which the English Demand Reparation from the United-Netherlands*. London: Brome, 1664. (p. 33)

14. Ceba, Ansaldo. *Rime*. Rome: Zannetti, 1611. (p. 29)

15. Cecchi, Giovanni Maria. *Lezione Overo Cicalamento Di Maestro Bartolino Dal Canto De' Bischeri, Letta nell' Accademia della Crusca, sopra'l Sonetto. Passere, e Beccafichi magri arrosto*. Florence: Manzani, 1583. (p. 29)

16. [Charles II, King of England]. *Speech to both Houses of Parliament*. London: Bill & Barker, 1664. (p. 38)

17. Chas, J. *Réflexions sur l'Angleterre*. Paris [1803]. (p. 32)

18. [*Commonefactio*]. *Ad Potentissimos ac Serenissimos Reges, Principes, reliquosq[ue]; amplissimos Christiani orbis Ordines . . . Commonefactio*. N.p. 1583. (p. 29)

19. *Considérations sur l'Artillerie de . . . Seigneurs Etats Generaux des Provinces-Unies des Pays-Bas*. St. Christophe 1786. (p. 38)

20. *Constitutional Queries, Humbly Addressed to the Admirers of a late Minister*. London: Davis, ca. 1762. (p. 32)

21. *Convention, The, between the Crowns of Great Britain and Spain, concluded at the Pardo [sic] on the 14th of January 1739*. London: Buckley, 1739. (p. 33)

22. [Dod, John]. *A Plaine And Familiar Exposition Of The Tenne Commandements*. [Leyden: Pilgrim Press], 1617. (pp. 38–39)

23. [Douglas, John]. *A Letter Addressed to Two Great Men on the Prospect of Peace*. London: Millar, 1760. (p. 33)

24. [Eden, Morton, Lord Henley]. *Reflections on the Present State of Affairs on the Continent, as Connected With the Question of a General and Permanent Peace*. London: Ridgway, 1814. (p. 31)

25. Fioravanti, Leonardo. *Della Fisica . . . in Libri Qvattro*. Venice: Sessa, 1582. (p. 36)

26. Grégoire, Pierre. *De Repvblica Libri Sex*. Frankfurt A/M: Hoffman, 1609. (pp. 29–30)

27. [Grose, Francis]. *Advice to the Officers of the British Army. With the Addition of some Hints to the Drummer and Private Soldier*. London: Kearsley, 1783. (pp. 32–33)

28. Hutten, Ulrich von. *Holz Guaiacum.* Strasbourg: Grüninger, 1519. (p. 36)

29. *Intérets De L'Imperatrice Reine, Des Rois de France, et D'Espagne . . . aux avantages de leurs Couronnes . . . négligés dans les Articles Préliminaires, signés a Aix-la-Chapelle . . . 1748.* N.p. 1748. (p. 33)

30. Interiano, Paolo. *Ristretto delle Historie Genovesi.* Lucca: Busdrago, 1551. (p. 28)

31. Jackson, Robert. *A Systematic View of the Formation, Discipline and Economy of Armies.* London: Stockdale, 1804. (p. 32)

32. Josephus, Joannes Henricus. *Propositiones Mathematicae ex Geographia de Aestu Maris.* Breslau: Baumann, [1665]. (p. 37)

33. Keckermann, Bartholomaeus. *Meditatio de Insolito et Stvpendo Illo Terrae-Motv, Qvo Anno praeterito, VIII. Septembris . . . tota pene Europa & Asiae . . . contremuit. Tractata.* Heidelberg: Voegelin, 1602. (p. 35)

34. Lamarca, Luis. *Teatro Histórico, Politico, y Militar.* Valencia: Mestre, 1690. (p. 30)

35. Le Couteulx de Canteleu, Jean Barthélemy. *Discours et Motion Sur Le Plan De Banque Nationale du premier ministre des finances.* Paris: Baudouin, 1789. (p. 31)

36. Loaisel de Tréogate, Joseph-Marie. *Florello, Histoire Méridionale.* Paris: Moutard, 1776. (p. 35)

37. Locke, John. *A Collection of Several Pieces . . . Never before printed.* London: Bettenham for Francklin, 1720. (p. 37)

38. Louis XV, King of France. *Ordonnance . . . Portant déclaration de guerre contre le Roi d'Angleterre. Du 9 Juin 1756.* [Paris 1756]. (p. 33)

39. Louvet, Pierre. *Le Mercvre Hollandois, ov L'Histoire De La Répvbliqve Des Provinces Unies des Pays-Bas.* Lyons: Baritel, 1674–76. (p. 32)

40. Loyer, Godefroy. *Rélation du Voyage du Royaume D'Issyny, Côte d'Or, Pais de Guinée, en Afrique.* Paris: Seneuze & Morel, 1714. (p. 31)

41. [Lynar, Heinrich Casimir Gottlieb von]. *Nachricht von dem Ursprung und Fortgange . . . von der gegenwärtigen Verfassung der Brüder-Unität.* Halle: Curt, 1781. (p. 38)

42. McKinnon, Charles. *Observations on the Wealth and Force of Nations.* Edinburgh: Balfour & Smellie, 1782. (p. 32)

43. Maffeius, Raphael Volterranus. *Commentariorvm Vrbanorvm . . . octo et Triginta Libri.* Paris: Badius Ascensius, 1515. (pp. 27–28)

44. [Mailly, Chevalier de]. *Principales Merveilles de La Nature . . . Par M. ***.* Rouen: Machuel, 1728. (p. 35)

45. Mainoldus, Jacobus. *De Titvlis Philippi Avstrii Regis Catholici Liber.* Bologna: Bonardus, 1573. (p. 28)

46. [Maupertuis, Pierre Louis Moreau de]. *Vénus Physique*. N.p. 1746. (p. 38)

47. Mavelot, Charles. *Nouveau Livre de différens Cartouches*. Paris 1685. (p. 34)

48. Mercier, Louis Sébastien. *L'Homme Sauvage*. Amsterdam: Zacharie, 1767. (p. 35)

49. *Notice Biographique . . . sur Mgr. Le Duc d'Orléans, Appelé en 1830 au Trône de France*. Paris: Barba, 1830. (p. 31)

50. Palissy, Bernard. *Oeuvres*. Paris: Ruault, 1777. (p. 38)

51. Panciroli, Guido. *Rerum Memorabilium Libri Duo*. Amberg-Frankfurt: Forster-Vetter, 1612–17. (p. 29)

52. Passerinus, Petrus Franciscus. *Schedarivm Liberale*. Piacenza: Bazachius, 1659. (p. 29)

53. Philip II, King of Spain. *Het Secreet des Conings van Spangien achterghelaten aen zijnen Soone Philips de derde*. N.p. [1598]. (p. 29)

54. [Piarron de Chamousset, Claude Humbert]. *Vues d'un Citoyen*. Paris: Lambert, 1757. (p. 37)

55. Placet, François. *La Corrvption dv Grand et Petit Monde*. Paris: Alliot, 1668. (p. 38)

56. *Rapport des Commissaires de la Société Royale de Médecine, sur le Mal Rouge de Cayenne ou Éléphantiasis*. Paris: Imprimerie Royale, 1785. (p. 38)

57. *Rates, The, of the Excize of New Impost . . . to be Paid and Collected from the 21 Day of December, 1649*. London: Husband, 1649. (p. 36)

58. [Reboul]. *Essai sur Les Moeurs du Temps*. London & Paris: Vincent, 1768. (p. 31)

59. *Remarks upon the Present Negotiations of Peace begun between Britain and France*. London 1711. (p. 32)

60. [Spangenberg, August Gottlieb]. *A Concise Historical Account of the Present Constitution of the Unitas Fratrum; or, Unity of the Evangelical Brethren*. London: Lewis, 1775. (p. 38)

61. Tarapha, Franciscus. *De origine, ac rebus gestis Regum Hispaniae liber*. Antwerp: Steelsius, 1553. (p. 28)

62. Tasso, Torquato. *Gervsalemme Liberata*. Casalmaggiore: Canacci & Viotti, 1581. (p. 28)

63. Teluccini, Mario. *Artemidoro*. Venice: Guerra, 1571. (p. 27)

64. [Valori, Filippo]. *Termini Di Mezzo Rilievo E D'Intera Dottrina tra Gl'Archi Di Casa Valori In Firenze*. Florence: Marescotti, 1604. (p. 29)

65. [Villegagnon]. Richer, Pierre. *Libri Dvo Apologetici ad Refvtandas Naenias, & coarguendos blasphemos errores, detegendaque mendacia Nicolai Durandi qui se*

Villagagnonem cognominat. Hieropolis [Geneva]: Thrasybulus Phoenicus, 1561. (pp. 30–31)

66. Waldenfels, Christophorus Philippus de. *Selectae Antiquitatis Libri XII. De Gestis primaevis, item de Origine Gentium Nationumque migrationibus . . . collecti.* Nuremberg: Endter, 1677. (p. 27)

67. Watt, Joachim von. *Epitome Trivm Terrae Partivm, Asiae, Africae et Evropae.* Zurich: Froschauer, 1534. (p. 29)

FEMINISM IS COLLECTIBLE

BOOKS BY WOMEN

1. Andreini, Isabella. *La Mirtilla Pastorale*. Bergamo: Ventura, 1594. (p. 58)

2. Berners, Juliana. *The boke of Saint Albans*. St. Albans 1486. A facsimile reproduction was made in 1905 with introduction by William Blades. (p. 58)

3. [Bernhardt, Sarah]. *Bibliothèque De Mme Sarah Bernhardt*. Paris: Le Clerc, 1923. (p. 58)

4. *Carmina Novem Illvstrivm Feminarvm*. Antwerp: Plantin, 1568. [Includes work of Corinna and Telesilla of Argos]. (p. 57)

5. Catharine II, Empress of Russia. *Instructions Adressées Par Sa Majesté L'Impératrice De Toutes Les Russies A la Commission établie pour travailler à l'exécution du projet d'un Nouveau Code De Lois*. Petersburg [Yverdon] 1769. (p. 59)

6. Chapone, Hester. *Letters on the Improvement of the Mind, addressed to a Young Lady*. London: Hughes, 1773. (p. 59)

7. Clarke, Mary Anne. *Les Princes Rivaux*. Paris: Buisson, 1813. (p. 56)

8. Colonna, Vittoria. *Rime*. [Venice: Salvionus], 1539. (p. 56)

9. [Cowley, Hannah]. *The Poetry of Anna Matilda. . . . To which are added Recollections . . . by General Sir William Waller*. London: Bell, 1788. (p. 57)

10. Craven, Elizabeth. *Somnambule*. Strawberry Hill 1778. (p. 58)

11. Dawbarn, Mrs. *The Rights of Infants*. Wisbech: White, 1805. (p. 59)

12. Falconia Proba, Valeria. *Centonis . . . excerptum e Maronis Carminibus*. Venice: Tachuinus de Tridino, 1513. (pp. 55, 70)

13. Farnham, Eliza W. *California, In-Doors and Out; or, How we Farm, Mine, and Live generally in the Golden State*. New York: Dix, Edwards, 1856. (p. 58)

14. Farnham, Eliza W. *Life in Prairie Land*. New York: Harper, 1855. (p. 58)

15. Fell, Margaret. *An evident Demonstration to Gods Elect*. London: Simmons, 1660. (p. 59)

16. Fidelis, Cassandra. *Epistolae & Orationes Posthumae*. Padua: Bolzetta, 1636. (pp. 55–56)

17. Fuller, S. Margaret. *Summer on the Lakes, in 1843*. Boston, New York: Little & Brown, Francis, 1844. (pp. 58, 69)

18. Labé, Louise. *Euures*. Lyons: De Tournes, 1555. (p. 57)

19. La Fayette, Marie Madeleine Pioche de la Vergne de. *La Princesse de Clèves.* Paris: Barbin, 1678. (p. 56)

20. [Lavallée, Joseph]. *The Negro Equalled by Few Europeans . . . . to which are added, Poems on Various Subjects . . . By Phillis Wheatley.* Philadelphia: Woodward, 1801. (p. 57)

21. [Lee, Rachel Fanny Antonina]. *An Essay on Government. By Philopatria.* London: Gillet, 1808. (p. 59)

22. Leslie, Mrs. Frank. *California A Pleasure Trip from Gotham to the Golden Gate.* New York: Carleton, 1877. (p. 58)

23. Macauley, Elizabeth Wright. *Effusions of Fancy; consisting of The Birth of Friendship, The Birth of Affection, and the Birth of Sensibility.* London: For the Author, 1812. (p. 58)

24. [Mazarelli, Claire Marie, Marquise de La Vieuville de Saint-Chamond]. *Eloge de René Descartes.* Paris: Duchesne, 1765. (p. 59)

25. Morata, Olympia Fulvia. *Opera omnia.* Basle: Perna, 1580. (p. 56)

26. Necker, Suzanne Curchod. *Réflexions Sur Le Divorce.* Lausanne: Ravanel, 1794. (p. 59)

27. Philips, Katherine. *Poems. By . . . the Matchless Orinda.* London: Herringman, 1667. (p. 57)

28. Pilkington, Mary Hopkins. *A Mirror for the Female Sex. Historical Beauties for Young Ladies.* Hartford: Hudson & Goodwin for Cooke, 1799. (p. 59)

29. [Pix, Mary]. *The Czar of Muscovy. A Tragedy.* London: Lintott, 1701. (p. 58)

30. Sforza, Isabella. *Della Vera Tranqvillita dell' Animo.* Venice: Sons of Aldus, 1544. (p. 56)

31. [Smith, Julia Evelina], tr. *The Holy Bible . . . Translated Literally from the Original Tongues.* Hartford: American Publishing Company, 1876. (pp. 59–60)

32. Squire, Jane. *A Proposal to Determine our Longitude.* London: For the Author, 1743. (p. 59)

33. Stael, Anne Louise Germaine Necker de]. *Réflexions sur Le Suicide.* London: Deconchy, 1813. (p. 59)

34. Stephens, Ann. *Malaeska: the Indian Wife of The White Hunter.* New York: Beadle, 1860. (p. 56)

35. Stern, Madeleine B., ed. *Behind a Mask: The Unknown Thrillers of Louisa May Alcott.* New York: Morrow, 1975. (pp. 56–57)

36. Stern, Madeleine B., ed. *Plots & Counterplots: More Unknown Thrillers of Louisa May Alcott.* New York: Morrow, 1976. (pp. 56–57)

37. Stern, Madeleine B., ed. *Women on the Move*. Nieuwkoop & New York: De Graaf, Schram, 1973. Reprints of # 13, 14, 17, 22. (p. 58)

38. Terracina, Laura. *Discorso . . . Sopra il principio di tutti i Canti d'Orlando Furioso*. Naples: Bulifon, 1698. (p. 57)

39. Trimmer, Sarah. *The Oeconomy of Charity*. London: Bensley, 1787. (p. 59)

40. Wheatley, Phillis. *Poems on Various Subjects, Religious and Moral*. London: Bell, 1773. (p. 57)

FEMINIST JOURNALS

41. *Anglo Saxon Review, The*. London & New York: June 1899–September 1910. (pp. 60–61)

42. *Dial, The: A Magazine for Literature, Philosophy, and Religion*. Boston: July 1840–April 1844. (pp. 61, 69)

43. *Forerunner, The*. New York: November 1909–December 1916. (p. 61)

44. *Free Enquirer, The*. New Harmony, Ind.: March 4, 1829–June 28, 1835. [Began as *The New-Harmony Gazette*, October 1, 1825]. (p. 61)

45. *Lowell Offering, The: A Repository of Original Articles on Various Subjects, Written by Factory Operatives*. Lowell, Mass.: October, December 1840, February, March 1841, & 1841–1845. (p. 61)

46. *Revolution, The*. New York: January 8, 1868–February 17, 1872. (p. 61)

47. *Woodhull & Claflin's Weekly*. New York: May 14, 1870–June 10, 1876. (p. 61)

BOOKS ABOUT WOMEN

48. Agnelli, Cosmo. *Amorevole Aviso alle Donne, circa alcvni loro Abusi*. Ferrara: Mammarello, 1592. (p. 62)

49. Agrippa, Henricus Cornelius. *De Nobilitate & Praecellentia Foeminei sexus* [& other works]. Cologne 1532. (p. 62)

50. Alberti, Marcello. *Istoria Delle Donne Scientiate*. Naples: Mosca, 1740. (p. 61)

51. Algarotti, Francesco, *Sir Isaac Newton's Philosophy explained for the use of the Ladies*. London 1739. [Translated by Elizabeth Carter]. (p. 65)

52. Ballard, George. *Memoirs of Several Ladies of Great Britain, Who Have Been Celebrated for Their Writings or Skill in the Learned Languages Arts and Sciences*. Oxford: Jackson, 1752. (p. 62)

53. Boccaccio, Giovanni. *Libri de Mulieribus Claris*. Ulm: Zainer, 1473. (p. 61)

54. [Bouchet, Jean]. *Les Trivmphes De La Noble Dame Amoureuse*. Louvain: Bogard, 1563. (p. 66)

55. Cabei, Giulio Cesare. *Ornamenti Della Gentil Donna Vedova*. Venice: Zanetti, 1574. (p. 64)

56. [Camposanpiero, Alvise Antonio]. *Discorsi Accademici di Varj Autori Viventi Intorno agli Studj delle Donne*. Padua: Manfre, 1729. (p. 65)

57. [Canning Elizabeth]. *The Case of Elizabeth Canning Fairly Stated*. London: Cooper, 1753; Fielding, Henry. *A Clear State of the Case of Elizabeth Canning*. London: Millar, 1753; Hill, John. *The Story of Elizabeth Canning Considered*. Dublin: Faulkner, 1753. (p. 63)

58. Capaccio, Giulio Cesare. *Illvstrivm Mvliervm, et Illvstrivm Litteris Virorvm Elogia*. Naples: Carlino & Vitale, 1608–9. (p. 61)

59. *Caractère, Le, d'une Femme sans Education*. Cologne: Rentrok, ca. 1700. (p. 65)

60. [Clairon, Mlle.]. [Gaillard de La Bataille, Pierre Alexandre]. *Histoire de Mademoiselle Cronel dite Fretillon, Actrice de la Comédie de Rouen. Ecrite par elle-même*. The Hague: Compagnie, 1740. (p. 63)

61. [Combault, Charles de]. *Blanche Infante De Castile*. Paris: Sommaville, 1644. (p. 62)

62. Darwin, Erasmus. *A Plan for the Conduct of Female Education in Boarding Schools*. Dublin: Chambers, 1798. (p. 65)

63. Dolce, Lodovico. *Dialogo Della Institvtion Delle Donne*. Venice: Giolito, 1553. (p. 62)

64. Domenichi, Lodovico. *La Nobilta delle Donne*. Venice: Giolito, 1551. (p. 61)

65. Doré, Pierre. *La Tovrtrelle De Vidvité*. Paris: Ruelle, 1574. (p. 64)

66. Erasmus, Desiderius. *A ryght frutefull epystle in laude and prayse of matrymony*. London: Redman, [1530?]. (p. 65)

67. Fénelon, François de. *Education Des Filles*. Paris: Aubouin, 1687. (p. 65)

68. Guyon, Jeanne Marie. *The Life of Lady Guion, Written by herself*. Bristol: Farley, 1772–73. (p. 63)

69. [Joan, Pope]. Allatius, Leo. *Confvtatio Fabvlae de Ioanna Papissa*. Cologne: Kalcovius, 1645; Blondel, David. *De Ioanna Papissa*. Amsterdam: Blaeu, 1657; Cooke, Alexander. *Pope Joane. A Dialogve betweene a Protestant and a Papist*. London: Blunt & Barret, 1610; Raemond, Florimond de. *Errevr Popvlaire de la Papesse Iane*. Lyons: Rigaud, 1595. (p. 63)

70. Juncker, Christian. *Schediasma Historicum, De Ephemeridibus Sive Diariis Eruditorum, In Nobilioribus Europae partibus hactenus publicatis.* Leipzig: Gleditsch, 1692. (p. 62)

71. Landi, Giulio. *La Vita di Cleopatra Reina d'Egitto.* Venice: [Aldine Press], 1551. (p. 63)

72. Le Moyne, Pierre. *La Galérie des Femmes Fortes.* Paris: Sommaville, 1647. (p. 61)

73. [Matilda, Countess]. Fiorentini, Francesco-Maria. *Memorie Di Matilda La Gran Contessa.* Lucca: Bidelli, 1642; Mellini, Domenico. *Trattato . . . Dell' Origine, Fatti, Costvmi, E Lòdi di Matelda, La Gran Contessa D'Italia.* Florence: Giunta, 1589; Razzi, Girolamo. *La Vita, O Vero Azzioni Della Contessa Matelda.* Florence: Sermartelli, 1587. (p. 63)

74. Ménage, Gilles. *Historia Mulierum Philosopharum.* Lyons: Posuel, 1690. (p. 62)

75. [Morata, Olympia Fulvia]. Noltenius, Georgius Ludovicus. *Comment. Hist. Critica de Olympiae Moratae Vita, Scriptis, Fatis Et Lavdibvs.* Frankfurt: Straus, 1775. (p. 63)

76. Moser, Friedrich Carl von. *L'Ambassadrice et ses Droits.* Berlin: Bourdeaux, 1754. (p. 64)

77. Nagge, Wilhelmus. *Schola Foeminarvm septem Classibus.* Deventer: Wermbouts, 1622. (p. 62)

78. [Noel, C.M.D.]. *La Triomphe des Femmes, ou il est montré Par plusieurs & puissantes raisons, que le Sexe Feminin, est plus noble & plus parfait que le masculin.* Antwerp: Sleghers, 1700. (p. 66)

79. Pancrace, Le Docteur. *Lettre du Docteur Pancrace . . . A La Signora Vittoria, sur la préeminence de l'Homme sur la Femme.* Bound with: *Réponse de la Signora Vittoria . . . Le Sexe Vengé, ou La Préeminence de la Femme sur l'Homme.* Bross 1755. (p. 65)

80. Passi, Giuseppe. *I Donneschi Diffetti.* Venice: Somascho, 1601. (p. 65)

81. [Pisan, Christine de]. Thomassy, Raimond. *Essai Sur Les Ecrits Politiques de Christine De Pisan.* Bound with: Gautier, A.F. *Notice sur Christine De Pisan.* Paris-Bordeaux: Debecourt-Faye, 1838–44. (pp. 63–64)

82. Postel, Guillaume. *Les Tres-Merveilleuses Victoires des Femmes du Nouveau Monde.* Sur l'imprimé A Paris: Ruelle, 1553 [Rouen 1738]. (p. 66)

83. [Poulain de La Barre, François]. *De L'Education Des Dames.* Paris: Du Puis, 1674. (p. 65)

84. [Prémoy, Geneviève]. [M, M***]. *Histoire de La Dragone.* Paris: Auroy, 1703. (p. 63)

85. S.I.E.D.V.M.W.A.S. *Hippolytus Redivivus id est Remedium contemnendi sexum muliebrem.* N.p. 1644. (p. 65)

86. [Santa Rosa of Lima]. Nobili, Francesco de. *Il Giobbe Nell' inuitta patienza di Santa Rosa Di Santa Maria Limana.* Bologna: Monti, 1678. (p. 63)

87. [Seton, Elizabeth Ann Bayley]. Barberey, Hélène Bailly de. *Elizabeth Seton et Les Commencements de L'Eglise Catholique.* Paris: Poussielgue, 1868. (p. 63)

88. Strong, James. *Joanereidos: Or, Feminine Valour; Eminently discovered in Western Women, At the Siege of Lyme.* [London] 1674. (p. 62)

89. Tasso, Torquato. *Discorso della Virtv Feminile, E Donnesca.* Venice: Giunti, 1582. (p. 62)

90. *Truth Triumphant: or, Fluxions for the Ladies.* London: Owen, 1752. (p. 65)

91. Vives, Juan Luis. *L'Institvtion de la Femme Chrestienne . . . Auec l'office du Mary.* Paris: L'Angelier, 1555. (p. 65)

92. Weppling, Johann Bernhard. *Dissertatio Academica . . . De Sexu Seqviori Eruditionis Fama Corusco.* Rostock: Weppling, [1707]. (pp. 61–62)

MILITANT FEMINIST LITERATURE

93. *American Spectator, The, or Matrimonial Preceptor. A Collection . . . of Essays . . . relating to the Married State . . . adapted to the State of Society in the American Republic.* Boston: Manning & Loring for West, 1797. (p. 66)

94. [Astell, Mary]. *A Serious Proposal to the Ladies, For the Advancement of their true and greatest Interest. By a Lover of Her Sex.* London: Wilkin, 1694. (p. 67)

95. Blackwell, Elizabeth. *A Curious Herbal.* London: Harding, 1737. (p. 68)

96. Coudray, Angélique Marguerite Le Boursier du. *Abregé De L'Art Des Accouchements.* Chalons-sur-Marne: Bouchard, 1773. (pp. 67–68)

97. *État, L', De Servitude Ou La Misère Des Domestiques.* Troyes: Garnier, [1711]. (p. 67)

98. [Flores, Juan de]. *L'Histoire d'Avrélio, Et Isabelle En Italien Et François.* Paris: Bonfons, 1581. (p. 66)

99. Fowler, Orson S. *Tight-Lacing, or the Evils of Compressing the Organs of Animal Life.* N.p. [1849]. (p. 67)

100. Fuller, Margaret. *Woman in the Nineteenth Century.* New York: Greeley & McElrath, 1845. (pp. 68–70)

101. Gassaud, Louis Prosper Geraud. *Considérations Médicales sur Les Corsets dont les femmes font usage.* Paris: Gassaud, 1821. (p. 67)

102. Hatfield, Miss. *Letters on the Importance of the Female Sex: with Observations on Their Manners and on Education.* London: Adlard for the Author, 1803. (p. 67)

103. [Lambert, Anne Thérèse de Marguenat de Courcelles, Marquise de]. *Réflexions Nouvelles sur les Femmes, par une Dame de la Cour de France.* London: Coderc, 1730. (p. 67)

104. *Lawes, The, Resolvtions of Womens Rights; or, The Lawes Provision for Women.* London: More & Grove, 1632. (p. 66)

105. [Manly, Mary]. *Secret Memoirs and Manners of Several Persons of Quality, of Both Sexes. From the New Atalantis, an Island in the Mediterranean.* London: Morphew & Woodward, 1709. (p. 68)

106. Marinella, Lucrezia. *La Nobilta, Et L'Eccellenza delle Donne, Co' Diffetti, et Mancamenti De gli Huomini.* Venice: Sanese, 1601. (p. 67)

107. Millett, Kate. *Sexual Politics.* New York: Doubleday, 1970. (p. 70)

108. Petit, Pierre. *De Amazonibus Dissertatio.* Amsterdam: Wolters & Haring, 1687. (pp. 66–67)

109. [Pringy, Mme. de]. *Les Différens Caractères des Femmes du Siècle.* Paris: Coignard & Cellier, 1694. (p. 67)

110. Prynne, William. *The Vnlouelinesse, of Loue-Lockes.* London 1628. (p. 67)

111. [Scudéry, Madeleine de]. *Les Femmes Illvstres.* Paris: Courbe, 1661. (p. 67)

112. Stanton, Elizabeth Cady, Anthony, Susan B., & Gage, Matilda Joslyn, eds., *History of Woman Suffrage.* New York-Rochester: Fowler & Wells-Anthony, 1881–1922. (p. 70)

113. Stern, Madeleine B. *We the Women: Career Firsts of Nineteenth-Century America.* New York: Schulte, 1963. (p. 68)

114. Stern, Madeleine B., ed. *The Victoria Woodhull Reader.* Weston: M & S, 1974. (p. 70)

115. Wollstonecraft, Mary. *Thoughts on the Education of Daughters.* London: Johnson, 1787. (p. 68)

116. Wollstonecraft, Mary. *A Vindication of the Rights of Woman.* London: Johnson, 1792. (p. 68)

117. [Wright, Frances]. *Views of Society and Manners in America . . . By An Englishwoman.* New York: Bliss & White, 1821. (p. 70)

BOOKS THAT SWING THE PENDULUM

1. *Act, An, Declaring and Constituting the People of England to be a Commonwealth and Free-State*. London: Husband, 1649. Broadside. (pp. 104–105)

2. Alantsee, Ambrosius. *Tractatus qui intitulatur Fedus Christianu[m]*. Augsburg: Otmar for Rynmann, 1504. (pp. 99–100)

3. Althusius, Joannes. *Politica*. Herborn 1614. (p. 97)

4. [American Peace Society]. *Prize Essays on a Congress of Nations . . . Together with a Sixth Essay, comprising the substance of the Rejected Essays*. Boston: Whipple & Damrell for the American Peace Society, 1840. (p. 102)

5. [Ascham, Antony]. [*Greek title*], *The Original & End of Civil Power: . . . By Eutactus Philodemius*. London 1649. (p. 98)

6. Bakunin, Mikhail Aleksandrovich. *Dieu Et L'Etat*. Paris: Pessaux, 1892. (p. 107)

7. [Beffroy de Reigny, Louis Abel]. *La Constitution De La Lune, Rêve Politique Et Moral. Par le Cousin-Jacques*. Paris: Froulle, 1793. (pp. 102–103)

8. [Bèze, Théodore de]. *De Ivre Magistratvvm In Svbditos, et Officio subditorum erga Magistratus*. Lyons: Mareschal, 1576. (p. 98)

9. [Bignon, Jérome]. *La Grandevr De Nos Roys et De Levr Sovveraine Puissance*. Paris 1615. (p. 95)

10. Bodin, Jean. *Les Six Livres de la République*. Paris 1576. (p. 96)

11. Botero, Giovanni. *Della Ragione Di Stato Libri Dieci*. Rome: Pellagallo, 1590. (p. 94)

12. [Burnet, Gilbert]. *A Compleat Collection of Papers, In Twelve Parts: Relating to the Great Revolutions in England and Scotland*. London: Clavel, 1689. (p. 106)

13. [Charles II, King of England]. [*Declaration of Breda*]. *A Common-Councell Holden The first day of May 1660*. London: Flesher, 1660. (p. 105)

14. Choppin, René. *De Priuilegiis Rusticorum: Lib. III*. Paris: Chesneau, 1574. (p. 98)

15. *Common-VVealth, A, Or Nothing: Or, Monarchy and Oligarchy Prov'd Parallel in Tyranny. In XII. Queries*. London: Chapman, 1659. (p. 98)

16. Condorcet, Marie Jean Antoine Nicolas Caritat, Marquis de. *Outlines of an Historical View of the Progress of the Human Mind*. Philadelphia: Carey and others, 1796. (p. 99)

17. *Congres des Amis de la Paix Universelle, Réuni à Bruxelles en 1848.* Brussels: Lesigne, 1849. (p. 102)

18. *Congres des Amis de la Paix Vniverselle Reuni a Paris en 1849.* Paris: Guillaumin, 1850. (p. 102)

19. *Congres, Le, Des Bêtes.* London: Thomson, 1748. (p. 102)

20. Contarini, Pier Maria. *Compendio Vniversal Di Repvblica.* Venice: Contarini, 1602. (p. 94)

21. *Defence, A, of the Resolutions and Address of the American Congress, In Reply to Taxation No Tyranny. By the Author of Regulus.* London: Williams, [1775]. (p. 107)

22. [Defoe, Daniel]. *A Free Discourse wherein the Doctrines which make for Tyranny are Display'd.* London: Lawrence & Baldwin, 1697. (p. 99)

23. Du Plessis, Philippe de Mornay, Seigneur. *Vindiciae contra Tyrannos . . . Stephano Ivnio Brvto Celta, Avctore.* Edimbvrg [Basle] 1579. (p. 97)

24. Du Plessis, Philippe de Mornay, Seigneur. *De La Pvissance Légitime Dv Prince Svr le Pevple, et du peuple sur le Prince.* N.p. 1581. (p. 97)

25. [Goudar, Ange]. *La Paix de L'Europe . . . ou Projet de Pacification Générale.* Amsterdam: Chatelain, 1757. (p. 101)

26. Grotius, Hugo. *De Ivre Belli ac Pacis Libri Tres.* Paris: Buon, 1625. (pp. 100–101)

27. Harrington, James. *The Common-Wealth of Oceana.* London: Streater for Chapman, 1656. (pp. 103–104)

28. Henry VIII, King of England. *Assertio Septem Sacramentorvm aduersus Martinu[m] Lutheru[m].* N.p. 1523. (p. 104)

29. [Hollingworth, Richard]. *An Exercitation concerning Usurped Powers: Wherein The Difference betwixt Civill Authority and Usurpation is stated.* [London] 1650. (p. 99)

30. Hotman, François. *Francogallia.* [Geneva]: Stoer, 1573. (p. 96)

31. James I, King of England. *Déclaration Povr Le Droict Des Rois & indépendance de leurs Couronnes.* Iouxte la coppie Imprimée à Londres: Bill, 1615. (p. 95)

32. Jay, William. *War and Peace: the Evils of the First, and a Plan for Preserving the Last.* London: Ward, 1842. (p. 102)

33. Lenin, Nikolai. *Die Naechsten Aufgaben Der Sowjet-Macht.* Berne: Promachos, 1918. (p. 107)

34. [Louis XIV, King of France]. *An Edict of the French King . . . Wherein he Recalls, and totally Annuls the . . . Edict given at Nantes.* [London]: G.M., 1686. (p. 105)

35. Mably, Gabriel Bonnot de. *Des Principes Des Négociations, pour servir d'introduction au Droit Public de L'Europe, Fondé sur les Traités*. The Hague 1767. (p. 101)

36. Mackenzie, Sir George. *Jus Regium: Or, The Just and Solid Foundations of Monarchy*. London: Chiswell, 1684. (p. 95)

37. Marx, Karl. *Capital*. London: Swan Sonnenschein, Lowrey, 1887. (p. 107)

38. Meinardus, Franciscus. *Regicidivm Detestatvm, Qvaesitvm, Praecavatvm*. Paris: Libert, 1610. (p. 96)

39. Mettais, H. *L'An 5865*. Paris: Librairie Centrale, 1865. (p. 103)

40. [Milton, John]. *Théorie de la Royauté, d'après la Doctrine de Milton*. N.p. 1789. (p. 97)

41. [Mirabeau, Honoré Gabriel Riqueti, Comte de]. *Essai sur le Despotisme*. London 1775. (p. 99)

42. [Nalson, John]. *The Countermine*. London: Edwin, 1678. (p. 95)

43. Palliot, C. *Les Cérémonie[s] Observées à La Solennisation de la Paix, en l'église Nostre-Dame de Paris, 21. Iuin. 1598*. Paris: Binet, 1598. (p. 105)

44. [Parker, Henry]. *Jus Populi. Or, a Discourse Wherein clear satisfaction is given, as well concerning the Right of Subjects, as the Right of Princes*. London: Bostock, 1644. (p. 98)

45. Paruta, Paolo. *Della Perfettione Della Vita Politica*. Venice: Nicolini, 1579. (p. 94)

46. [Pelletier, Pierre]. *De L'Inviolable Et Sacrée Personne Des Rois. Contre tous Assassins & Parricides qui oz attenter sur leurs Maiestez*. Paris: Huby, 1610. (p. 96)

47. *Pragmatica Sanctio et Co[n]cor[data]*. Lyons: Crespin, 1530. (p. 105)

48. Proudhon, Pierre Joseph. *Les Démocrates Assermentés et les Réfractaires*. Paris: Dentu, 1863. (p. 107)

49. Pufendorf, Samuel. *De Officio Hominis & Civis, Juxta Legem Naturalem Libri Duo*. Cambridge: Hayes, 1682. (p. 98)

50. Pufendorf, Samuel. *Of the Law of Nature and Nations*. Oxford: Lichfield, 1703. (p. 101)

51. [Rabaut de St. Etienne, Jean Paul]. *Considérations sur Les Interets Du Tiers-Etat*. N.p. 1788. (p. 98)

52. Revocation of the Edict of Nantes. Collection of Seventy Decrees: *Arrets, Déclarations, Edicts* and *Ordonnances* relating to the Revocation of the Edict of Nantes. Paris 1679–85. (p. 105)

53. Rousseau, Jean-Jacques. *Du Contract Social; ou, Principes du Droit Politique.* Amsterdam: Rey, 1762. (pp. 97–98)

54. Rousseau, Jean-Jacques. *Du Contrat Social.* Paris: Mourer & Pinpare, 1797. (pp. 97–98)

55. Rousseau, Jean-Jacques. *Discours sur l'Origine et les Fondemens de l'Inégalité parmi les Hommes.* Amsterdam: Rey, 1755. (p. 99)

56. Rousseau, Jean-Jacques. *Extrait du Projet de Paix Perpetuelle de Monsieur L'Abbé De Saint-Pierre.* N.p. 1761. (p. 101)

57. Saavedra, Diego Fajardo de. *L'Idea del Prencipe Politico Christiano.* Venice: Pezzana, 1678. (pp. 94–95)

58. Sansovino, Francesco, ed. *Propositioni, overo Considerationi in materia di cose di stato, sotto titolo di Auuertimenti, Auuedimenti Ciuili, & Concetti Politici, di M. Francesco Guicciardini. M.Gio. Francesco Lottini. M. Francesco Sansouino.* Venice: Salicato, 1583. (p. 94)

59. Savaron, Jean. *De La Sovveraineté dv Roy.* Paris: Mettayer, 1620. (p. 95)

60. [Sexby, Edward]. *Killing no Murder: . . . By Col. Titus, alias William Allen.* N.p. 1689. (p. 96)

61. Sidney, Algernon. *Discourses Concerning Government.* London: Darby, 1704. (p. 97)

62. Sully, Maximilien de Bethune, Duc de. *Memoires des Sages et Royalles Oeconomies D'Estat, Domestiqves, Politiqves Et Militaires de Henry Le Grand.* Amstelredam [*sic*]: Chez Aletinosgraphe de Clearetimelee, [1638]. (p. 101)

63. Vialardi, Francesco Maria. *La Grandissima Pompa Fvneral Fatta a Parigi . . . Del . . . Enrico il grande Re di Francia, e di Nauarra.* Venice: Marcello, 1610. (pp. 95–96)

64. Voltaire, François Marie Arouet. *A Treatise on Religious Toleration.* London: Becket & De Hondt, 1764. (pp. 106–107)

CURIOUSER AND CURIOUSER

1. Aconzio, Jacopo. *Stratagematvm Satanae libri octo.* Basle: Perna, 1565. (pp. 131–132)

2. Albaret, D'. *Différens Projets Relatifs Au Climat Et A La Manière La Plus Convenable De Batir Dans Les Pays Chauds, Et Plus Particulierement Dans Les Indes Occidentales.* [Paris] 1776. (p. 129)

3. Allen, Nathan. *An Essay on the Connection of Mental Philosophy with Medicine.* Philadelphia: Waldie, 1841. (p. 134)

4. Allen, Nathan. *The Opium Trade; including a Sketch of Its History, Extent, Effects, Etc. as carried on in India and China.* Lowell: Walker, 1853. (p. 136)

5. *Alphabet Artificiel Attribué au Celèbre Pascal.* N.p. 1787. (p. 126)

6. *Alphabet des Cris de Paris.* Paris: Marchand, ca. 1850. (p. 126)

7. *Alphabet Grotesque.* Paris: Saussine, ca. 1890. (p. 126)

8. *Alphabet Militaire.* Paris n.d. (p. 126)

9. [Amelunghi, Girolamo & Others]. *La Gigantea Et La Nanea Insieme Con La Gverra De Mostri.* Florence: Guiducci, 1612. (p. 128)

10. *American Ice Company.* Glasgow: Pattison, 1845. (p. 125)

11. Anderson, James. *A Description of A Patent Hot-House.* London: Cumming, 1803. (p. 129)

12. *Art of Talking with the Fingers, The.* London: Darton, ca. 1840. (p. 126)

13. [Banchieri, Adriano]. *La Nobilissima Anzi Asinissima Compagnia Delli Briganti della Bastina.* Venice: Barezzi, 1611. (pp. 128–129)

14. Barailon, Jean François. *Projet sur Le Costume Particulier à donner à Chacun des Deux Conseils Législatifs, et à tous les fonctionnaires publics de la République Française.* Paris: Imprimerie Nationale, [1794/1795]. (p. 130)

15. Barra, Pierre. *L'Usage de La Glace, De La Neige Et Dv Froid.* Lyons: Cellier, 1675. (p. 131)

16. Becker, Daniel. *Cultrivori Prussiaci Curatio singularis.* Leyden: Maire, 1640. (p. 131)

17. Berrettarius, Elpidius. *Tractatus de Risu.* Florence: Giunti, 1603. (p. 136)

18. *Bibliothèque Imaginaire De Livrets, Lettres, et discours imaginaires.* [Paris] 1615. (p. 135)

19. Bisset, James. *Dandyism Displayed, or the Follies of the Ton . . . Female Dandies.* London: Duncombe, n.d. (p. 130)

20. [Boileau, Daniel]. *Papyro-Plastics, or the Art of Modelling in Paper.* London: Boosey, 1824. (p. 135)

21. Bottifango, Giulio Cesare. *Lettera Dell' Elefante.* Rome: Corbelletti, 1630. (p. 129)

22. [Bourgeois, Dominique François]. *Mémoire Sur une Nouvelle manière d'éclairer, pendant la nuit, les rues de Paris.* [Paris]: Gueffier, 1765–66. (p. 131)

23. Breitkopf, Johann Gottlieb Immanuel. *Über den Druck der geographischen Charten.* Leipzig: Breitkopf, 1777. (p. 135)

24. Brewster, Sir David. *Letters on Natural Magic. Addressed to Sir Walter Scott.* New York: Harper, 1839. (p. 133)

25. [Brunet, Gustave]. *Livres Perdus Essai Bibliographique sur les livres devenus introuvables par Philomneste junior.* Brussels: Gay & Doucé, 1882. (p. 135)

26. [Buoni, Tommaso]. *Della Compagnia De' Tagliacantoni, Descrittione Vniversale.* Venice: Guarisco, 1601 (1600 at end). (p. 136)

27. Canonhiero, Pietro Andrea. *De Cvriosa Doctrina, Libri Quinque.* Florence: Germanus, 1607. (p. 123)

28. [Caraccioli, Louis Antoine]. *L'Ecu de Six Francs.* Geneva & Paris: Esprit, 1778. (p. 136)

29. Cardano, Girolamo. *La Métoposcopie.* Paris: Jolly, 1658. (p. 133)

30. Carwitham, John. *Floor-Decorations of Various Kinds, Both in Plano & Perspective . . . in XXIV Copper Plates.* [London]: Caldwell, [1739]. (p. 129)

31. Castelli, Petrus. *De Hyaena Odorifera.* Frankfurt: Sande, 1668. (p. 129)

32. *Catalogue Of Curious but Prohibited Books, & c. Chiefly Modern, A.* London: Lion, ca. 1750. (p. 135)

33. Chassanion, Jean. *De Gigantibvs, Eorvmqve Reliqviis, Atqve ijs, quae ante annos aliquot nostra aetate in Gallia reperte sunt.* Basle 1580. (p. 136)

34. Ciampoli, Giovanni Battista. *Poesia in Lode dell' Inchiostro Dedicata al Signor Georgio Coneo Gentilhvomo Scozzese.* Rome: Mascardi, 1626. (p. 135)

35. Clairian, L.J. *Recherches Et Considérations Médicales Sur Les Vêtemens des Hommes, Particulièrement Sur Les Culotes.* Paris: Aubry, 1803. (pp. 130–131)

36. [Coquelet, Louis]. *L'Eloge de Quelque Chose Dedié A Quelqu'un.* Paris: Heuqueville, 1730. (p. 123)

37. [Coquelet, Louis]. *L'Eloge de Rien dedié A Personne.* Paris: Heuqueville, 1730. (p. 123)

38. Cordus, Valerius. *De Halosantho sev Spermate Ceti vvlgo dicto, Liber.* Zurich 1565. (p. 129)

39. Cosimo II de Medici. *Bando Che Non si Givochi per le Strade et Piazze. Publicato di 23. d'Agosto. 1566.* Bound with: Cosimo II de Medici. *Bando Contro Li Contraventori De Bandi di Tener Givochi, E Biscazze. E Prohibizione di alcuni altri giuochi di carte, cioe trentuno, e quaranta bassetta.* Bound with: Ferdinand II de Medici. *Bando Et Prohibizione De' Givochi E, Biscazze. Bandito il di 18. di Maggio 1579.* Florence: Pignoni, 1615–17–39. (p. 124)

40. Daneau, Lambert. *Les Sorciers, Dialogve Très-Vtile . . . povr ce temps.* [Geneva]: Bourgeois, 1574. (p. 132)

41. [Délaisement]. *Dissertation Sur le commencement Du Siècle Prochain, Et la Solution Du Problème, Savoir laquelle des deux années 1700. ou 1701. est la première du Siècle.* [Paris 1699?]. (p. 131)

42. Della Bella, Stefano. *Cartes des Rois [& Reines] de France.* Paris: Le Gras, [1644]. (pp. 126–127)

43. *Description of the Field of Battle, and disposition of the Troops engaged in the Action . . . near Waterloo . . . in the Panorama, Leicester-Square.* [London] 1816. (p. 126)

44. Digby, Sir Kenelm. *Discovrs Fait En Vne Célèbre Assemblée . . . Tovchant La Gvérison des Playes par la Poudre de Sympathie.* Paris: Courge & Moet, 1658. (p. 134)

45. Edwards, James. *A Catalogue of The Valuable Library of James Edwards, Esq.* [London]: Bulmer, 1815. (p. 135)

46. *Elliot's Grand and Correct Panorama of the Coronation Procession of Queen Victoria, On June 28th, 1838.* London: Elliot, 1838. (p. 126)

47. Engelbrecht. *Christ Scourged in the Temple.* Germany late 17th century. (p. 126)

48. *Ephemerides Cvm Praedictionibvs. Anno Trinodi numinis. 1544.* N.p. [1545]. (pp. 125–126)

49. *Explanation Of the famous and renowned Glas-Work, Or painted windows, in the fine and eminent Church at Gouda.* Gouda: Van der Klos, 1790. (p. 129)

50. *Explanation of the Works of the Tunnel under the Thames from Rotherhithe to Wapping, An.* London: Warrington, 1840. (p. 129)

51. Eynatten, Maximilian ab. *Manvale Exorcismorvm.* Antwerp: Plantin-Moretus, 1648. (p. 132)

52. Falcone, Ippolito. *Narciso Al Fonte . . . Diviso In Dve Parti.* Venice: Hertz, 1675. (p. 134)

53. Fendius, Michael. *Penna Scriptoria.* Neuberg: Danhauser, 1618. (p. 135)

54. Ferrarius, Franciscus Bernardinus. *De Vetervm Acclamationibvs Et Plausv Libri Septem.* Milan 1627. (p. 136)

55. Fienus, Thomas. *De Viribvs Imaginationis Tractatvs.* Leyden: Elzevier, 1635. (p. 134)

56. Francesco I de Medici. *Bando Et Ordinatione Che Le Strade Pvbliche Si Mantenghino Sempre In Bvono Essere.* Florence: Giunti, 1578. (p. 124)

57. Francesco I de Medici. *Bando contro li Giocatori, Dannatori, discoli & insolenti.* N.p. [1589]. (p. 124)

58. Francis II, King of France. *Ordonnance svr le Défence De ne porter Chausses Chicquetées & bouffantes de taffetas, Dagues, Espées ne autres bastons offensibles.* Paris: Nyverd, 1559. (p. 124)

59. [Frederick II, King of Prussia]. *Dissertation Sur L'Ennui.* Berlin: Decker, 1768. (p. 136)

60. Fregoso, Antonio. *Opera.Nova . . . laquale tracta de doi Philosophi.* Venice: Rusconi, 1513. (p. 136)

61. [Gauden, John]. *A Discourse of Artificial Beauty . . . Between Two Ladies.* London: Royston, 1662. (p. 130)

62. Genin, John Nicholas. *An Illustrated History of The Hat.* New York 1848. (p. 130)

63. Gohorry, Jacques. *De Vsu & Mysteriis Notarum Liber.* Paris: Sertenas, 1550. (p. 133)

64. Hall, J. Sparkes. *The Book of the Feet.* London: Simpkin, Marshall, n.d. (p. 130)

65. Harring, Harro. *Rapport entre le Magnétisme et la Sphéreologie.* London, Brussels, Rio de Janeiro 1856. (p. 134)

66. Howard, Thomas. *On the Loss of Teeth and Loose Teeth; and on the Best Means of Restoring Them.* London: Simpkin & Marshall, 1861. (p. 127)

67. *Interrogatoire de Maistre Vrbain Grandier Prestre . . . Avec les confrontations des Religieuses possédées contre ledit Grandier. Ensemble la liste & les noms des Iuges députez par sa Majesté.* Paris: Hebert & Poullard, 1634. (p. 132)

68. *Jargon, Le, ou Langage De L'Argot Réformé.* Troyes: Garnier, [1728]. (p. 136)

69. [Johnson, Samuel]. *Proposals for Printing, by Subscription, the Two first Volumes of Bibliotheca Harleiana.* In: *The Gentleman's Magazine for 1742.* London: Cave, 1742. (p. 125)

70. [Johnson, Samuel]. Boucher, Jonathan. *Proposals for Printing, by Sub-*

scription, in Two Volumes, Quarto, A Supplement to Dr. Johnson's Dictionary. [London]: Hanfard, [1802]. (p. 125)

71. Koops, Matthias. *Historical Account of the Substances which have been used to Describe Events, And To Convey Ideas, from the Earliest Date to the Invention of Paper . . . Printed on Paper Manufactured of Straw Alone.* London: Jaques, 1801. (p. 135)

72. Lachmund, Fridericus. *De Ave Diomedea Dissertatio.* Amsterdam: Frisius, 1674. (p. 129)

73. La Mesnardière, Hippolyte Jules Pilet de. *Raisonnemens . . . Svr La Natvre Des Esprits Qvi Servent Avx Sentimens.* Paris: Camusat, 1638. (p. 134)

74. *Life, The, of That Wonderful and extraordinarily heavy man, Daniel Lambert, from his Birth to the Moment of his Dissolution; with an Account of Men noted for their Corpulency, and other interesting matter.* New York: Samuel Wood & Sons, 1815. (p. 131)

75. Lorichius, Joannes. *Aenigmatvm Libri III.* Frankfurt: Eginolph, 1545. (p. 136)

76. [Louis XIII, King of France]. *Ordonnance . . . Portant défenses a tous . . . de porter ny vser d'oresenauant d'aucuns passements, poincts couppez & dentelles, tant en leurs collets & manchettes, qu'en tout leur autre linge.* Paris: Morel, Mettayer & Estiene, 1626. (p. 124)

77. Ludlow, Fitz Hugh. *The Hasheesh Eater: being passages from the Life of a Pythagorean.* New York: Harper, 1857. (p. 136)

78. Maillard, Firmin. *Les Publications de la Rue pendant La Siège et La Commune. Bibliographie Pittoresque et Anecdotique.* Paris: Aubry, 1874. (p. 136)

79. [Marchand, Jean Henri]. *Les Mémoires de L'Eléphant, Ecrits sous sa Dictée, Et traduits de l'Indien par un Suisse.* Amsterdam & Paris: Costard, 1771. (p. 129)

80. Melanchthon, Philipp. *Eine Warhafftige Nye Tiding van deren Kindern de sick so seltzam vnd wuenderlick holden mit Dantzen vnd Springen dach vnd nacht.* N.p. ca. 1555. (p. 131)

81. Menghi, Girolamo. *Compendio Dell' Arte Essorcistica.* Bologna: Rossi, 1590. (p. 132)

82. *Metamorfosi del Giuoco detto l'Enimma Chinese.* Florence: Landi, 1818. (p. 129)

83. Montagu, Henry de. *Daemonis Mimica In Magiae Progressv Tvm in Sectis Errorvm.* Paris: Rigaud, 1612. (p. 133)

84. *Moyen pour Connoitre L'Amitié ou Inimitié des Personnes, procédant des Influences Célèstes qui les enclinent.* Sur l'imprimé, A Lyon: Guynand, 1687. (p. 133)

85. Nancrede, Joseph and Barnard B. Macanulty. *Proposals for Publishing, by Subscription, A New System of Geography, Ancient and Modern. By J. Tytler.* Salem 1802. (p. 125)

86. Nausea, Fridericus. *Ad Sacratissimvm Caesarem Ferdinandvm . . . Exploratio.* N.p. 1531. (p. 133)

87. Niphus, Augustinus. *De Auguriis Lib. II . . . . His adiecimus Ori Apollinis . . . de hieroglyphicis notis Lib. II.* Basle: Hervagius, 1534. (p. 133)

88. Nobili, Giacinto. *Il Vagabondo overo Sferza De Bianti, E Vagabondi.* Venice: Grifei, 1646. (p. 136)

89. Nozzolini, Tolomeo. *Sogno in Sogno, ouero Il Verme da Seta.* Florence: Pignoni, 1628. (p. 129)

90. *Nugae Venales, Sive Thesavrvs Ridendi & Iocandi.* Bound with: *Stvdentes sive Comoedia de Vita Studiosorum autore Ignoto Peerdeklontio.* Bound with: *Pvgna Porcorvm per P. Porcivm, Poetam.* Bound with: *Crepundia Poetica Somniata.* 1642–62. (p. 129)

91. Perréaud, François. *Démonologie ov Traitté des Démons et Sorciers . . . Ensemble L'Antidémon de Mascon.* Geneva: Aubert, 1653. (p. 132)

92. Peucer, Caspar. *Commentarivs, De Praecipvis Divinationvm Generibvs, In Qvo A Prophetiis, Avthoritate Diuina traditis.* Frankfurt: Wechel, 1593. (p. 133)

93. [Pona, Francesco]. *L'Antilvcerna Dialogo di Evreta Misoscolo.* Ferrara: Gironi, 1648. (p. 136)

94. Psellus, Michael. [Greek title] *De Operatione daemonum Dialogus.* Paris: Drovart, 1615. (p. 132)

95. Puteanus, Erycius. *Democritvs: Sive De Risv Dissertatio Satvrnalis.* Louvain: Elavius, 1612. (p. 136)

96. Quérard, Joseph Marie. *Livres Perdus et Exemplaires Uniques.* Bordeaux: Lefevbre, 1872. (p. 135)

97. Rantzovius, Henricus. *Catalogvs Imperatorvm, Regvm ac Principvm Qvi Astrologicam Artem amarunt.* Antwerp: Plantin, 1580. (p. 133)

98. *Récit Véritable de ce Qvi S'Est Passé à Lovdvn.* Paris: Targa, 1634. (p. 132)

99. Rizza Casa, Giorgio. *Prédictions ov Discovrs . . . sur les Merveilleux effects que les influxions célestes monstrent deuoir aduenir par l'Europe, les années 1586. 87. 88. 89. 90.* Lyons: Petit-Jean, 1588. (p. 133)

100. Rorarius, Hieronymus. *Quod Animalia bruta ratione utantur melius Homine. Libri Duo.* Amsterdam: Ravestein, 1666. (p. 129)

101. [Sala, George Augustus]. *Grand Processions Against Papal Aggression.* London ca. 1851. (p. 126)

102. Sala, George Augustus. *The House That Paxton Built*. London: Ironbrace, Woodenhead, 1851. (p. 126)

103. Schulze, Ioannes Ludovicus. *Dissertatio Philosophica de Somniis*. Halle: Franck, [1758]. (p. 134)

104. Senguerd, Wolferdus. *Tractatus Physicvs De Tarantula*. Leyden: Gaasbeeck, 1668. (p. 129)

105. Spach, Isaac. *Theses Medicae De Somno Et Vigilia*. Strasbourg: Bertram, 1597. (p. 136)

106. Stathmion, Christopher. *Practica auff das M.D.XLvii. Jar*. N.p. [1547]. (p. 133)

107. Stern, Madeleine B. *Sherlock Holmes: Rare-Book Collector A Study in Book Detection*. New York: Schulte, [1963]. (p. 135)

108. *Tesoro di Scienze Nominato Corona Pretiosa*. Rome: Fortunato, 1564. (p. 133)

109. [Wise, Thomas James]. *Poems and Sonnets. By Percy Bysshe Shelley. Edited by Charles Alfred Seymour. Member of the Phila. Hist. Soc.* Philadelphia 1887. (p. 127)

110. Witlich, Matthias. *Avrora Carmine*. Cologne: Birckman, 1565. (p. 136)

CATALOGUES ISSUED BY
LEONA ROSTENBERG—RARE BOOKS*
1946–1978

1. *A Catalogue for the Easter Term containing divers matters relating to the History of the Book.* 1946. 100 items. With list of references and index.

2. *The House of Elzevier A Seventeenth-Century Retrospect.* 1947. 165 items. With list of references and index.

List 1. *A Miscellany Of English Literature Art Science And History.* 1947. 70 items.

List 2. *A Miscellany Of Continental Art Literature And Philosophy Science, History And Theology.* 1947. 100 items.

3. *Science And Philosophy.* 1947. 50 items. With subject index.

4. *History Law & Political Theory.* 1947. 50 items. With subject index.

5. *Renaissance & Reformation.* 1948. 50 items. With subject index.

6. *Language & Literature.* 1948. 50 items. With subject index.

7. *Art & Illustrated Books.* 1948. 50 items. With indexes of subjects and artists.

8. *Typography & Bibliography.* 1948. 60 items. With index.

9. *The Italian Renaissance.* 1948. 75 items. With subject index.

10. *Science & Natural History.* 1948. 90 items. With subject index.

11. *Law & Political Theory.* 1949. 40 items.

12. *English History.* 1949. 60 items. With subject index.

13. *The French Renaissance.* 1949. 60 items. With subject index.

14. *The Art & Craft Of The Book.* 1949. 133 items. With index.

15. *The Mid-Century 1450-1950.* 1950. 66 items. With indexes of subjects and authors.

16. *Russia Hungary Turkey & Cathay.* 1950. 82 items. With subject index.

17. *History Biography & Memoirs.* 1950. 203 items.

18. *Four Centuries of Fine Books 1507–1900.* 1950. 324 items. With author index.

19. *History Of Printing/Art & Illustrated Books.* 1951. 100 items.

*Occasional Lists are not included.

20. *Book-Notes 1500-1700*. 1952-53. Issued semi-monthly. 34 parts. 690 items. With prospectus.

   I The Renaissance: The New Learning; Germany & The Empire; Italy; France; The Ottoman Conquest; Knowledge of the New World; The Republic of Letters; Philosophy; Science & Superstition; Art

  II The Reformation: Rome & The Papacy; Luther & Germany; The French Reformation; Tudor England

 III The Counter Reformation: 16th-Century Political Thought; England under Elizabeth & James I; France under Henry IV; The Low Countries; The New Republic of Letters

 IV The Thirty Years War: The Imperial Background; France under Richelieu; The Continental Struggle; Charles I & Cromwell; Mazarin & Spain; The United Provinces; Philosophy & Political Theory; Science & The Humanities

  V The Age of Louis XIV: Government & The Court; Wars & Foreign Policy; Arts & Letters

 VI The Restoration & The Glorious Revolution: England under Charles II; James II & William of Orange

VII Russia & Central Europe

VIII Science & Philosophy In The Seventeenth Century

21. *Holiday List Twenty-Five Beautiful Books*. 1953. 25 items.

22. *The Man Of The Renaissance*. 1954. 425 items. With index.

23. *The Century Of Conflict 1600-1700*. 1955. 550 items. With index.

24. *Political Theory/Economics/Historical Ephemera*. 1956. 518 items.

25. *The Book A Survey of its History, Art, Science & Social Impact*. 1957. 256 items. With author and title index.

26. *La Belle France*. 1958. 632 items. With index.

27. *The Renaissance World*. 1959. 555 items. With index.

28. *Italy*. 1960. 515 items. With index.

29. *Persons & Places*. 1960. 518 items. With index.

30. *England*. 1961. 600 items. With subject index.

31. *Literature*. 1962. 835 items. With index.

32. *The Renaissance*. 1963. 578 items. With index.

33. *Books Of Three Centuries 1500-1800 The Renaissance/The Baroque/The Age Of Reason*. 1964. 430 items. With subject index.

Unnumbered. *Books Published During Shakespeare's Lifetime 1564–1616*. 1964. 117 items.

34. *One Hundred Years Of France 1547–1652 A Documentary History*. 1965. 755 items. With preface and subject index. [En bloc collection].

35. *Books With Illustrations 1500–1800*. 1965. 443 items. With index of authors and titles and index of engravers.

36. *Four Hundred Books Of Four Centuries*. 1966. 400 items. With subject index.

37. *The French Revolution*. 1966. 1659 items. With foreword. [En bloc collection].

38. *The Reformation Its Influence Upon History, Thought & Literature*. 1967. 451 items. With index.

39. *The Aldine Press*. 1967. 258 items. With foreword, Aldine chronology, bibliography, index of authors and titles and index of editors and translators. [En bloc collection].

Unnumbered. *A Fair Catalogue of Rare Books*. 1967. 171 items.

40. *France & Italy*. 1968. 534 items. With index.

41. *Drama & The Stage*. 1968. 4 parts. 190 items plus 30 *Early Novels*.

42. *Germany & Austria*. 1968. 200 items.

43. *English Books and Pamphlets*. 1968. 285 items.

44. *Fare for the Fair*. 1968. 119 items.

45. *Renaissance & Reformation*. 1968. 264 items.

46. *Literature*. 1968. 357 items.

47. *Statecraft/Political Theory/Law*. 1969. 286 items.

48. *Rare Books for the Antiquarian Book Fair*. 1969. 140 items.

49. *Exotic Lands*. 1969. 105 items. With *Supplement* of 50 items.

50. *France History—Political Theory—Law*. 1969–70. 3 parts. 312 items.

51. *Drama*. 1970. 104 items.

52. *French Literature*. 1970. 124 items.

53. *Italian Literature & Drama*. 1970. 117 items.

54. *100 New Acquisitions On The History Of Old France*. 1970. 100 items.

55. *England*. 1971. 369 items.

56. *100 for the Fair*. 1971. 100 items.

57. *Reform & Revolution*. 1972. 100 items.

58. *The Italians*. 1972. 269 items.

59. *Thirty Old Books For The New Year.* 1972. 30 items.

60. *Judaica—Hebraica & The Influence Of Jewish Thought.* 1973. 40 items.

61. *A Fair Exchange.* 1973. 128 items. With index.

62. *300 Fine Books.* 1974. 300 items. With index.

63. *Rare & "Fair."* 1974. 163 items. With index.

64. *Nineteenth-Century Nostalgia.* 1975. 70 items.

65. *Central Europe—Near & Far East/Fates & Facts.* 1975. 80 items.

66. *France.* 1975. 102 items.

67. *Old & Rare.* 1975. 157 items. With index.

68. *Political Theory.* 1975. 3 parts. 97 items.

69. *1776 Causes & Effects.* 1976. 251 items. With index.

70. *Center-Pieces.* 1976. 81 items.

71. *May Fair.* 1976. 95 items.

72. *Old & Rare.* 1976. 169 items. With index.

73. *Europe & America.* 1977. 202 items. With index.

74. *Pictures Of The Past.* 1977. 72 items.

75. *Plums at the Plaza.* 1977. 180 items. With index.

76. *The Renaissance.* 1978. 434 items. With index.

77. *The Court of Louis XIV.* 1978. 85 items.

INDEX

Index